Lesson Plans for Creative Dance

CONNECTING WITH LITERATURE, ARTS, AND MUSIC

Sally Carline, MA

Human Kinetics

Library of Congress Cataloging-in-Publication Data

Carline, Sally.
    Lesson plans for creative dance : connecting with literature, arts, and music / Sally Carline.
        p. cm.
    ISBN-13: 978-1-4504-0198-2 (soft cover)
    ISBN-10: 1-4504-0198-8 (soft cover)
    1. Dance--Study and teaching. 2. Movement education. 3. Dance for children. 4. Lesson planning. I. Title.
    GV1753.5.C37 2011
    372.86'8--dc22

                                        2010045128

ISBN-10: 1-4504-0198-8 (print)
ISBN-13: 978-1-4504-0198-2 (print)

The Web addresses cited in this text were current as of February 11, 2011, unless otherwise noted.

Acquisitions Editor: Gayle Kassing, PhD; **Developmental Editor:** Bethany J. Bentley; **Assistant Editor:** Derek Campbell; **Copyeditor:** Jan Feeney; **Permission Manager:** Martha Gullo; **Graphic Designer:** Nancy Rasmus; **Graphic Artist:** Kathleen Boudreau-Fuoss; **Cover Designer:** Keith Blomberg; **Photographer (cover):** Gang Tao; **Photographers (interior):** Dr. Qingbin Li (pp. 3, 17, 62, 74, 95, 100, 173, 186), Gang Tao (pp. 13, 14, 33 (right), 34, 47, 50, 53, 55, 57, 59, 64, 65, 67, 69, 71, 75, 89, 130, 135, 150, 152, 165, 169, 176, 187), Jo Vickers (pp. 6, 8, 16, 21, 33 (left), 39, 76, 81, 83, 92, 101, 111, 113, 121, 127, 137, 140, 142 (top and bottom), 143, 157, 166); **Photo Production Manager:** Jason Allen; **Art Manager:** Kelly Hendren; **Associate Art Manager:** Alan L. Wilborn; **Illustrations:** © Human Kinetics; **Printer:** United Graphics

We thank the University of Alberta, Edmonton, for assistance in providing the location for the photo shoot for this book.

Printed in the United States of America   10 9 8 7 6 5 4 3 2 1

The paper in this book is certified under a sustainable forestry program.

Human Kinetics
Web site: www.HumanKinetics.com

United States: Human Kinetics
P.O. Box 5076
Champaign, IL 61825-5076
800-747-4457
e-mail: humank@hkusa.com

Canada: Human Kinetics
475 Devonshire Road Unit 100
Windsor, ON N8Y 2L5
800-465-7301 (in Canada only)
e-mail: info@hkcanada.com

Europe: Human Kinetics
107 Bradford Road
Stanningley
Leeds LS28 6AT, United Kingdom
+44 (0) 113 255 5665
e-mail: hk@hkeurope.com

Australia: Human Kinetics
57A Price Avenue
Lower Mitcham, South Australia 5062
08 8372 0999
e-mail: info@hkaustralia.com

New Zealand: Human Kinetics
P.O. Box 80
Torrens Park, South Australia 5062
0800 222 062
e-mail: info@hknewzealand.com

E5299

This book is dedicated to the Joeys,
Jens, Ginas, and Jackies,
and all children who dance.

CONTENTS

PART III Dances With Music

PREFACE

I have taught dance as part of the physical education program at both primary and secondary levels and have spent many years working with university education students in the areas of curriculum and instruction of creative dance and physical education. At the same time, I had the good fortune to work with Dr. Joyce Boorman in a creative dance program on Saturdays and then to run that program—a total of 34 years to date. Working weekly with classes of children aged 4 to 13 years has provided the drive to continue to develop new materials.

Many of the children dance in our program for eight consecutive years. This has provided me the opportunity to learn about their growth and development in dance, to discover what concepts they understand and when, and to know how much complexity children can deal with at each age. It has also showed that with regular, well-prepared dance classes over time, children can become proficient, confident movers. Dance becomes part of their lives.

This book is a creative dance resource for teachers of children ages 4 to 12 years. This includes classroom teachers responsible for all subjects including physical education; specialists in dance, physical education, or music; university students in teacher-training programs; and instructors in schools of dance where creative dance is taught.

Over the years at in-services and workshops for teachers, it became apparent that many teachers wanted to teach more creative dance. They had the teaching skills but lacked the time in their demanding work schedules to find appropriate music and to develop and plan their own material. My hands-on ideas were useful because each teacher could adapt them to suit the needs of their own classes. Given the resources with concepts to be explored and the teaching progressions described, teachers could select and develop lesson plans to fit their gymnasium time and sometimes find connections between ideas in dance and other curricular areas.

It was time to organize some materials from my experience in teaching into more than a few pages for an in-service. The format of the resulting book is significant because it is divided into three major parts: activities for the warm-up part of the class; a variety of means of exploring dance through words, rhymes, poetry, and rhythm; and ways of exploring dance through stories and music. In part III, accessible music is visualized with notations so that those with or without a music background can follow while listening and then readily see how the story or image and the dynamic, spatial, and relationship concepts all tie together before moving on to the teaching progressions that follow.

Each dance is based on solid movement principles. The suggested teaching processes challenge children to think as they work on their physical responses. This combination of cognition and physical exploration, together with the affective and social involvement inherent in the ideas, means that the children are actively engaged in their learning.

All the dance ideas presented in this book have been tested with classes of children with a range of experience and from different socioeconomic and ethnic groups. Edmonton, where I teach, is a multicultural city. Despite initial resistance to dance from some children (Edmonton is also an ice-hockey city), they become increasingly interested and engaged once challenged physically and mentally. In part, this might be due to the choice of content: It was right for the children affectively and allowed them to see that it is as physically demanding as other areas of physical education. An additional factor is that dance is experiencing new respect as a result of the athleticism shown by both men and women on television series such as *So You Think You Can Dance* and *Dancing With the Stars*.

The organization of the book makes it an easy tool for planning creative dance lessons. Part I provides a review of the movement concepts on which the dances are based and offers some tips for assessment. Chapter 2 includes many possibilities for rhythmic traveling actions and information about developing them as warm-up activities for the first few minutes of each class. (See appendix A for information on accessing the music referenced in chapter 2.) You can read the section devoted to the appropriate age group and follow the progressions aided by diagrams to clarify the use of space.

Part II presents ways to explore creative dance through action words, rhymes, poetry, and rhythm. Some of these ideas may take a relatively short time to develop; others can develop into longer dances. There are opportunities here for you to link the learning in dance with work in language arts.

Part III includes four dances with music and stories for each age group. (See appendix B for information on accessing the music referenced in part III.) These dances are intended to be developed over a series of classes.

To use the materials effectively, you can select a traveling action from part I to use for the first few minutes of several consecutive classes. Then you can develop another traveling action for the next few, and so on. Later in the year, you may revisit some earlier actions and put them into a more complex situation, such as one involving a partner relationship.

After the warm-up, you can select an idea from one of the chapters in part II. Again, you would review and develop it in subsequent classes. Or you may decide to start work on a dance with story and music from part III after the warm-up. Fortunate children whose classes run for 35 to 40 minutes may be able to experience a warm-up (part I), a short time with some aspect of part II, and some work on a dance from part III during one session.

Once you have decided on the content, you can make a lesson plan incorporating the teaching progressions that are given throughout the book. You can copy the relevant tables, poems, and so forth from the book to go with your plans.

Working and developing dances over time are valuable for the children's involvement and long-term learning. Some ideas may be completed in a shorter time, and others will take longer. But introducing, reviewing, and developing materials from class to class are key.

From the outcome of the first lesson, the second lesson will develop. What skills and concepts do you need to review, and how? What ideas should you add? With help from the materials in the book, you can provide your classes with a variety of creative dance experiences, thus meeting the needs of the children—and enjoying this rewarding experience yourself.

A good dance lesson has variety. The children need to experience a range of actions so that various body parts and muscles are worked. They need to work sometimes intensely at great speed and with power, sometimes slowly and gently. They need to use lots of space and to learn to work in a group. They also need to develop their peripheral vision, spot an open space, dodge an object or classmate, and come to an abrupt halt. They need to dance alone at times, and at other times sort out their ideas with a partner or in a small group.

Children need to dance about many things—real, imaginary, funny, happy, and sad. Mostly they need to develop their ideas over time to let things gel physically and mentally—and to change their minds.

ACKNOWLEDGMENTS

My gratitude is extended to the people who helped in various ways to shape this book:

Dr. Joyce Boorman taught me much about children and dancing over many years.

Jackie Best-Walushka, my co-teacher, helped me to clarify the teaching processes, and contributed some delightful dances.

Dr. Tim Hopper triggered the writing of the book by insisting that I put some of my resources onto paper.

Jo Vickers, Dr. Qingbin Li, and Gang Tao captured the photographs of the children dancing—a difficult task in a room full of moving bodies!

Sheila MacMillan made all the text additions and corrections on the computer; noticing errors that I missed.

John Carline showed great patience when I needed material to be scanned or photocopied "now."

Gayle Kassing, Bethany Bentley, and the staff at Human Kinetics took a rough manuscript and helped me to give it form.

All the children I work with every week whose energy and delight in dancing inspire me to continue to develop new ideas.

PART I

Introduction to Teaching Creative Dance

Chapter 1, Teaching and Assessing Creative Dance, has two purposes: to introduce and describe movement analysis and to offer some general guidelines for assessing creative dance. The dance material in this book is based on Rudolf Laban's analysis of human movement. Chapter 1 explains the content and meaning of body awareness, dynamic awareness, spatial awareness, and relationship awareness. When you are planning a lesson and need further information about the concepts involved in a particular dance in later chapters, this movement analysis should provide clarification. The second part of the chapter offers some insights into the challenges of assessing children in creative dance, followed by observation tips and the benefits of using rubrics to evaluate how your students are progressing in their knowledge and performance of dance.

Chapter 2, Introductory Activities, describes age-appropriate rhythmic traveling activities to use in the first few minutes of a class. Teaching progressions are included. Developed over a series of classes, each warm-up increases the children's heart rates, channels their energy, and improves their footwork and rhythmic skills for creative dance.

Teaching
and Assessing
Creative Dance

Some of my distinct memories as a new teacher, with potentially good ideas but little knowledge of teaching process, are of panic! Many faces looked expectantly my way, but I wasn't sure how to proceed. I still experience feelings of worry, excitement, and nervous anticipation prior to starting a new term, but I have come to the conclusion that this is part and parcel of being a teacher.

The best preparation for teaching creative dance is to know your material thoroughly and have a lesson plan with key ideas to explore, including steps for processing those ideas with the students. Know exactly what you are going to do the moment the students enter the room, and have the music ready. This eases the somewhat hurried transition from, for example, moving from a language arts class to the gymnasium a few moments later. I learned to have extra material ready in the event of a breakdown of a plan or in case I rushed too quickly through my lesson, a tendency in new teachers.

In those days I did not have many resources at my disposal and spent a great deal of time listening to music, searching for pieces that I could use. (I still do that, but I enjoy it.) The abundance of material in this book, along with the music resources suggested, should provide a jumping-off point for new teachers and perhaps extend possibilities for those with experience.

Even if a dance idea was not working very well, I had the feeling that it would if only I could clarify my teaching process. Some classes develop better than others. I honestly think it is important to think "What could I have done better or differently?" rather than thinking the children are at fault.

So, I persisted. The reactions of the children who clearly remembered concepts explored during the previous class, together with their desire to continue convinced me that teaching creative dance was worth the effort. Watching as they became involved in a story and became confident enough to take risks was exciting. Watching them develop their skills and ability to express ideas was rewarding.

Gradually, my fear of trying new ideas faded. Now I am excited when I am starting new dances. Teaching creative dance requires belief in what you are doing. In turn, the students will believe in what they are learning.

The first part of this chapter describes the four areas of movement analysis, which are important for understanding both the teaching process and the learning possibilities in creative dance. The vast information in this section will be useful for developing lessons based on material in the chapters that follow. The latter part of this chapter introduces some ideas for assessment and provides sources of further information.

Movement Analysis

The dance material in this book is based on Rudolf Laban's (1879-1958) analysis of movement. This framework can be a guide when planning, teaching, and assessing progress in creative dance. If you know exactly which concepts are important for exploration in each dance idea, the children will be challenged over time to extend the range and quality of their movement. Those same concepts will also be the focus for the movement aspects of assessment.

There are four areas in movement analysis:

1. Body awareness: what the body is doing
2. Dynamic (or effort) awareness: how the body is moving
3. Spatial awareness: where the body is moving
4. Relationship awareness: with whom or with what the body is moving

These four areas are interrelated as you help children to explore action words selected for a particular dance idea by emphasizing aspects of dynamics, space, and relationships. This process opens up possibilities within movement cognitively and physically and provides choices for the children.

Body Awareness

What the body is doing

Creative dance is the expressive area of physical education, and its action vocabulary is large. Whereas in games a player runs or shuffles to project, receive, or guard a ball, a space, or another player, in dance there are many ways and reasons to travel. Rush, flee, and dart are all runs, but each is used for a unique purpose and to convey a unique meaning. There are shades of meaning as each action is altered by the way it is performed dynamically, spatially, and in relationship with others.

The focus of body awareness is on the use of the body as actions are explored. These may be whole-body actions (such as jump, spin, and freeze) or isolated actions of a particular part of the body (such as reach, punch, or kick).

Dynamic (Effort) Awareness

How the body is moving

Laban divided effort into four categories: weight, time, space, and flow. With younger or less experienced children, I concentrate more on the areas of weight and time.

Weight: Firm to Fine

Weight, the degree of bodily tension required for performing an action, is measured on a continuum from firm to fine. Firm tension involves tight and powerful muscles. Fine tension involves a light tension in the muscles and soft touch. In daily life, we tend to operate somewhere in the middle—neither totally powerful nor very fine. The intent in dance development is to help the children to extend their dynamic range, so often the dances will explore the contrast between firm movement and fine movement.

Some actions are essentially firm, such as punch and explode. Others are fine, like tremble and float. However, many actions may be either firm or fine, so lots of exploration can occur with these words. Spin and open are good examples of this. In the Battle of the Seasons dance for 6- to 8-year-olds (see page 123), the children work on the difference between turning powerfully and turning lightly to contrast the cold of winter and the warmth of spring.

Time: Sudden to Sustained

Actions are also performed along a time continuum from sudden to sustained. Sudden involves an immediate, often surprising, action. At the other end of the continuum, the body takes time to execute a single action; the movement is sustained, lingering, and ongoing. In the vocabulary, some actions are sudden, such as freeze, bounce, and stamp; others are sustained, like settle and sink. Many can be explored at either end of the continuum. The Changes dance for 9- to 11-year-olds (see page 168) helps children to explore with a partner and a rubber band the action opposites of open and close, expand and contract, and rise and sink with sudden and sustained movement.

Some children are naturally sudden movers, while others have to work at moving suddenly, so the intent is to extend their range. Young children have a hard time sustaining an action because it requires control and concentration.

All actions have both weight and time. Skipping is sudden (lots of skips) and may be fine, but if the intent is to show power or anger, it becomes sudden and firm in the body (but with light feet). A turning action has room for exploration. It could be sudden and firm, sudden and fine, sustained and firm, or sustained and fine, depending on the context of the dance.

Contrasting opening and closing with a rubber band in the Changes dance.

Space: Curved or Linear

The spatial factor within effort is more difficult for younger, less experienced children, but it's something that can be introduced as their understanding of movement develops. An arm gesture, for example, can move away from the body in a curved (roundabout) fashion, or it can move directly outward in a linear (direct) way. The sparkle jumps so enjoyed by children from the age of 8 or 9 require the arms to thrust directly from the chest until fully extended above the body, then to return directly inward. This takes practice because many tend to fling their arms around and out instead. The Wizards dance for 7- to 9-year-olds (see page 132) works with direct extensions into space as the children try to remember the order of a spell.

Flow: Free or Bound

The body can move freely in a continuous motion, or movement can be interrupted and come to an abrupt halt, binding the flow. During the last part of the Miners dance for 10- to 12-year-olds (see page 183), the children whirl in what appears to be an unstoppable motion, then bind their movement, interrupting the flow. The older children enjoy this difficult challenge. You can introduce the concept of flow by exploring speedy tumbling with the body close to the floor and then suddenly halting the movement, binding it in unexpected positions. This requires good muscle control.

Spatial Awareness
Where the body is moving

Where the body moves has many possibilities for explorations:

- Personal and general space
- Directions

- Pathways
- Levels
- Body bases
- Body shapes
- Spatial prepositions
- Extensions into space

TIP

Choose a specific type of pathway to explore with the class, because the open-ended statement of "Make a pathway" causes random responses without conscious thought from the children.

Personal and General Space

Nonlocomotor actions occur in the children's personal space. They can shiver, rise, spin, pause, or sink within their personal bubbles around their bodies. Traveling actions, many jumps, and often turning actions are examples of movements into general space.

The ability to move more freely and safely in general space develops as a result of practice and with regular reminders from you, the teacher. You might notice that when a child has been working on mastering a traveling action and starts to show good quality of movement, the quality is compromised once he is asked to focus on moving along a particular pathway. With reminders and ongoing practice, the what and where come together.

Directions

The use of directions (forward, backward, sideways, up, and down) is exciting for young children. The body is designed for forward travel, so if a child is asked to run or skip or creep, she will go forward. Just as toddlers are delighted when they discover that (with great concentration) they can walk backward, the 4- to 6-year-olds enjoy mastering backward skipping.

It helps if young children establish the rhythm of skipping forward and then change to a backward skip rather than starting from a standstill. In this case, they learn to change direction first. Traveling backward is tricky because of a child's high center of gravity, and they tip over easily. Plenty of reminders are needed about checking for an empty space behind them. The dance Pattern to Cure a Headache for 5- to 7-year-olds (see page 103) is about doing everything backward, and children in this age group love it!

Pathways

A pathway is the pattern made on the floor when traveling (a person can make a pathway in the air with gestures too). It may be a direct, straight line; a series of short, straight lines; an organized pattern of straight lines with sharp corners (zig-zags); a curved, meandering path; or a circle. In northern climates, children can relate to pathways in the context of footprints left in the snow; similarly, those familiar with beaches and deserts know about tracks in sand. Imagining dipping feet in bright red paint, thus leaving footprints, helps children to think about making a particular pathway.

If a pathway is a key element in a dance with story, there is a reason for using that particular path that the children will remember. In the Queen's Guards dance for 4- to 6-year-olds (see page 85), the guards skip in circular paths around their sentry boxes, and this idea helps the children to skip in a circle. The Snowstorm (a dance for 5- to 7-year-olds; see page 99) explores meandering pathways as the gentle wind blows the snowflakes before the onset of a blizzard. The path may be specifically linear as in the Archers for 7- to 9-year-olds (see page 128), where each archer, loaded with an imaginary quiver and arrows, pursues a foe.

With younger children, it is better to focus on either an aspect of direction or a pathway in one dance. Trying to involve both tends to be confusing. They need plenty of experience before they can concentrate on executing a particular pathway while also changing direction.

Levels

Levels are a concept that young children can grasp, especially for times of stillness (for example, skipping along and then freezing in a high or low shape). As with early language comprehension, it pays to work with the opposites of high and low before adding the medium level.

Some actions, such as darting, are at a medium level. Jumps can take the body high, whereas tumbles take the body over the floor at a low level. Much of the action vocabulary, such as twirl, wobble, or release, can be explored with the use of different levels. It is through this exploration that children learn that there are choices and will begin to use these possibilities at opportune times. One example is when a child discovers that he can rise from a low to a medium level instead of the more common low to high level.

Body Bases

An area of space exploration that uses different levels is that of body bases. Children 6 to 8 years of age can understand and enjoy playing with making shapes that are standing, sitting, kneeling, or lying. A standing shape can involve one or both feet touching the floor. Children can be guided in experimenting with interesting ways of achieving this: A crouch balancing on one foot with the other leg extended is one way of making a low standing shape. Sitting shapes must have only part of the buttocks in contact with the floor; non-weight-bearing parts can be extended or tucked. Kneeling requires balance on one or both knees, and many body shapes are possible. Lying shapes allow only part of the trunk to take the weight, and these shapes require awareness of bodily tension in order to be interesting.

A dance idea called Building Castles that I sometimes work on with 6- to 8-year-olds shows the thinking involved when exploring body bases. The bricks are variations of standing, sitting, kneeling, and lying shapes. At different points in the dance, the children rush together quickly in groups (not prearranged) and attach to one another as they attempt to build a castle. When they rush into a group of four, a brick of each body base must be represented. In other words, one child must be standing, one sitting, one kneeling, and one lying. It is fascinating to watch how quickly some of them make shape adjustments to make it work.

Stretching into a low, wide shape.

Body Shapes

As a dance student, I remembered the four basic body shapes as wall, ball, pin, and screw. In other words, the body can be wide in a variety of shapes, at different levels, and on different bases. Round shapes curl around the center of the body. Narrow shapes are as long and thin as possible, whether vertical, horizontal, or even diagonal. A twist requires the trunk to face more than one front so that if the lower body faces one way, the upper body faces another. The Sheriff and the Cowboy dance for 10- to 12-year-olds (see page 174) involves jumping over and then hiding behind wide, round, narrow, and twisted features in a ghost town.

Spatial Prepositions

Prepositions that represent spatial concepts, such as over and under, above and below, and close to and far from, make for interesting explorations for children aged seven and older. They have to be helped to see and feel the difference between just being low and being under something, for example. The Mirage dance for 9- to 11-year-olds (see page 164) works with the idea of being over the space below, under the space above, and surrounding the space behind; then it gives the sense of hiding away from space.

Extensions Into Space

Parts of the body can reach into spaces above, below, in front, behind, and to either side, often causing a limb to be out of its normal position. A delightful early exploration of extensions happens when a young child discovers that she can balance on two hands and one foot and purposely extend the free leg above and behind. The Space Stealers for 7- to 9-year-olds (see page 136) explores filling spaces around the body by making three-dimensional shapes. Exploration of this concept makes children aware of their extremities and body shapes in space.

Relationship Awareness
With whom and with what the body moves

In dance, a relationship can be with a partner, with two others, or with a group. The possibilities of leading and following, meeting and parting, splitting, mirroring, contrasting, and being in canon and unison are enormous. Some dances, especially for very young children, are individual with no direct relationship other than moving safely in a space occupied by a whole class. As they mature socially, children can start simple meeting-and-parting or leading-and-following relationships with partners. When there are two or more children dancing in a relationship, there is an opportunity for working on contrasting levels, shapes, and bases. In Rice Krispies for ages 4 to 6 years (see page 88), each of the three rice krispies is at a different level in the cereal bowl, even when they pop and change their shapes. Older children enjoy the give-and-take of composing dances in small groups, usually within a set of parameters.

A dance may be individual but with an imaginary partner. In the 5- to 7-year-olds' dance The Snowstorm (see page 99), the wind is the imaginary force that triggers first the gentle and later the vigorous movements of the snowflakes. In the Archers dance for 7- to 9-year-olds (see page 128), the escaping foe is imaginary but can almost be seen as the result of the actions of his real partner.

A relationship can also exist between a child and an object—though this again may be an imaginary one. Props need to be selected with an eye toward safety because situations in which many children are moving quickly with objects could pose a problem. I have used props such as light fabric scarves, paper plates, wands, small boxes, umbrellas, rubber bands, jester sticks, periscopes, stars, bells, and dowel sticks (with experienced children). The majority of props are homemade so that they are light and free of sharp edges.

Assessing Creative Dance

Each school board has its own criteria and language for assessment for the program of studies, and you will need to know these criteria and terms from the outset. Following are general guidelines for assessment of your classes.

Even when a child reaches the mature stage of motor skill development, increasingly complex use of these skills continues far beyond elementary schooling. In most

TIP
Explore the movement content of a dance with the class before introducing a prop (the same applies to individual work leading into partner relationships). Once their bodies have a sense of the movement concepts involved, the prop can enhance the movement and give a new focus for a dancing body.

subject areas, the written or drawn pieces of work can be evaluated and compared to later efforts. In creative dance, children are on the move and it is difficult even for an experienced teacher to observe each child all the time, especially if the class is large. The children's dances cannot be put in a binder, displayed on the wall, or taken home for further reflection.

These characteristics of creative dance make assessment challenging. At the same time you are learning to recognize the various stages of motor skill development, you are learning which aspects of the children's movement to evaluate. It is comforting to know that practice helps! As you continue to work with your classes, your observation skills will improve, making assessment easier.

In our dance program, many children start at the age of 4 and remain with us until they are 12 or 13. Teaching the same child over an 8-year period has been a good lesson in reserving judgment. Time and again, an apparently less-talented child has surprised us, often as late as the age of 10, by suddenly putting it all together and emerging as a keen and capable dancer.

The question of what to evaluate often arises. There are motorically delayed children who have difficulty with skipping, despite plenty of encouragement and practice. Yet some of those children show strength in other areas: original body shaping, control, good movement memory, comprehension of concepts, focus, and expression. Once they catch up motorically, they are in good stead because they have not been judged on motor skills alone and their self-concept is intact. Assessment should be ongoing, gathered in a variety of contexts, and gathered through the use of various strategies. It should reflect a child's ability in relation to curricular goals up to the time of reporting. Assessment practices should be used in encouraging a child to learn.

Here are some suggestions for accurate observation and assessment of children:

• Select two to four children to observe in detail during one class. The children concerned need to remain unaware of any assessment or they might behave differently than usual. If time permits, anecdotal notes can be made during class and reviewed later. If not, you can jot down notes as soon as possible after the class.

• If possible, ask a colleague to videotape as you teach a class. This offers two benefits. First, you can watch the recording more than once, allowing you to note behaviors that you might have missed during the live version. Second, a recording can be a great help in evaluating aspects of your teaching process. You might be alerted to some strategies of your teaching process that you need to rethink.

• Children should be aware of the parameters for a dance that will be assessed before they work on it. Those parameters become your foci for assessment.

• When older children perform dances that will be assessed, it is beneficial if each group can show it twice. This lets you know if they can replicate the dance and allows a second chance to observe aspects that you might have missed during the first performance.

A rubric is an assessment tool for creative dance that allows you to describe each level of quality of comprehension, performance, partner or group work, and effort at points along a continuum from the very best to the poorest work. This assessment strategy shows the child and parent what each of these levels looks like and encourages the child to strive for improvement (see table 1.1).

With a rubric as a basis, you can insert the particulars for any dance. Strategies for involving the children in developing their ability to observe others objectively are suggested at various points during the teaching process of dance ideas in this book.

Dr. Tim Hopper, associate professor in the school of exercise science, physical and health education at the University of Victoria in British Columbia, has some excellent tools on his Web site: http://education2.uvic.ca/Faculty/thopper/Dance/Dance.htm. I had the pleasure of working with Dr. Hopper when he was a doctoral student at the

TABLE 1.1 Sample Rubric

	Excellent	Proficient	Minimal	Insufficient
Dance content	Demonstrates in-depth understanding of dance concepts involved.	Demonstrates strong understanding of dance concepts involved.	Demonstrates limited understanding of dance concepts involved.	Demonstrates insufficient understanding of dance concepts involved.
Dance performance	Always shows confidence, expression, accuracy.	Generally shows confidence, expression, accuracy.	Is less confident and expressive. Often has errors.	Lacks confidence and ability to express. Has many errors.
Partner and group work	Always works well as a group member. Able to lead and to follow. Contributes and motivates.	Generally works well as a group member. Often leads and follows. Often contributes and motivates.	Sometimes works well as a group member. Occasionally leads and follows. Occasionally contributes and motivates.	Rarely works well as a group member. Rarely leads or follows. Rarely contributes or motivates.
Effort	Applies extra effort (student initiated).	Consistently applies effort (student and teacher initiated).	Effort is inconsistent (teacher initiated).	Rarely applies effort.

University of Alberta. Dr. Hopper's expertise is in teaching games for understanding. His enthusiasm and knowledge in that area provided a good foundation for extending his knowledge of creative dance. When he took a position at the University of Victoria, Dr. Hopper took some of my dance materials to use with his education students, and his Web site contains clips of preservice teachers performing each section of task progression up to the final completed dance with their classes. Also included are music files, assessment documents, and assessment ideas for creative dance, so the Web site functions as a practical resource in your teaching.

It is important to remember that each child has different strengths and progresses at a different pace, thus the need for a variety of assessment strategies implemented over the course of the school year.

Introductory Activities

The activities described in this chapter are meant to be done in the first few minutes of each class. When children enter the gym space, they want to go, to move quickly. The activities that take place at the start of the class set the pace for the rest of the lesson and help to channel the children's energy and focus them on some of the action vocabulary of the lesson—in this instance, dance. If you waste no time in starting the activity, the children become accustomed to being active immediately. One method is to start with a rhythmic traveling pattern: Select a traveling action appropriate for the age group and gradually develop it by exploring a spatial or dynamic aspect and possibly add a partner relationship.

This is one time in teaching when I have the children travel from one end of the space to the other. This allows enough room for the children to repeat an action (at speed) several times in order to establish a rhythm. And many of the traveling actions involve exploring new floor patterns, which require a clear space. This method of working also allows children to develop their sense of timing. Gradually, with practice and age, the children learn to be ready to move a set number of beats (such as two or four) after the children ahead of them. This kind of work helps them musically, which benefits their development of dances with complex pieces of music in another part of the lesson. It is also a challenge that they enjoy.

A vigorous introductory activity gets the children's bodies moving and their minds thoroughly awakened so that they are ready to work freely during the exploration that will take place in the main part of the lesson. One way you can develop an introductory activity is to select a traveling action appropriate for the age and developmental level of the children. Over time (a few minutes at the start of each class), you can add an aspect that will make it more complex, challenging, and interesting. The trick is to do this gradually; first be sure that the children are fluent with the action itself before increasing the level of difficulty by adding, for example, a spatial aspect, such as a pathway. If the children perform the traveling action fluently, they can focus on where they are going. Next, you can introduce a relationship aspect. If a child is fluent with the action and has mastered a new pathway, he can focus on dealing with another person. You need to add these levels of difficulty gradually over time by working on a traveling action for a few minutes at the start of each class. You can judge when to introduce the next stage. Of course, the extent to which any traveling pattern may be developed depends on several factors; an important factor is the age of the children. You would not, for example, expect 5-year-olds to master a combination traveling pattern (e.g., run 4 strides, bounce 4 beats) in a consistent zigzag floor pattern while matching a partner! But, with appropriate

Growing from a small shape and ready to travel.

experiences, you can set the foundation for more complex ideas that students can try at a later (often a *much* later) date.

You should select high-quality music with the right tempo for the traveling action and for the size of the children. It is very difficult for a young child to adjust the speed of movement if the music is too fast or too slow. An older child can, at times, add height or distance to an action in order to stay with the rhythm. A younger child might not be able to adjust her natural traveling speed to an inappropriate tempo. I have suggested music that is appropriate for each introductory activity. See appendix A for information on where to find the music referenced in this chapter.

It is best for the children to practice the action individually at first, even if the activity will be done eventually with a partner. When practicing the action first, remember that any action (skip, gallop, bounce, run) is made more difficult with the addition of the following elements:

Space

- A change of direction (backward, sideways)
- A focus on pathways (curves, zigzags)
- A change in levels (high to low)

Effort

- A change of time (sudden or sustained)
- A change of weight (firm or fine tension)
- A change of flow (bound or free)
- A combination of actions (e.g., run for 4, bounce for 4)

Relationship

- A relationship (e.g., meeting and parting)
- A combination of any of the previous elements (e.g., skip in a zigzag pathway while matching a partner)

Once the chosen action is fairly fluent, you can add one of the complicating factors if it is developmentally appropriate, then add another element later. Here are examples:

- Skip (action)
- Skip forward and backward (action and change of direction)
- Skip with change of direction while meeting and parting with a partner (action, change of direction, and relationship)

You may work with the children on one traveling pattern at the start of several classes, then move on to developing another one for a few classes, preferably involving a different action. You can revisit the previously learned material at a later date.

The children remember and look forward to practicing the introductory activity they are currently exploring. When they hear the music cue, they can enter the gym and get going. It is rewarding when, for example, 5- to 7-year-olds who have been working on skipping backward turn around as they cross the threshold of the gym and enter backward! Likewise, you can see the joy in 8- to 10-year-olds who rush to the end of the gym to find partners and start galloping, changing the front every 4 beats.

The following materials suggested for introductory activities are cumulative and reflect what children can learn to do physically, cognitively, and socially during that particular year.

Each year new things become possible—sometimes a new action, sometimes a new way to use an old action. Look at the ideas for the previous grade, and use your own

TIP

The children will learn better and enjoy the process more if they spend a short but intense time on an introductory activity at the start of each dance class. The learning is cumulative, so distributing progressions over several lessons allows the children time to internalize, allows time for review (a very important aspect of learning), and ensures that a child who is absent for a session does not miss out on the development of a complex pattern. In addition, too much time spent on one activity causes physical and mental fatigue, frustration, and a reduction in the quality of the movement. Short, frequent attempts with maximum focus and energy lead to long-term learning.

Partners trying to match their gallops.

ideas as well. For example, between the ages of 4 and 6, children develop the ability to skip backward. Later in the year, they can use this newfound skill in a meeting-and-parting relationship with a partner. This activity is not described for 5- to 7-year-olds, though it could be very appropriate at the start of the year. The activities for ages 5 to 7 are those that now become possible but were not previously possible.

Previously covered skills and concepts can be explored in more open contexts, such as in the development of a dance. Notice that Pattern to Cure a Headache, a dance for 5- to 7-year-olds, is all about backward movements: stepping slowly, spinning quickly, and bouncing to a rhythm. At ages 4 to 6 years, it was enough just going backward!

The following introductory activities contain teaching progressions for rhythmic traveling actions constituting the warm-up for the first few minutes of each class. This high level of activity should cause the children's heart rates to rise. Then they will be ready to concentrate on whatever you have selected to do next. This may be to start a new dance or to review and continue with one from the previous class. For each activity, music suggestions are listed, followed by the name of the music artist. For example, for the skipping activity, "Baby Beluga" is the name of the song, and Raffi is the name of the artist.

Introductory Activities for Ages 4 to 6

The range in terms of development and previous experience at this age is evident. Some children can skip and gallop, others pick up quickly given the opportunity, and a few might not be developmentally ready to skip until partway through the year. All the children can still enjoy trying to go backward or meeting and parting with a partner. Given encouragement, time, and opportunity, the action will come once a child is developmentally ready.

Actions
- Skip (rhythmic, high knees, light feet)
- Gallop (sideways, legs meeting in the middle of each upward action)

SKIPPING

MUSIC SUGGESTIONS

Baby Beluga: Raffi

Pennywhistle Jig: James Galway and Henry Mancini

TEACHING STRATEGIES

First focus on the quality of the action so that the children skip with energy, bringing the knees high in front of the body and always landing lightly on the feet. At the beginning of the year, some of the children might not have developed a skipping action. With opportunity for practice and a focus on lifting the knees high, each child will learn to skip as soon as he or she is developmentally ready.

From here, you may introduce several ideas over time:

- Add a relationship: leading and following.
- Add a change of direction: backward and forward.
- Add a relationship: changing direction with a partner.
- Add a relationship: meeting and parting.
- Add a pathway: corners.

Add a Relationship: Leading and Following

This is one of the earlier relationships that children should develop because the focus is on the action and the fact that each child is either being followed or following. It demands that the children start accommodating a partner because one child may cover more ground with each skip and lose the partner! Each child needs to experience being both leader and follower. At a later date, you may introduce changing from one role to the other without stopping. When the leader wants to become the follower, he turns around (180 degrees) and the following child responds by doing the same, thus becoming the leader. With practice, the children will learn to do this without interrupting the flow of their skipping.

Skipping with knees high in front of the body.

Add a Change of Direction: Backward and Forward

Let the children skip forward to establish a rhythm and then try skipping backward. This is more difficult than it sounds because a young child has a high center of gravity and has difficulty with balance when moving backward. To compensate, emphasize pulling knees away from the floor and leading the action with the buttocks. Practice moving from forward into backward and backward into forward so that the children learn to make smooth transitions from one direction into another.

Add a Relationship: Changing Direction With a Partner

When the children appear to be ready, they can practice traveling backward and forward with a partner. Two children face each other fairly close together. One child starts to skip forward, causing the other to skip backward. They decide when to reverse the procedure. To avoid collisions, it helps to have all the pairs facing north and south for this at first.

Add a Relationship: Meeting and Parting

For this relationship, the partners start away from each other, skip forward to meet, then skip backward to part. An excellent piece of music for this is "Les Petites Marionettes" by Raffi.

Add a Floor Pattern: Corners

Skipping diagonally from one corner to another sounds so easy, but several factors get in the way. Young children are still developing their perception of space, and few young children skip in a straight line!

(continued)

SKIPPING (continued)

DESCRIPTION

Start the children at one corner of the space, and point to the diagonally opposite corner. Skip to that corner with them, then up the side of the room, to arrive at a new corner (see figure 2.1).

Next, send two or three children off at a time, then eventually one at a time every few beats. Try from the new corner. When it appears that the children understand the concept and the movement, they can start in two groups, one at each corner (see figure 2.2).

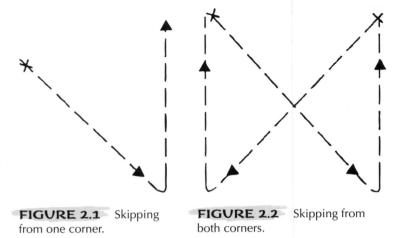

FIGURE 2.1 Skipping from one corner.

FIGURE 2.2 Skipping from both corners.

GALLOPING SIDEWAYS

TEACHING STRATEGIES

Work at first on the quality of the action so that the children learn to travel with one side of the body leading and with their legs meeting in the middle of the action (rather than crossing). They should practice leading with each side of the body and stop fairly effectively by bending the knees.

Add a Relationship: Matching

This is easier than matching a skip (see the skill for children 6 to 8 years of age) because the children are facing each other and can see their partners. Two children face each other in a ready-to-gallop position, knowing which way they will travel by stretching the leading foot to that side. As they gallop, they try to match each other as their legs snap together in the middle of each galloping action. Later they can learn to gallop one way for 8 beats, freeze and clap for 8 beats, gallop the other way for 8 beats, and so on.

Add a Floor Pattern: Corners

The progression should follow that for skipping: First all the children gallop from one corner diagonally to the opposite corner (see figure 2.1). When they are ready, they can start in two groups, one on each corner (see figure 2.2).

Introductory Activities for Ages 5 to 7

The awareness of space and relationships is more developed at this age. This means the children are ready for more interesting pathways and can observe a partner as they try to match a galloping action. They can start and stop more readily, so a combination action pattern is introduced. You may wish to use some suggestions for the 4- to 6-year-olds, plus the following activities.

Actions

- Skip (rhythmic, high knees, light feet)
- Gallop (sideways, legs meeting in the middle of each upward action)
- Run (rhythmic, feet coming high behind thighs, on toes)
- Bounce (two feet to two feet, light landings)

SKIPPING

MUSIC SUGGESTIONS

Oats and Beans and Barley: Raffi

Pennywhistle Jig: James Galway and Henry Mancini

TEACHING STRATEGIES

After a quick skipping practice with reminders for quality, you may do the following:

- Add a pathway: zigzags.
- Add a pathway: small circles.

Add a Pathway: Zigzags

This is easier if there are some parallel lines on the gym floor to help the children learn the length of each zig (see figure 2.3). If necessary, use chalk or tape.

Encourage maintenance of a high-quality skipping action and sharp turns to change the pathway. At these ages, a consistent zigzag can be achieved with 4 skips for each zig and 4 skips for each zag. When they are older, the children can experiment with uneven patterns and other variations.

Add a Pathway: Small Circles

Add spatial aspects of small circles (pathways) and a combination of actions: skip and skip and turn (see figure 2.4).

This pathway involves skipping for 4 and skipping while turning a tiny circle (on the spot) for 4, skipping again for 4, and skipping while turning a tiny circle for 4, but turning the other way.

Some children might turn one way only at first but can learn to recognize, by watching, when another child turns first one way, then the other way. This tends to be less confusing than left and right at this age.

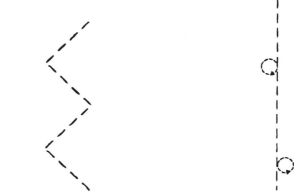

FIGURE 2.3 Zigzag skips.

FIGURE 2.4 Skipping and then turning on the spot.

GALLOPING

After a quick review of galloping individually, add a relationship: matching. By now, children should have a more fluent sideways galloping action and can start by facing a partner and galloping a fair distance. Encourage them to watch each other so that they can match when their legs are apart and together. When they reach the end of the space, the two can separate and peel off, galloping alone to return to the starting point (see figure 2.5).

In this way, their pathway will not interfere with other pairs who are galloping down the space. At some later date, experiment with timing. Set each pair off 8 beats after the preceding pair while the next pair gets ready. Several pairs of children may travel down the space at one time, depending on its width.

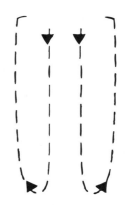

FIGURE 2.5 Peeling off.

RUNNING

This is an even, rhythmic run involving a slight spring so that the children learn to take a running step to each beat of the music.

As they try this to a rhythm set with claves or drums, encourage the children to work on their toes, with light landings. Also encourage keeping the chest up (so that they do not lean too far forward) and kicking each foot behind the body, pointing the toe. Some children might be unaware of what is happening to their legs and toes once those body parts are out of sight behind the body, so learning and remembering to kick behind while extending the ankles require practice, reminders, and even a visual check by each child. Often, a quick demonstration by a few children who are light, rhythmic, and bodily aware can help other children.

BOUNCING

This action is a jump from two feet to two feet and may be on the spot or traveling in a variety of pathways. Encourage a springy action with extension of legs and toes in the air and bending of the ankles, knees, and hips for silent landings. As with the run, the children enjoy practicing this to a beat.

VARIATIONS

- Add a combination of actions: run, bounce. In their own spaces, with your guidance of a clear, steady rhythm, the children can practice running for 7 beats, landing softly on two feet for the 8th beat. When they have the idea, they can add a bounce to make a repetitive pattern (see figure 2.6). The children can do this easily in general space as they find open spaces to run in. And as with some of the other traveling introductory activities, they can also do this action down the length of the room.
- Add a relationship: matching. A later development is working in pairs. Starting next to (but not holding on to) a partner, the children can run (travel) for 8 beats and bounce (on the spot) for 8 beats, run again, and so on while keeping level with a partner. This involves adjusting how far each child travels while running in order to remain level with the partner. They derive a lot of satisfaction from this and from the light, springy pattern itself. Again, the pairs may peel off at the end of the space and return (still doing the pattern) out of the line of traffic.

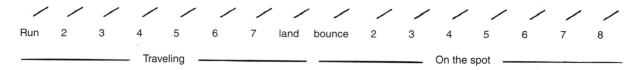

FIGURE 2.6   Run for 8 beats, bounce for 8 beats.

Introductory Activities for Ages 6 to 8

The children enjoy more complex partner relationships at this age in part because they are able to adjust their actions to accommodate another person's possibly slower or faster pace. Now, with a clear teaching process, they can combine pathways and relationships. You may wish to use some suggestions used for the 5- to 7-year-olds, plus the following activities.

Actions

- Skip (rhythmic, high knees, light feet)
- Gallop (sideways, legs meeting in the middle of each upward action)
- Run (rhythmic, feet coming high behind thighs, on toes)
- Bounce (two feet to two feet, light landings)

MUSIC SUGGESTIONS

New River Train: Raffi

Pennywhistle Jig: James Galway and Henry Mancini

TEACHING STRATEGIES

After a review of skipping lightly with high knees, you may do the following:

- Add a relationship: matching knees.
- Add a floor pattern and relationship: zigzags and crossing.
- Add a floor pattern and relationship: zigzags and matching.

Add a Relationship: Matching Knees

You can introduce this by asking the children to stand next to their partners and try to skip along so that their knees match. There are two possible ways to do this, so the success rate is high! A pair can match by having their left knees up at the same time, then the right, or by having the inside knees (or closest) up at the same time, then outside knees (or farthest). After some experimenting, the children could watch a pair showing one answer, verbalize what they saw, then try it. Do the same with the other response. Because you are able to adjust your skips, you can clarify the process by partnering with a child to demonstrate while verbalizing the action.

Matching knees involves considerable adjustment between the children. Some children skip higher or farther than others because of differences in springiness, stride length, or size. In order to match, one or both partners have to be aware of what the other is doing and make adjustments accordingly. Also, it is hard to get going from a standstill, but trial and error, observation, and your guidance give them the tools to solve the problem!

Some children might not be totally ready to adjust their movement to that of a partner. If the partner *is* aware, she will do the adjusting and may help the other child to understand what is going on. Occasionally a child will be oblivious to the task of matching for several sessions but catch up once she is developmentally ready. You may judge when to try this introductory activity according to the developmental progress of the group.

Partners skipping, matching right then left knees.

(continued)

Add a Floor Pattern and a Relationship: Zigzags and Crossing

Before adding a partner, the children should have recent experience of skipping in zigzags (see the activity for ages 5 to 7 years). The children sometimes need to see this pattern (figure 2.7) because it is difficult to verbalize it with few words!

In opposite zigzags, if two children start facing the same way but about four feet (a little over a meter) apart (a pair of parallel lines on the gym floor helps), and the two skip forward at the same time in a diagonal path to the opposite line, thus passing each other, this is one zig. Then, each turns sharply and skips across to the previous line, and so on. If you are one of the pair, you can adjust the skipping to match that of the child so that the others may learn from a clear example.

Let the children try this down the length of the space, returning up the sides. As with other partner relationships in a matching situation, each has to adjust the size of the skip to make it work. One suggestion that helps those performing crossing zigzags is that the partners take turns crossing in front and behind each other. In this way, if one child is about to zoom ahead, he may shorten the length of the skip when it is the partner's turn to cross in front. I sometimes draw the pattern on the chalkboard (a piece of chalk in each hand) so the children can *see* the shape a series of crossing zigzags makes (it's diamonds!).

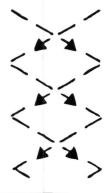

FIGURE 2.7 Opposite zigzags.

Add a Floor Pattern and Relationship: Zigzags and Matching

After a review of skipping in a zigzag pattern individually, the children can try to match each other as they skip along the same pathway (see figure 2.8). This involves some of the adjustments necessary for crossing zigzags. Now the child on the outside of the corner turn must increase his skip length while the inside child has to make her steps closer together. Practice and experience solve many problems!

FIGURE 2.8 Matching zigzags.

GALLOPING

After a short review of galloping sideways, you may do the following:

- Add a change of front.
- Add a change of front and relationship of matching.

Add a Change of Front

Start the class at one end of the room, spaced out across its width, all facing one way (wall). Ask the children to travel down the room, seeing if they can switch partway so that they continue down the room but facing the other wall. This requires a little experimentation, so allow a few tries, encouraging the children to turn sharply so that the flow of galloping is not interrupted. As they catch on (remember that a clear demonstration from a child accompanied by your verbalization often helps), encourage maintenance of a high-quality gallop. Advise holding the arms out to the sides of the body, drawing them in sharply on the 180-degree turn, then extending them again. Once the children master the change of front, try it every 8 beats if there is sufficient space in the room. Traveling on a diagonal pathway from corner to corner adds distance.

Add a Relationship: Matching

Now the children start facing a partner. They gallop opposite each other for 8 beats, change front, and gallop facing away from each other for the next 8 beats, change again, and so on (see figure 2.9).

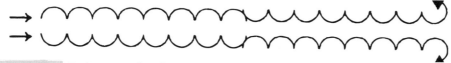

FIGURE 2.9 Facing toward and away.

RUN AND BOUNCE

(Combination of Actions)

After a practice of light rhythmic running and light springy bouncing, link the two to form alternating phrases of 4 runs, 4 bounces, 4 runs, and so on.

Add a Relationship: Matching

Starting side by side with a partner (not too close), the pair can try running for 4, bouncing on the spot for 4, and so on, while they remain level with each other. This requires more control than the 8 and 8 pattern for 5- to 7-year-olds.

Introductory Activities for Ages 7 to 9

In this age range, multiple patterns become possible. Motorically, the children should be reaching the mature stage of their fundamental skills. You can introduce the exciting action of the skip change of step. New patterns can be developed with the old actions of skip, gallop, run, and bounce now that the children are able to focus on quicker changes of front, enter 4 beats after the previous person or group, make increasingly complex floor patterns, and concentrate on more precise footwork. You may wish to use some suggestions used for the 6- to 8-year-olds, plus the following activities.

Actions

- Skip (rhythmic, high knees, light feet)
- Gallop (sideways, legs meeting in the middle of each upward action)
- Skip change of step (alternating so that the lead leg changes)
- Run (rhythmic, feet coming high behind thighs, on toes)
- Bounce (two feet to two feet, light landings)
- Heel–toe (place one heel gently on floor, lift knee, place toe gently on the same spot)

SKIP CHANGE OF STEP

MUSIC SUGGESTION

Radetzky March: Johann Strauss Sr.

TEACHING STRATEGIES

This is an exciting new pattern for this age group, but for many of the children, it needs to be introduced in parts rather than as a whole.

Briefly practice a sideways gallop first, then change to a forward gallop so that the children can feel the similarity of the rhythm but see the difference in the action. Then ask the children to choose which leg will be the leader and which will be the follower. Giving them a regular rhythm on the drum or claves, ask them to travel forward lightly through the space with a galloping action so that one leg always goes first and the following leg catches up but does not overtake the movement. Try this with the other leg as the leader (or bossy leg).

(continued)

Next, as they travel, ask them to change the bossy leg every now and again so that a child may gallop forward with one leg leading for 4 or 5 gallops, then, without interrupting the flow, the other leg takes over. Gradually encourage them to reduce the number of steps they take before switching the leading leg. The takeover step will be a skip; the knee of the following leg lifts as it comes through to become the leading leg. Eventually the children will be able to switch the leading leg after every pattern:

Right leg leads, left catches up, right leg leads.

Skip, left leg leads, right catches up, left leg leads.

Skip . . . and so on.

Watching a couple of children whose footwork is clear can help the others, but it is better to let each child progress at his or her own rate rather than foster a feeling of incompetence by pushing the development too quickly.

Over time, and always after a review of the skip change of step, you may do the following:

- Add a relationship: matching.
- Add a relationship: leading and following.
- Add a pathway: line, curves, circles.

Add a Relationship: Matching

Starting next to a partner, children decide which leg will lead for the first pattern and try to match each other. They may decide to change the leading leg every two patterns or every pattern.

Add a Relationship: Leading and Following

Children explore ways in which the follower can take over as leader without interrupting the flow of the traveling. One way is for the follower to increase the distance covered with one pattern and overtake the leader. In another method, the leader would turn sharply (180 degrees) during the skip part, causing the follower to turn also and become the leader.

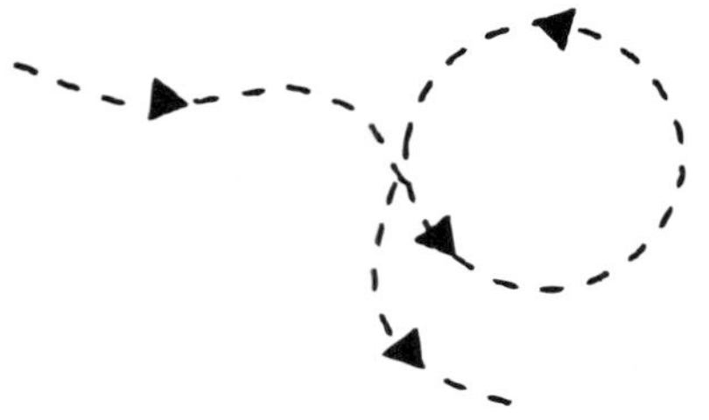

Add a Pathway: Lines, Curves, and Circles

Individually, let the children experiment with traveling in straight lines, turning sharply in order to go into a new space. Then let them experiment with curved pathways and large circles (see figure 2.10).

FIGURE 2.10 Curved pathway.

When the children show that they are making clearly chosen pathways rather than traveling randomly, add the relationship of leading and following again. This would obviously be introduced at a later date than the original leading and following of the second option, where the focus was on learning how to lead and follow. Now the children must be capable of leading and following (adjusting the size of their steps to stay behind the leader and being able to change leaders easily) in order to focus on the pathway.

GALLOPING

MUSIC SUGGESTION

Pie in the Face Polka: Henry Mancini and James Galway

TEACHING STRATEGIES

After a quick review of light individual galloping sideways and a review of change of front (see suggestions for ages 6 to 8 years), experiment with changing front every 4 gallops.

Add a Relationship: Matching

Children start by facing a partner at one end of the space. They gallop (matching) for 4 counts, change front so that the two are back to back as they travel for the next 4 gallops, and so on, all the while continuing on the same line of direction down the room.

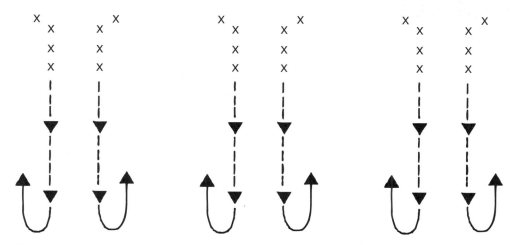

FIGURE 2.11 Matching gallops in pairs. Several groups can work simultaneously.

By now, the children should be able to set themselves off with each successive pair starting 4 beats after the pair ahead. So that they have plenty of practice and exercise, you may organize several groups to operate at once (see figure 2.11).

SKIPPING

After a quick review of skipping to emphasize clear, light footwork, do the following:

- Add a pathway: zigzag and a partner relationship of crossing.
- Add a pathway: zigzag and a partner relationship of meeting and parting.
- Add a variety of pathways: new zigzags.
- Add new zigzags and a partner relationship: matching, crossing, or meeting and parting.

Add a Pathway and Partner Relationship: Zigzag and Crossing

Review a spatial aspect of zigzag with 4 skips to every zig (see instructions for ages 5 to 7 years), then add the partner relationship of crossing (see instructions for ages 6 to 8 years). Reviewing this previously learned pattern may help the children with the following variations.

Add a Pathway and Partner Relationship: Zigzag and Meeting and Parting

In this variation, the pair stands facing the same way but a few feet apart. They skip forward along a diagonal toward each other for 4 skips, turn sharply, and skip along a diagonal away from each other for 4 skips (see figure 2.12). This is more complex than the previous zigzag because the partners cannot see each other for much of the time, so they have to be accurate with their diagonals and their length of skips.

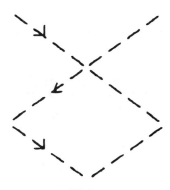

FIGURE 2.12 Zigzags meeting and parting.

Add a Variety of Pathways: New Zigzags

At this age the children can experiment with uneven zigzags individually at first. Drawing a few possibilities on the chalkboard (taken from what the children do as well as new ones) helps them to clarify their ideas (see figure 2.13). Notice that some patterns are uneven, causing the pathway to drift across the floor; others are even.

(continued)

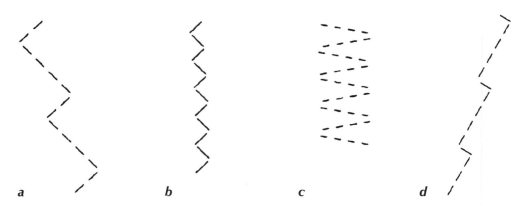

FIGURE 2.13 *(a)* 2 skips, 4 skips; *(b)* 1 skip, 1 skip; *(c)* 4 skips, 4 skips; *(d)* 1 skip, 4 skips.

Add New Zigzags and Partner Relationship: Matching, Crossing, Meeting, and Parting

At a later date, partners could work together in developing a new pattern that could involve matching with an uneven path, crossing with an even path, or meeting and parting with an even path (see figure 2.14).

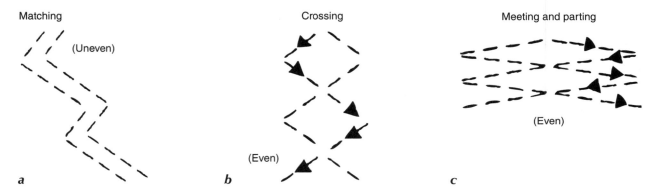

FIGURE 2.14 *(a)* Matching with uneven path; *(b)* crossing with even path; *(c)* meeting and parting with even path.

RUNNING AND BOUNCING

(combination of actions)

MUSIC SUGGESTION

Pie in the Face Polka: Henry Mancini and James Galway

TEACHING STRATEGIES

After a review of running and bouncing for 4 beats each, with reminders about working on the balls of the feet and pointing each toe as it kicks behind the body during the run, instruct children to do the following:

- Add a pathway: zigzags.
- Add a relationship: crossing, matching, or meeting and parting.

Add a Pathway: Zigzags

Starting in their own spaces, and to a clear rhythm, let the children experiment with running for 4 beats, then bouncing on the spot for 4 beats (repeat), making a zig during the first run and a zag during the second (see figure 2.15). Give time for several patterns so that the children can establish a pathway. The children will learn that they have to turn slightly with each bounce, ready to face the new diagonal.

Add a Relationship: Crossing, Matching, or Meeting and Parting

If the children have had experience with these relationships (see Skipping for 7- to 9-year-olds), each pair could choose from the outset which relationship to try. If not, you will need to process them one at a time and let the children choose later (see figure 2.16).

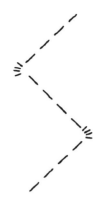

FIGURE 2.15 Zigzags alternating 4 runs and 4 bounces.

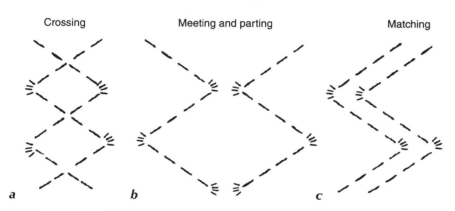

Crossing   Meeting and parting   Matching

a   b   c

FIGURE 2.16 *(a)* Crossing; *(b)* meeting and parting; *(c)* matching.

RUNNING AND STOPPING
(combination of actions)

MUSIC SUGGESTION

Pie in the Face Polka: Henry Mancini and James Galway

TEACHING STRATEGIES

This sounds as though it should be easier than the previous pattern, but it is not! To do this, the children have to learn to land and hold, ready for the next run. With an 8 and 8 pattern, let them practice running lightly and rhythmically for 7 beats, landing on two feet for the 8th beat. They need to keep a light tension in the body during the stop of 8 beats, then spring from two feet back into a run. Practice this using the whole space, then when the children are ready (able to feel the rhythm rather than count it and able to cue the changes themselves), they can start to do this pattern with a partner (matching).

Add a Relationship: Matching

Two children start side by side and travel parallel to each other, matching their running strides. The children can travel the length of the space and peel off as shown for galloping. At a later date, focus on a timing relationship. Starting at one end of the space (several groups), the first child of each group runs for 8, and as he or she lands to stop for 8 beats, the next child of each group starts to run. In this manner, 2 catches up with 1, and as 2 lands, 1 is off running again. This continues down the room as 3 starts, then 4, and so on! It's tricky, but fun.

HEEL-TOE RUNS

(combination of actions)

MUSIC SUGGESTION

Pie in the Face Polka: Henry Mancini and James Galway

TEACHING STRATEGIES

You can practice the new heel–toe skill, combine it with running, and gradually put it into contexts of matching, leading and following, and timing (as in the run–step pattern).

To learn heel–toe, ask the children to start in a space with the weight mainly on one foot and to place the heel of the other foot on a spot next to but a few inches away from the toes of the weight-bearing foot. This is clear when shown to the children, so a verbally described visual demonstration helps. The ankle should be flexed so that the toes reach as far away from the floor as possible and the knee is straight. Then, lifting the knee, the toe can be placed gently on the same spot previously occupied by the heel with the foot extended (pointed) and the knee bent. Repeat this several times, then try with the other foot. Give a clear rhythm so that the children can try a series of heel–toe actions on each foot, learning to transfer the weight each time they change to the opposite foot. Next, establish a pattern of 4 heel–toe actions, followed by a light run for 8 beats, 4 heel–toes on the opposite foot, 8 runs, and so on (heel–toe, heel–toe, heel–toe, heel–toe, run, run, run, run, run, run, run, run). With practice, the children will learn to jump slightly as they land so that they can alternate which foot is ready to heel–toe. Listen to the first few bars of the music to establish the pace, then let the children try the pattern while you cue the changes with a drum or claves.

Add a Relationship: Matching

Starting side by side, two children can travel parallel with each other during the running phrase, and heel–toe next to each other on the spot. Some pairs might be ready to decide whether to heel–toe with each of them using the same side foot (right or left) or to have outside feet working at the same time, then inside. For some, it is enough to make smooth transitions from running into heel–toe and back into running, so the question of which foot should not be pushed as a major issue at this time.

Add a Relationship: Leading and Following

Using the general space, with the partners starting one behind the other, let the children try to heel–toe run as one leads and the other follows. After a few patterns, stop and change leaders. Using the whole space will require the leader to think about where he or she is going in order to move into open spaces.

When the children are fairly proficient, you may wish to use this traveling pattern from the end of the space with each child setting out 8 beats after the previous child (see the timing description for 7- to 9-year-olds in the Running and Stopping activity).

Introductory Activities for Ages 8 to 10

By age 8, children will have had plenty of experience with many of the actions, but the quality of the movement and the distance and height (where appropriate) can always be improved. Regular practice is necessary for their growing bodies so that they can maintain body awareness through to the ends of their limbs and provide opportunities for their increasing strength. Without rhythmic traveling, children tend to get sloppy; they forget how to maintain appropriate tension in their bodies in order to stop suddenly, go suddenly, and make good transitions from one action to the next. They need to increase their endurance. A vigorous few minutes of continuous traveling and jumping, followed by the body of the dance lesson, will help with this aspect of fitness. In addition, the children should engage in activities that cause them to be alert and to think ahead. You may use some suggestions for 7- to 9-year-olds, plus the following activities.

Actions

- Skip (rhythmic, high knees, light feet)
- Gallop (sideways, legs meeting in the middle of each upward action)
- Run (rhythmic, feet coming high behind thighs, on toes)
- Bounce (two feet to two feet, light landings)
- Skip change of step
- Heel–toe (place one heel gently on floor, lift knee, place toe gently on same spot)
- Oranges and bananas (an extension of a skipping action with a curled, then arched, spine)

GALLOPING

Review a sideways gallop, aiming for good height. As always, use light landings. Work on leading with either side of the body, then practice changing front (see instructions for 6- to 8-year-olds for method), but now experiment with changing front every 2 gallops. If this seems to be a problem, offer the choice of changing front either every 4 gallops or every 2 gallops without making either choice appear to be inferior or superior. In this way, each child may be challenged.

Add a relationship of matching, in which the pairs start facing each other and travel,

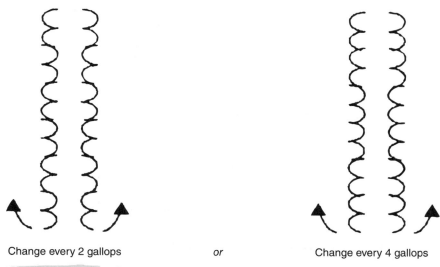

Change every 2 gallops   *or*   Change every 4 gallops

FIGURE 2.17   Change every 2 gallops or change every 4 gallops.

matching their gallops, while changing front (so facing each other, then facing away; see figure 2.17). In 8- to 10-year-olds, the children's timing should be good, so they can tackle the partner relationships *plus* start to travel 4 beats after the previous pair.

HEEL-TOE RUNS

(combination action)

MUSIC SUGGESTION

Pie in the Face Polka: Henry Mancini and James Galway

TEACHING STRATEGIES

After a review of the heel–toe action (see instructions for 7- to 9-year-olds) and rhythmic running, work toward sequences of 4 and 4: heel–toe, heel–toe, run, run, run, run. This is more difficult than the younger age group's

(continued)

8 and 8 because the pattern changes so quickly. You may decide to offer choice initially so that some children work on 8 and 8, others on 4 and 4.

Over time you could do the following:

- Add a relationship of matching or leading and following.
- Add a pathway of zigzags and work toward a partner relationship.
- Add a change of direction: forward, sideways.

Add a Relationship: Matching or Leading and Following

With a partner, the children can travel down the space, matching their heel–toe running pattern and choosing whether to have the right and then left legs in unison or the inside and then outside legs matching. As usual, for traveling down the space, they can peel off at the end. By this stage, the 8- to 10-year-olds will be capable of working with the music, each pair starting 8 or 4 beats after the previous pair.

FIGURE 2.18 Heel–toe for 8 beats, run for 8 beats.

Using the general space, the children can start in 2s, one behind the other, and use the traveling pattern to lead and follow. They can experiment with various ways of changing leaders. One possible method is for the leader to run more or less on the spot when he wishes to switch, allowing the follower to run past and take over. Another way is for the leader to turn 180 degrees during the 4 runs, causing the follower to turn also, becoming the leader. As the children become proficient, continue to encourage good use of the space.

Add a Pathway: Zigzags and Work Toward a Partner Relationship

The pathway is a familiar one, but it becomes challenging again with the heel–toe pattern. Individually at first, try either an 8 and 8 or a 4 and 4 pattern of heel–toe runs in a zigzag pathway (see figures 2.18 and 2.19).

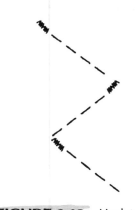

FIGURE 2.19 Heel–toe for 4 beats, run for 4 beats.

At a later date, the children can work in twos and try traveling side by side or meeting and parting or crossing, with the heel–toe runs in a zigzag pathway (see figure 2.20). These choices use familiar pathways and relationships but with a more complicated traveling pattern.

Add a Change of Direction: Forward and Sideways

Experiment with just the running at first. Establish a light, rhythmic run forward to the rhythm with a drum or claves. Next try running toward the right, then left. As their skill improves, try a sequence of 8 runs forward, 8 to one side, and 8 to the other side (repeat).

Notice that 8 beats per phrase are used again rather than the 4 that were used in the leading and following and zigzag situations. Now, an added difficulty of change of direction is the focus, so a longer phrase will allow them time to think ahead and change direction effectively.

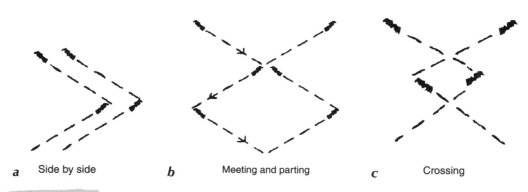

a Side by side   *b* Meeting and parting   *c* Crossing

FIGURE 2.20 *(a)* Side by side; *(b)* meeting and parting; *(c)* crossing.

Developing their own sequences of running with change of direction and then working with a partner is a whole area that can be explored without the heel–toe. To return to the combination action, link the stationary heel–toes with the runs. Initially it might be helpful for you to choose the order. Here is an example:

8 runs to one side, 4 heel–toes

8 runs forward, 4 heel–toes

8 runs to one side, 4 heel–toes

8 runs to other side, 4 heel–toes (repeat)

Later the children can develop their own order, as long as all directions are used.

RUNNING AND BOUNCING

(combination action)

After a review of each action, then combining the two (see instructions for 7- to 9-year-olds), you can introduce a new idea. Instead of bouncing on the spot 4 times facing one way, ask the class to try doing 2 bounces facing one way and the remaining 2 facing another way. This will take a little practice as they find out how much force is needed to execute a quarter turn without losing the rhythm.

Make sure that they can turn to both the left and the right. Give a rhythm and allow time for practice, giving the children any necessary reminders about maintaining the quality of the jump itself. Now, link this with the run: run, run, run, run, bounce, bounce–turn, bounce, bounce.

Add a Relationship

This is an idea that began as an introductory activity but developed into a dance. It integrates the run–bounce combination, the image of robots, and the music "Second Rendez-Vous" by Jean Michel Jarre. As we worked on the quarter turn between the second and third bounces, it struck me that the children looked sloppy. So I suggested that they stay very erect and keep their heads still, staring ahead all the time. This caused them to make their bounces more precise and use the power from their legs to turn and remain straight. We put this robotic bounce, bounce–turn, bounce, bounce back into sequence with the runs—also robotic and good with the music—taking care to move into open spaces. Later, the children started in their own spaces, and I asked about a third of them (scattered throughout the space) to start the pattern while the other two-thirds waited.

Those who began (the switched-on robots) could travel for no more than three patterns, ending purposely next to a stationary, or switched-off, robot. At the end of that bounce pattern, the stationary robot switched on promptly and started the pattern with the run, while the first one switched off. In this way, some were traveling, some were stationary, and all were charged with traveling to different people so that everyone switched on and off regularly.

Another day, to increase the challenge, we changed the point at which the active robot switched off and an inactive one started (see figure 2.21). Now, it was between the second and third bounces! The Jarre music is helpful because it has a robotic, precise sound and rhythm.

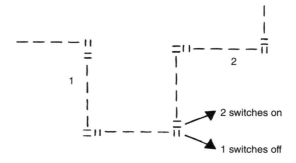

FIGURE 2.21   As 1 switches off, 2 switches on.

SKIP CHANGE OF STEP

For a description of this combination action, see page 23 in the activities for children ages 7 to 9 years.

MUSIC SUGGESTION

Radetzky March: Johann Strauss Sr.

TEACHING STRATEGIES

After a review of the action individually using the whole space, then working briefly in twos leading and following with a focus on pathways (see instructions for 7- to 9-year-olds), you can introduce the following.

Add a Relationship: Traveling in Groups

Working in groups of 3, 4, or 5, with each group member taking turns as the leader, let them practice traveling as a group, making sure that their footwork matches (left or right foot leading). Once they have sorted this out, suggest traveling as a pack rather than in a long line (which they tend to do when following a leader).

Experiment with traveling in a direct pathway, then in a curved one. Then let the groups see what they can do.

Another day, try the idea of entering and exiting the space in their groups. Each group starts ready to go, at the edge of the space (see figure 2.22). Now the challenge is to ensure that there is always at least one group traveling in the space at any time, but not too many groups at once. The current leaders decide (by watching the space and other groups) when to take their group into the space, what pathway to make, and when and where to exit the group. This is good for their observation skills because each decision depends on the activities of the other groups and the situation constantly changes.

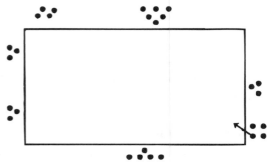

FIGURE 2.22 Groups ready to enter the space.

ORANGES AND BANANAS

(combination action)

The name for this liberating traveling action was coined many years ago by Dr. Joyce Boorman.

MUSIC SUGGESTION

L'ouverture-Éclair: André Gagnon

TEACHING STRATEGIES

This is one of the most enjoyable traveling actions for the 8- to 12-year-olds because it allows the children to fly.

To develop the action, ask the children to keep their arms close to their sides and skip all over the space. Next, they choose which knee will always be, as usual, high in front of the body. The other leg, instead of coming in front on the next skip, extends behind the body. So the legs alternate: one in front, one behind with a skipping rhythm. The children should experiment with this for a while to establish the rhythm, then try with the other leg leading to see if this feels more comfortable. Once the rhythm is present, add the arms, asking the children to see what they want to do. This might produce a variety of results, but usually some children will try to extend their arms up and out each time the leg extends behind.

To clarify the action, ask the children to stand on one leg, other knee high in front of the body and with a curled back, head down, and arms tucked in. As the high knee steps down, the body extends up and back, head is up, arms swing up and out, and free leg extends behind the body. The children can use this pattern in traveling the length of the room or across diagonally (corners) to give room to establish the rhythm and aim for height and distance. This action takes a while to develop and will come and go in some people. Given feedback and encouragement and short intense practices, the children learn to maximize the round body shape of the orange and thrust strongly up and out on the banana. Once a child has felt a true stretch, she will try to achieve it again because it feels good and assists in a sense of flight.

Orange (tucked arms and rounded spine).

Banana (arched spine).

Introductory Activities for Ages 9 to 11

Children 9 to 11 years of age can benefit from regularly revisiting a variety of traveling actions during the introductory part of their dance classes, and the material for 8- to 10-year-olds is useful here too. In every instance, you should encourage improvement in the quality of the movement and give refining tasks, focusing on aspects that need attention. When ready, the children may be further challenged by the addition of more complicating factors such as these:

- Continue to expand their vocabulary of rhythmic, precise whole-body jumps. The oranges and bananas action introduced for ages 8 to 10 is an example in which the upper body has a specific role. A new example is sparkle jump.
- Work with shorter phrases of each action within a combination pattern (e.g., run, run, bounce, bounce, run, run). This demands clear footwork and thinking ahead, which should be expected at this age.
- Add a new variable to an old pattern.
- Use a traveling pattern as the basis for working in small groups (such as galloping with a change of front or traveling in groups of 3, 4, or 5). This demands that the children find a mutual height or distance as they gallop, as well as select a group formation and pathway.
- Work with a combination action and a change of effort and direction (e.g., running forward quickly into stepping backward slowly).

Actions
- Skip (rhythmic, high knees, light feet)
- Gallop (sideways, legs meeting in the middle of each upward action)
- Run (rhythmic, feet coming high behind thighs, on toes)
- Bounce (two feet to two feet, light landings)
- Skip change of step

- Heel-toe (place one heel gently on floor, lift knee, place toe gently on floor on same spot)
- Oranges and bananas (an extension of a skipping action with a curled and then arched spine)
- Sparkle jump (two feet to one foot, upward thrust)

SPARKLE JUMP

MUSIC SUGGESTIONS

Pennywhistle Song: Hans Zimmer

Pour Les Amants: André Gagnon

TEACHING STRATEGIES

A new action that can be explored at this age is a sparkle jump, which, like oranges and bananas, focuses on the specific use of arms.

First, with the children in their own spaces, ask them to push upward from two feet into the air (no running preparation) and land on *one* foot before allowing the second foot to touch the floor. Let them experiment with this for a while, encouraging a directly upward thrust rather than trying to move forward. Suggest that they alternate the landing foot so that the pattern becomes two feet to one foot, other foot touches down, push from two feet to other foot, second foot touches down. Or, if you prefer, two feet to right foot, left touches down, push from two feet to left foot, right touches down.

As the children get the rhythm and aim for height, there will be time (and it will happen naturally) for the free leg—the one that does not land first—to extend behind the body.

Now they will need their arms to counteract the leg action and complete the extension. Ask them to stand still and place their hands close to their chests, palms facing outward, elbows tucked in to their sides (a demonstration will help here). Keeping their feet planted on the floor for now, they should try shooting the arms upward until they are fully extended but reaching slightly to one side.

They will bring the arms back down, elbows leading, and shoot the arms directly upward to the other side.

Now they alternate this, reaching to one corner of the space above with a firm, direct thrust, then to the other. Add this to the jump. When the thrust is to the right, the left leg will extend and vice versa. The children will travel a little with each jump, but the aim is for full upward extension each time, heads up, backs stretched, and a tilt to the right or left.

Reaching high with sparkle jumps.

Try this with music using the whole space, then from the end of the space with each child setting out 8 or 4 beats after the person ahead.

RUNNING AND BOUNCING

(combination action)

MUSIC SUGGESTION

Pie in the Face Polka: Henry Mancini and James Galway

TEACHING STRATEGIES

After a review of the rhythmic running action and bouncing, encouraging light landings in both cases, try alternating 2 runs and then 2 bounces. Once the children are fluent in this, the class can travel from the end of the space in twos, matching with a partner and peeling off at the end.

At another time, you may wish to use the whole space and work on pathways by adding a quarter turn during the second bounce: run, run, bounce, bounce–turn, run, run, and so on.

RUNNING AND STOPPING

(combination action)

MUSIC SUGGESTION

Second Rendez-Vous: Jean Michel Jarre

TEACHING STRATEGIES

This combination was introduced for 7- to 9-year-olds but with longer phrases of 8 runs and a stop for 8 beats. Now you may wish to try a pattern of 4 runs landing on two feet from the last run, then hold a still, alert position for 4 beats, springing onto one foot to start the next running phrase (see figure 2.23).

Initially the children can practice this in the general space; then, over time, they can develop it in several ways.

- The children can travel from the end of the space individually, each child starting 4 beats after the previous person. In this way, the catch-up effect will occur (see figure 2.24).

- At another time, the children can work in twos or threes using the whole space. Starting in a close line, child 1 runs 4 strides. As she stops for 4 counts, child 2 follows with a run for 4 strides. As 2 stops for 4 counts, 1 runs again and 3 starts the run. As one child catches up, the previous child travels ahead. Fun!

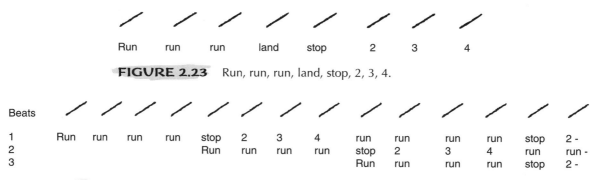

Run   run   run   land   stop   2   3   4

FIGURE 2.23   Run, run, run, land, stop, 2, 3, 4.

Beats														
1	Run	run	run	run	stop	2	3	4	run	run	run	run	stop	2 -
2					Run	run	run	run	stop	2	3	4	run	run -
3								Run	run	run	run	stop	2 -	

FIGURE 2.24   The catch-up effect.

HEEL-TOE RUNS
(combination action)

MUSIC SUGGESTION

Pie in the Face Polka: Henry Mancini and James Galway

TEACHING STRATEGIES

For 8- to 10-year-olds, a change of direction was suggested as a challenge to the heel–toe, run pattern, and the children worked individually to develop their own sequences. Now, after a review of the heel–toe, run action and doing it forward and sideways, they can work with a partner. First try matching. Each pair can develop a sequence of 4 and 4 (heel–toe, heel–toe, run, run, run, run), choosing their own order of directions. Here's an example:

Forward, left, forward, right
or
Right, left, right, forward

Once a pair has decided on a plan of action, they can repeat it several times with the music.

Another way to explore this pattern is by not matching, or by matching for part of the time. Here's an example: forward matching, parting as one child travels left and the other right, meeting as they reverse the sideways travel, forward matching, and so on (see figure 2.25).

FIGURE 2.25 Matching, then parting.

ORANGES AND BANANAS

MUSIC SUGGESTION

L'ouverture-Éclair: André Gagnon

TEACHING STRATEGIES

This delightful jump to a skipping rhythm can stand frequent repetitions as the children become more powerful from experience and growth. After an individual review, they can work with a partner so that both parts of the action—the curled orange and the extended banana—match. This is exciting because it produces a lovely feeling of unison when two children fly down the space in time with each other. As with many partner-work situations, the two have to experiment and cooperate to find a good way of starting out so that they match (shall we extend first, or curl first?), and then adjust their height and distance in order to remain together. The partners can see each other peripherally without actually turning their heads, which helps. If the children are traveling in pairs from the end of the space, several pairs may work at once, and each successive pair starts 4 beats after the previous one. This keeps them focused and ensures plenty of activity.

GALLOPING

MUSIC SUGGESTION

Pennywhistle Jig: James Galway and Henry Mancini

TEACHING STRATEGIES

This activity uses a traveling pattern as the basis for working in small groups. Galloping has been a regularly used introductory activity: individually, matching, then with a change of front individually into matching in twos.

Now the children can try traveling in groups of 3, 4, or 5. First, they need to gallop as a small group without changing front to become accustomed to the amount of force each group member needs to exert to travel as a unified group. When they are ready, they can try galloping with a change of front, first with 4 gallops, change of front, 4 gallops, and so on. Then, if they feel brave enough, they can use 2 gallops, change of front (repeat). Also, each group can decide whether its members all wish to face the same way as they travel and change or have one or more children back to back or facing the rest.

RUSHING AND STEPPING

MUSIC SUGGESTION

With Kate by the Sea: White Eisenstein

Or other music with clear alternating phrases of fast and slow

TEACHING STRATEGIES

This activity introduces working with a combination pattern and a change of effort and direction. By 9 years old, the children have enough control over their bodies to be able to change from sudden to sustained effort in an instant without losing rhythm.

Starting in their own spaces, children practice a light, fast running over the floor (a sense of rushing, but as lightly as possible) while weaving in and out of each other. Try it again, always starting high on toes, maintaining light tension throughout the body; take a deep breath and go. Repeat this several times until the children are traveling at speed, moving in and out of each other, and able to stop suddenly and quietly. (This kind of running is part of both The Mirage and Changes in chapter 12, Dances for Ages 9 to 11.) Next, ask them to run again; this time, at the end of the run, they change from moving very quickly to taking two slow, controlled steps backward. Practice this several times, aiming for a sudden, light run into two sustained, light backward steps. Now suggest that the children try turning 180 degrees as they take the first step so that the *steps* travel backward but the *children* continue on the same line of travel (see figure 2.26).

Listen to the first part of the music, which consists of 8 phrases of rush–step, step (see figure 2.27).

This will allow the children time to hear the rhythm and the points at which the change of time and direction occur. Then, back in the space, try with the music, encouraging movement into open spaces with each rush. Each child can use all 8 phrases or you may split the class into two groups, 1s and 2s, muddle them up in the space, letting the 1s take the first and alternating phrases, 2s the second and alternating phrases (see figure 2.28).

After the 8 phrases, the music changes. Several ideas could develop here. Both 1s and 2s could rock gently, transferring weight from foot to foot, or try rocking for part of the phrase, followed by a spin. Or, you and the children might have other ideas!

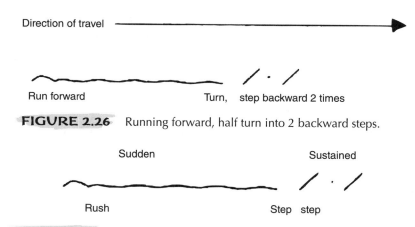

Direction of travel

Run forward — Turn, step backward 2 times

FIGURE 2.26 Running forward, half turn into 2 backward steps.

Sudden — Sustained

Rush — Step step

FIGURE 2.27 Contrasting a sudden rush into 2 sustained backward steps.

(continued)

RUSHING AND STEPPING (continued)

After this section, the rush–step, step phrases return. The musical form is simple: AABAABAABAA, but you can feel the change of time clearly.

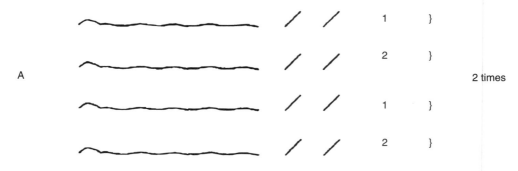

FIGURE 2.28   Traveling on alternating phrases.

Introductory Activities for Ages 10 to 12

The traveling patterns that 8- to 12-year-olds explore fall into two broad categories of movement. One category involves fine motor control and light body tension. This includes patterns such as heel–toe, run, run and bounce and run and stop within a rhythmic framework. The second category involves the explosive actions of the oranges and bananas and the sparkle jump, where the focus is on firm, powerful movement.

The 10- to 12-year-old children should experience both of these kinds of movements and can derive as much satisfaction from the light, precise movement patterns as from the power generated in the explosive actions. The body becomes educated through exploration of the full range of effort qualities. Naturally powerful movers need experiences with fine, delicate movement just as naturally inclined sustained movers need to use sudden movements where appropriate. This education takes place in introductory activities as well as in the development of dance ideas.

For 10- to 12-year-olds using traveling patterns involving both types of movement, the focus continues to be on relationships as they work with partners or in groups, and they continue to develop the aspect of timing that this age group so enjoys: starting and stopping 4 or 2 beats before or after another person. To this end, children ages 10 to 12 may practice and further develop these ideas and gradually add a few new twists. The new ideas are described, but you should revisit patterns involving galloping, heel–toe runs, and so on at intervals and develop them according to the needs and past experiences of the class.

Actions

- Skip (rhythmic, high knees, light feet)
- Gallop (sideways, legs meeting in the middle of each upward action)
- Run (rhythmic, feet coming high behind thighs, on toes)
- Bounce (two feet to two feet, light landings)
- Skip change of step
- Heel–toe (place one heel gently on floor, lift knee, place toe gently on floor on same spot)
- Oranges and bananas (an extension of a skipping action with a curled and then arched spine)
- Sparkle jump (two feet to one foot, upward thrust)

- Leap (one foot to the other, stretch in air, light landing)
- Tumble (transfer of weight over various body surfaces on the floor)

SKIPPING

MUSIC SUGGESTION

Pennywhistle Jig: James Galway and Henry Mancini

TEACHING STRATEGIES

A common action that has not been mentioned since the ideas for the 7-to 9-year-olds is skipping. At this age the children will be capable of varying the power of their skipping by gaining height or distance with each skip, or by skipping very fast. This ability allows them to accommodate to match the pace of a partner easily. Now skipping can be challenging with the addition of a few more complicating factors.

The children should experiment individually with skipping on an even zigzag pathway with 4 skips for each diagonal. Next, they can try to skip forward along the first diagonal, turn sharply, and skip backward along the second one, and so on.

Once they are clear with this pattern, the children can try traveling a parallel pathway in twos. For this, one child starts forward and the other backward so that they travel together but never face the same way.

The description makes this sound easy, but it's deceiving because each child, while adjusting to remain parallel with the partner, has to figure out which way to turn at each corner as well as be able to skip a straight backward pathway!

ORANGES AND BANANAS

(combination action)

MUSIC SUGGESTION

L'ouverture-Éclair: André Gagnon

TEACHING STRATEGIES

Group work is exciting at this age, and the children have the necessary motor skills to coordinate their actions to travel in unison.

Add a Relationship

The children will want a few minutes to practice this jumping traveling action on their own (see description for 8- to 10-year-olds). You should continue to help each child to improve the quality of the movement by focusing on aspects needing work. The children most commonly need reminders to extend their arms fully up to each corner on the banana part of the jump, and some might need to think about stretching the extending leg.

The 9- to 11-year-olds worked on matching the jumping with a partner. The

Three children flying as they match with oranges and bananas.

(continued)

10- to 12-year-olds can do oranges and bananas while traveling in groups of three, four, or five. The group members will have to decide on their group formation, where to go, and whether to start with the curled or extended part of the action so that they are all matching.

This is exciting for both the dancers and you because it feels good to travel through the space powerfully and in unison, and it is lovely to watch. After some practice in groups, you may wish to extend this idea to an entrance-and-exit situation (see ideas for skip change of step for 8- to 10-year-olds).

Add a Turn

At another time, the children could try to turn during the oranges and bananas pattern. Starting at the end of the space, ask the children to see if they can turn 360 degrees as they travel doing oranges and bananas down the space. This will produce a variety of results as they experiment. Somewhere along the line, a few children discover that it is easier to turn during the orange, or tucked, part of the action when the body can turn quickly. This is also something that children at this age will understand, even if they cannot master it immediately. It helps if the children can watch a couple who are turning effectively.

Remind the class to fix their focus on the far wall, start with the banana jump part of the action, then turn as they draw the body in for the orange part so that the next banana action once more faces the far wall. This is fun and develops with short practices over time.

SPARKLE JUMP

MUSIC SUGGESTIONS

Pennywhistle Song: Hans Zimmer

Pour Les Amants: André Gagnon

TEACHING STRATEGIES

The 9- to 11-year-old children started to work on the explosive sparkle jumping action as individuals. Now they can begin to match or mirror the sparkle jumps with a partner.

Add a Relationship

After an individual practice, with a focus on the quality of the action, the children can start to work with partners in a matching situation.

Starting at the end of the space and standing next to a partner (not too close together), the pairs can try to match their jumps so that they both sparkle to high right, then left, and so on. As usual in a partner matching situation, the children have to adjust their movement (timing and distance traveled with each jump) to work in unison. When the pairs are successful in matching, they can also use the musical beat to start 4 or 2 beats after the previous pair.

With several groups working from the end at once, the children will have time for plenty of practice and lots of exercise!

At another time, they could try not matching (also known as mirroring): The child on the right starts by shooting upward to the right, while the child on the left shoots upward to the left. In this manner, the two sparkle alternately away from, then toward, each other. It produces a feeling of unison similar to the matching pattern, but it looks quite different.

LEAP, SPIN, TUMBLE, FREEZE, CLAP, RUN

(action sequence in groups)

MUSIC SUGGESTION

Chanson Pour Petula: André Gagnon

TEACHING STRATEGIES

This introductory activity is a favorite because of a combination of factors: the music, the fast pace, the satisfaction of binding the flow, and the excitement of entering and exiting at just the right moment.

Starting in their own spaces, the children take a couple of preparatory steps, then leap (one foot to the other) as high as they can, landing lightly. Try this several times, reminding them to use their arms to help with height, to stretch in the air, and to bend each knee as they land. Leave this for a minute, and ask them to start in a shape that's ready to spin. Then they spin, traveling as they do so. Try this again, but this time take the spin lower as they travel, until their bodies are right down on the floor. Practice this, encouraging the children to bend their knees as they get lower so that they can transfer their weight onto their buttocks or sides without any bumps. As this transfer of weight improves, encourage more speed so that it is a fast spin to the floor. Now introduce the challenging part. Tell the children that you would like to see them spin really fast, but once they start to tumble over the floor, to stop absolutely and suddenly. As they practice, give reminders about exerting strong body tension in order to bind (stop) the flow of movement. Observing children who are doing so effectively may help others.

Next, ask them all to be ready to spin, and try the phrase together (spinning into open spaces). Verbalize the sequence as they work: "And spin—tumble—freeze."

Challenge the children to freeze at any point during the tumble. They may not be successful at first, but they will start to test themselves. This usually produces more innovative movement as children challenge themselves to bind the flow at any point of a tumble.

Link the leap to the spin, tumble and freeze, then gather to listen to the first part of the music (see figures 2.29 and 2.30).

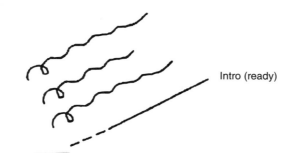

FIGURE 2.29 Ready for the introduction.

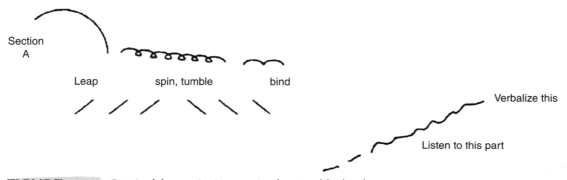

FIGURE 2.30 Part A of the music: Leap, spin, then tumble, bind sequence.

(continued)

After the introduction, where the children freeze ready to move, part A of the music occurs twice. At the start of each A phrase, they will "hear" the leap, spin, then tumble, bind. This is followed by 2 strong sets of 3 beats and a rushing sound.

As the children listen, verbalize the sequence they have practiced (leap, spin, then tumble, bind) and listen to the part that follows. Now, back into spaces, and practice a few times with the first part of the music, holding the binding action until just before the second leap.

Next, ask the children to clap to the rhythm they heard in the music after the bind (see figure 2.31).

From a frozen position on the floor (as if they have just tumbled and stopped), ask them to use the two clapping sets to clap as they rise back to their feet. Ask them to make each firm, sudden clap reach into a different area of space around them while they transfer their weight from the body or buttocks back to the feet. You need to explore this so that the children are changing body shape to reach into spaces and possibly clap the floor too!

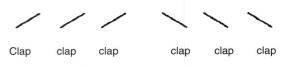

Clap   clap   clap   clap   clap   clap

FIGURE 2.31   Clap three times, clap three times.

Divide the class into two groups, 1s and 2s, and then scatter them into the space. Now 1s will take the first sequence (2s poised ready) and 2s the second. The sequence for each is jump, spin, then tumble, bind. Clap three times, clap three times, rush! (See figure 2.32.)

There are many ways of continuing to develop this. A popular method with the children is to start with 1s at one end of the space, spread along its width, and 2s at the opposite end. Now, 1s leap in, spin, tumble, bind the flow, clap three times, clap three times as they rise, and run to the opposite wall as 2s leap in toward them to start their sequence. This is exciting as the two groups pass through each other. Try this to the first two A sections of the music, then develop the B phrase. The B phrase can be fast, but do a light run from one end of the space to the other so that each group returns to its starting point (see figure 2.33).

The 1s run first, then 2s, each group turning around quickly as they reach the other end because immediately the 1s must be ready to leap back in as part A of the music returns.

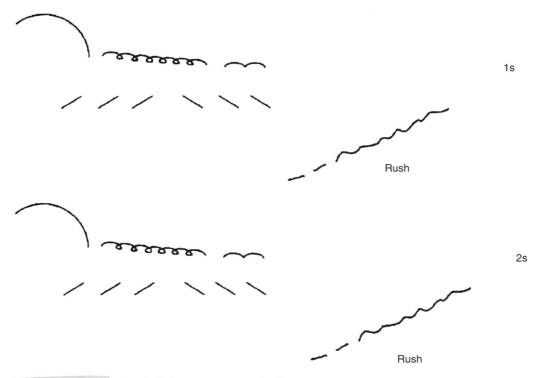

1s

Rush

2s

Rush

FIGURE 2.32   Part A of the music repeated twice.

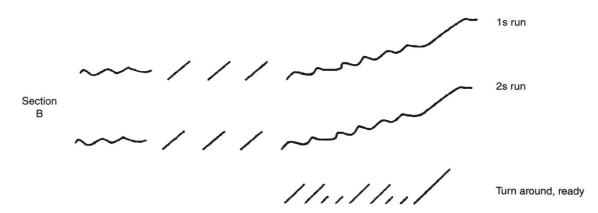

Section
B

1s run

2s run

Turn around, ready

FIGURE 2.33 Part B of the music.

The complete music form is AABAABAAB¹. The B¹ is about half the length of the previous B phrases. The class may decide to switch ends at the same time by running or to each run back into a space and freeze. The timing elements in this fast-paced piece make it both challenging and exciting.

As usual, this introductory activity should be developed over time, allowing for review, repetition, and consolidation. The children may have ideas for when and where the groups travel, but these will not emerge if the process is rushed, completed, and left behind.

PART II

Dances With Literature, Arts, and Rhythm

Once the children are warmed up and ready, it is time to move into the body of the lesson. This can be a good moment to work with action words, rhyme, poetry, and rhythm. Sometimes you can complete the explorations during one class period; other explorations may develop over a series of classes. I tend to follow work of this nature by either starting or continuing a dance with music. In this way, the children have a balance of activity and pace.

Chapter 3 offers ideas for working with action words, with suggestions for appropriate age groups and teaching progressions. A brief section toward the end of this chapter shows ideas for action words through visual aids.

Chapter 4 is about action words too, but now embedded in rhyme. These are fun to teach, easy to remember (for the children and for you), and the basis of short dances developed by each child with guidance from you.

Chapter 5 offers suggestions for poetry and creative dance. Unlike much of the work with action words and action rhymes, poetry involves the expression of images and feelings.

Chapter 6 is about rhythms in single words and phrases, some with images as well. Although carefully selected music could be played as a background for some of the ideas in part II, the majority of the dances evolve through the rhythm of body movement.

Dances
With Action Words
and Visual Aids

Children love to play with ideas in both movement and language and often shun boring words for ones that have more interest. Regularly as I review an idea with young children in which they have turned, they will tell me, "It twirled," even if I have not mentioned *twirl* at all! Older children enjoy exploring the nuances of more complex words, such as *suspend*, *release*, and *toss*, once they are old enough to understand them in a movement context and able to capture them with their bodies.

Because creative dance is expressive, there are many words to choose from in expressing an idea clearly. For example, the body can stop in various ways. *Freeze* implies a sudden, firm stop; *perch* gives a sense of stopping at a higher level on a small base; and *settle* takes time to come gently to a stop.

In table 3.1, the heading for each family of action words gives the intent of the words in the category. For example, all the traveling words take the mover from one place to another, but the action itself, the dynamics and spatial use, will vary depending on the word selected. Table 3.1 is useful as you prepare for classes. It can guide you in ensuring that various kinds of movements are being explored so that the children's movement vocabulary grows. It also helps you to choose appropriate words for the context of the dance.

You can develop a wealth of challenging dance material by exploring action words and linking them to form sequences of movement. You may select the words, or older children can choose the words from a list. Check to ensure the following:

- The words are within the children's level of comprehension both cognitively and physically.

- It is possible to link the words together. For example, *collapse* followed by *settle* would be a poor choice.

- The children will be able to work a variety of body parts.

- The words offer opportunity for contrast in an aspect of space (levels, pathways, directions, and personal and general) or effort (firm and fine, sudden and sustained, free and bound).

TABLE 3.1 Families of Action Words

Traveling actions		Vibratory actions		Jumping actions	
run	slither	shiver	shake	leap	hurl
skip	float	quiver	tremble	toss	bound
creep	gallop	wobble	vibrate	soar	bounce
rush	dart	patter	shudder	pop	fly
flee	slide				hop
skip change of step					

Turning actions		Stopping actions		Percussive actions	
spin	whirl	freeze	hold	stamp	punch
twirl	whip	hover	grip	explode	pound
swivel	tumble	perch	anchor	patter	clap
pivot		pause	suspend		
		settle			

Contracting actions		Expanding actions		Sinking actions	
shrink	shrivel	expand	reach	collapse	sink
close	narrow	grow	open	lower	drip
contract		release	extend	fall	
		spread			

Rising actions	
lift	rise

Adapted from J. Boorman, 1973, *Dance and language experiences with children* (New York: Harcourt Brace), 25.

Here is an example:

Here is an example:

    Traveling: dart

    Stopping: pause

    Jumping: pounce

These three words have potential for some exciting sequences. For a start, each is from a different family so will involve different kinds of movement. Second, there will be a change of effort from the sudden dart to the brief stillness of pause followed by the sudden pounce. Third, a contrast in levels could be developed. Dart travels at a medium level; pause may be low, medium, or high; and pounce may go from low or medium up to high and then finish low. In contrast, consider these words:

    Traveling: run

    Traveling: skip

    Traveling: gallop

These words are just a series of traveling actions, all on feet, all sudden. Boring! Consider this group of words:

    Sinking: fall

    Stopping: settle

    Contracting: shrinking

These would be limiting because once the child had fallen, it would be difficult to settle, an action normally associated with a downward movement. This sequence is interesting:

    Rising: rise

    Turning: spin

    Percussive: explode

The words are from different families; use a variety of body parts; and could involve a focus on change of time (sudden to sustained), weight (firm to fine), and levels.

To enjoy the exploration of movement possibilities within each word and how they may be linked to form a sentence (sequence), the children need a teacher-guided process. You need to awaken the thinking power of the children by progressively challenging them to try new things and to improve the quality of their movement. The children need to physically explore and understand the words and concepts to allow experimentation, discovery, and repetition to occur in order to develop a vocabulary of movement before they form their movement sentences.

EXAMPLE OF EXPLORATION: RISE, SPIN, EXPLODE

1. Explore Rise

Ask the children to start in their own spaces. Giving them several opportunities to have another go, help them to become conscious of what they are doing by asking questions such as these:

- What sort of starting shape did you use (e.g., folded, round)? On what part of the body did you begin (knee, foot, side)?

- Does it start very low, or could it start a little higher?

- Which parts of the body led the action? Where are you looking?

(continued)

> **TIP**
>
> The key to using words productively is for you to select a sequence (three or four words) that allow for contrast in terms of movement exploration through use of body, space, and effort.

EXAMPLE OF EXPLORATION: RISE, SPIN, EXPLODE (continued)

- Do you rise very quickly? Can you rise very slowly?
- How high are you when the action is complete? In what shape did your body finish?

During a few minutes of several attempts with guidance, the children will start to be conscious of what they are doing and how and where. They have to think about it. When they discover that they have choices, they are both cognitively and physically engaged.

2. Explore Spin

- What shape will you start in if you are going to spin? (Try several.)
- Can you spin on the spot? Can you spin while traveling?
- Is the spin all on one level, or could it go from low to high? From high to low? Or can it constantly change?
- Are you wide as you spin or narrow as you spin?
- Can you spin with a lot of power in your body or with a light tension?
- Is the spin always very fast? Can it be slower? Can it change speed?
- Do you have to spin on your feet?

3. Link Rise and Spin

Now choose a starting shape ready to rise. When you have finished rising, go into your spin showing (for example) which action is strong and which is light in your sequence. Freeze at the end. Repeat.

4. Explore Explode

- How will you start?
- Do you finish in a different place?
- Is it really strong and sudden (explosive)?
- What parts of the body help you to look like an explosion in the air? (Arms help in height and distance.)
- What happens if you turn in the air as you explode? What are your legs doing?
- Do both feet land at the same time, or one after the other?
- Hold your finishing shape each time.

Responses to the action word "explode."

5. Link Rise, Spin, Explode

Now be ready to rise and then spin, but this time add explode to your sequence. Find two or three ways to do it differently, *or* work on it so that you can repeat it twice in the same way.

With lots of attempts stimulated by your questions, the children can be exposed to new movement possibilities. With appropriate feedback, they can improve their movement quality. Then they can select from these ideas and form their own sequences. In this way, each child will have a slightly different answer.

The finished sequence may be the end of that particular piece of work or the basis for more exploration such as partner or group work.

Action Word Sentences
for Young Children (Ages 4 to 9)

You can decide on the main focus for the sentence (such as level changes) and bring this to the children's awareness through the exploration. The words should be printed on a board, card, or flip chart to help with their reading skills.

bounce whirl sink	(pathways or sudden and sustained contrast)
skip pause collapse	(directions or pathways)
spin stamp shrink	(firm and fine contrast)
grow creep twirl	(levels)

At first the whole class may develop sentences using one set of words. But once the children have a little experience, have developed some movement memory, and can read, you may explore several words with the whole class, then offer two or three choices of sentences. Task cards are useful here: The children enjoy taking one and then going off to explore it (see figure 3.1).

You are free to circulate, assist, challenge, and be prepared to answer questions ranging from "How do you say this word?" to "Can I do the bottom word first?" After a few minutes of experimentation and practice, you should ask the class to get into their starting shapes, do their sequences, and hold their finishing shapes. With 4- to 7-year-olds, one more repetition may be the end of that particular problem, but 8- to 10-year-olds could go one stage further:

- Find a partner, watch each other's sequence, and try to guess which words he or she used.

- Half the class gathers, watches the other half, and tries to spot someone using your words. Now the other half.

- All the children with the *skip pause collapse* cards gather to watch those using the *grow creep twirl* cards. Look for something interesting (connected with the main focus). Now the other group goes.

As long as the children have something clear to look for and spend a short time watching, this can be beneficial to their observational powers and learning. They are definitely not looking for the best one but for different solutions to a problem.

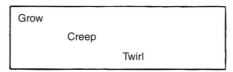

FIGURE 3.1 Sample task cards.

Action Word Sentences for Older Children
(Ages 8 to 12)

An action word for older children can be more challenging, suited to both their physical and verbal understanding. For example, the action "release" (let go) demands a higher level of ability than "grow," which is suited to younger children. Once the children have explored and developed their individual action sequences they can be used as a basis for work in small groups.

release skip hold	(firm and fine contrast)
toss shrivel rise	(sudden and sustained contrast)
whip explode lower	(levels)
spread gallop settle	(pathways)
wobble bounce collapse	(body shape)
open flee perch	(sudden and sustained contrast)
leap shrink lift	(body parts leading the movement)

As you did for the younger children, you should decide on the main focus for the exploration and clarify it during the guided exploration. More difficult words can be introduced as appropriate.

After the initial guided exploration followed by the development of the individual sequence, the children have the basis for more exploration. This can take many forms; you can make the following suggestions to the children:

- In a group of three, quickly review each other's sequences, then make a dance using your sequences where, for example, you start close together and finish far apart.

- In a group of three, after watching each other's sequences, make a dance where one of you will start a sequence, another person waits until person 1 has finished the first word, then person 2 starts, and 3 starts after 2 has finished his first word:

Canon

1. rise	spin	explode		
2.	rise	spin	explode	
3.		rise	spin	explode

- Will you start close together or far apart? Where will you finish?

- In a group of three, watch each other's sequences, then decide which word you would like to do twice as you develop your dance together. Here is an example:

rise	spin	explode	rise
rise	spin	explode	explode

If different action phrases are introduced, explored, and developed fairly regularly, the children become adept at making small but exciting group dances. The situation works well because each child in the group has a sequence developed, so each group member (rather than just the dominant characters) has a contribution to make. They have to work together with this material within whatever limitations you have set for the group dance. If the children work regularly in different groupings, they learn to cooperate and learn from each other.

So far, the process has been for sequences that you have chosen. Once the children have some experience, they can choose some words from a list that you select. Here is an example:

Traveling: rush creep gallop

Turning: spin whip

Expanding: reach release

Stopping: settle anchor

This list has been chosen so that children can explore a contrast between sudden and sustained movement as the main focus.

You guide the children through an exploration of some of the words (printed on a board) through a focus (in this example) of sudden and sustained movement. It is a good idea to link a couple of words occasionally to emphasize possible contrast:

rush	(sudden)
creep	(sustained)
anchor	(a strong and sudden stopping action using several body parts in contact with the floor)
settle	(a fine, gentle, sustained stopping action that, with forward-and-backward and side-to-side movements, takes the body from a higher to a lower place)

TIP
Sometimes I give a couple of examples and ask the children to tell me *why* I might have chosen them. Occasionally I ask the children to make their choices, then tell me quickly before shooting away to start work. In this way I can check for understanding by asking those children who may need clarification which words would be sudden, and so on.

Explore any new words or words that have not received recent attention in the context of sudden and sustained.

Then, from the list on the board, ask each child to choose three words, each from a different family, that could be used to make a sequence showing a clear contrast in time (sudden and sustained).

From this point, the process is similar to the ones previously described, but now the children have choices not only in how they make their sequences but also in the words and the order.

You may review and improve these individual sequences another day and use them as the basis for a partner or group situation. This is good for the children's movement memory, and it also teaches you how they think and remember. Sometimes a child will say, "I've forgotten one of my words, but I know what I did," indicating a kinesthetic memory. Once the child shows the movement, you can help to supply the forgotten word.

Holding her shape after "settling."

Action Sequences as a Basis for Working With Rhythm

There are many ways of working with rhythm. This particular method is described here because it is a progression from exploring action word sequences.

You can choose a poem that has a clear rhythm and is of interest to the children. Here are some possibilities: "Some One" by Walter de la Mare, "Allosaurus" by Dennis Lee, and "Eletelephony" by Laura E. Richards.

Introduce the Poem

The following process is based on an excerpt from Robert Browning's (1812-1899) "The Pied Piper of Hamelin" and developed with 9- to 12-year-olds.

Rats!

They fought the dogs and killed the cats,
And bit the babies in the cradles,
And ate the cheeses out of the vats,
And licked the soup from the cooks' own ladles,
Split open the kegs of salted sprats,
Made nests inside men's Sunday hats
And even spoiled the women's chats
By drowning their speaking
with shrieking and squeaking
In fifty different sharps and flats.

After some initial guided exploration, working on possible use of sudden and sustained contrast, I asked the children to choose one of the following sets of action words:

- drop tumble expand shake
- dart leap freeze swing
- rise creep spin hold

As the children made their choice, I asked that we have three fairly evenly sized groups so that each set of words could be represented. The children went off to develop their sequences with these parameters: They must use the words in the order given, and the contrast between sudden and sustained movement must be clear.

Review Sequences

During the next class, the children reviewed and improved their sequences until they knew them and could repeat them.

Next, the fun part! I asked the class to get into their starting shapes and told them that they would be given 16 beats (letting them hear the pace on the drum), at the end of which their sequences should be complete. This took some trial and error and repetition while each child found places in his or her sequence to make some actions even more sudden and others even more sustained so that the whole phrase could be complete at the end of 16 beats. This part of the process was a great deal of fun and very challenging, so when they were satisfied with the results, we watched each group.

The children gathered to listen to the excerpt of the poem, but only as far as the end of the sixth line (Sunday hats). They were delighted with the words, and by the next class one child knew the entire passage by heart, so a little research might have taken place.

As an intermediate stage to get used to working with the words, they all practiced their sequences to the first four lines of the poem, accompanied by the drum:

          /   /   /   /
They fought the dogs and killed the cats,

          /   /   /   /
And bit the babies in the cradles,

The sudden drop that precedes tumble, expand, shake—one of the action sequences in Rats!

<pre>   /   /   /   /
</pre>
And ate the cheeses out of the vats,
<pre>   /   /   /   /
</pre>
And licked the soup from the cook's own ladles,   (16 beats)

We left it at this point, moving on to other dance ideas in process. But during the next class we reviewed their sequences as previously, then tried them with the accompaniment of the words but with no drum.

Working in Canon

Next, we experimented with working in canon. Those children with the *drop tumble expand shake* phrase became 1s. *Dart leap freeze swing* were 2s, and *rise creep spin hold* were 3s. Each group would start their sequences 4 beats (one line of the poem) *after* the previous group. To increase confidence at this stage, each group was given a third of the space to start in, like groupings in a choir:

1s   They fought . . . ladles

2s   And bit . . . sprats

3s   And ate . . . hats

We experimented with this several times, often with false starts or unexpected breakdowns—frequently caused by me because I jumbled the words! However, the children knew what they were aiming for and knew that they could do it—so they did. When they were clear with their starting and stopping points and showed good quality in their sequences, the three groups muddled themselves up in the space. Now they were confident enough to work independently, knowing their part in the canon sequence.

Make a Plan

The children wanted to use the "rats!" word, so the next week, after a review, we tried various ideas and eventually settled on a plan. In their starting shapes, all the children said, "Rats!" then we inserted (with apologies to Robert Browning) "Rats!" at the end of each line (4 beats) and everybody said it whether they were moving or still. This added two extra beats to each line, so those moving at the time paused in the middle of whatever action they were doing to say, "Rats!" then continued moving:

Rats!

1	They fought the dogs and killed the cats—rats!
1, 2	And bit the babies in the cradles—rats!
1, 2, 3	And ate the cheeses out of the vats—rats!
1, 2, 3	And licked the soup from the cooks' own ladles—rats!
2, 3	Split open the kegs of salted sprats—rats!
3	Made nests inside men's Sunday hats—rats!

Make Adjustments

After this stimulating and challenging few lines of poetry, we decided to change the pace, in keeping with the theme, for the remaining four lines. With contributions from the children and several tested and rejected and tested and modified ideas, the following plan evolved:

- "And even spoiled the women's chats" was narrated very slowly as the children crept away, leaving a big hole in the space.

- In "By drowning their speaking/With shrieking and squeaking," the narration started low and slowly, increasing in pitch and speed as the children turned and then spun into a tight group.

- "In fifty different sharps and flats" was said briskly, emphasizing the beat as the children, a few at a time (some on each beat), leapt high and dropped suddenly into stillness. With a little practice, the children took over the words as well as the movement for these last five lines, so it was a pleasure to watch and listen to them.

Playing with action words on a regular basis helps the children to understand physically and cognitively that they can make choices when they dance. They enjoy being guided through exploration of new words and then choosing an order and deciding, for instance, which words could be sudden or sustained and firm or fine. They enjoy watching half the class showing their finished sequences and pointing out positive aspects, then in turn showing theirs.

Action Words With Visual Aids

As a contribution to the variety of approaches in dance education, occasionally we use visual task cards, which children enjoy very much. You may introduce visual task cards to any age group once the children have a little experience, vocabulary, and confidence to step out on their own.

The idea of seeing what they are doing is familiar to the children because I regularly gather them near the chalkboard to clarify a point visually. An example is the use of space, showing that a child may move into different areas of space each time she travels instead of continuing in one line (see figure 3.2).

Sometimes drawing can clarify a tricky transition in a piece of music or the form the music takes. Mozart's exciting "Turkish March" with its unpredictable repetitions comes to mind. The children enjoy watching me try to draw, especially with a piece of chalk in each hand as I endeavor to illustrate a pathway or a relationship created

Discussing the movement possibilities on a visual aid.

TIP
Working with action words without music or story as security can be intimidating. Start with short explorations, such as a sequence of three words. The exploration could follow the introductory activity when the children are still fresh and be followed by a review of a dance with music. With practice, you will gain confidence because it is exciting to watch the children develop skill in working with words.

by two people! Seeing the result on the board seems to help some of the children, presumably the strong visual learners, and they return to work with renewed vigor. This use of designs and pictures makes it seem sensible at times to use visual shapes as the stimulus for a problem to be solved.

For younger children, you should use simple clear patterns without too much detail (see figure 3.3).

Using one example, the objective must be set. Ask the children to look at the first pattern in figure 3.3a and then to find a space and see what they can do.

With that particular design, many children will spin, traveling as they do so.

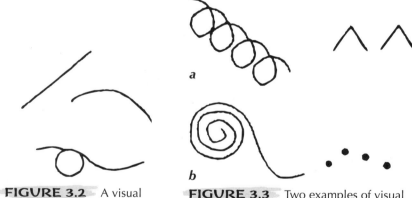

FIGURE 3.2 A visual representation of various pathways to travel.

FIGURE 3.3 Two examples of visual patterns.

These children see the design predominantly as an action. Others see it spatially and may skip along its outline showing the pathway. Often children come up with perfectly appropriate answers that have not occurred to me, teaching me about the flexibility of the young mind.

The pictures will tell them something about what action to do, how many repetitions to have, what pathway to travel, and sometimes how big or how small it should be. You function as a guide to improving the quality of their movement.

Later on in the term, you can give older children (7 years and up) a choice of two or three patterns drawn either on the board or from individual task cards. They can go off to experiment before making a sequence. Sometimes they may share the resulting work with half the class watching, then vice versa. Occasions like this teach me how observant children can be when a watching child says, "He did my card but he started at the other end." In other words, it had been read from right to left (see figure 3.4).

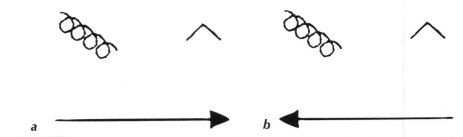

FIGURE 3.4 *(a)* Reading the card from left to right and *(b)* reading the card from right to left.

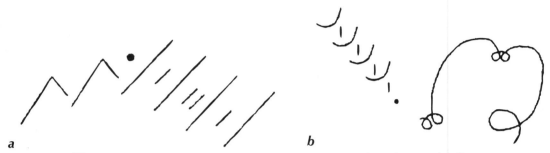

FIGURE 3.5 *(a)* One card with more details; *(b)* another example with more details.

As a later step, you may add mood words. So once children have created their sequences with the use of actions, space, and possibly size or rhythm if there is repetition in the design, they can now explore contrast in time and weight. For example, an action performed in a happy mood would probably be fairly light compared to one that was angry. The words can vary in complexity to suit the knowledge of the children. If the designs are on task cards, you may tailor them to meet individual needs in the class (see figure 3.5).

For children 6 to 10 years of age, work on the actions and use of space to make a sequence, and add contrasting weight and time (figure 3.6).

For 9- to 12-year-olds (figure 3.7), work on the actions and use of space to make a sequence, and add contrasting weight and time.

Here are some other possible combinations:

energetic	bold	delicate
lively	timid	dainty
anxious	soft	vigorous
boisterous	carefree	determined

In the classroom, the children may make their own cards, with the use of crayons, and choose contrasting adjectives to accompany each action.

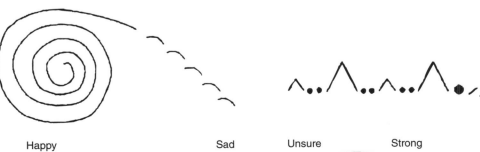

Happy   Sad

FIGURE 3.6 An example of adding two mood words to a card for 6- to 10-year-olds.

Unsure   Strong   Hurried

FIGURE 3.7 An example of a card with three mood words.

Dances With Action Rhymes

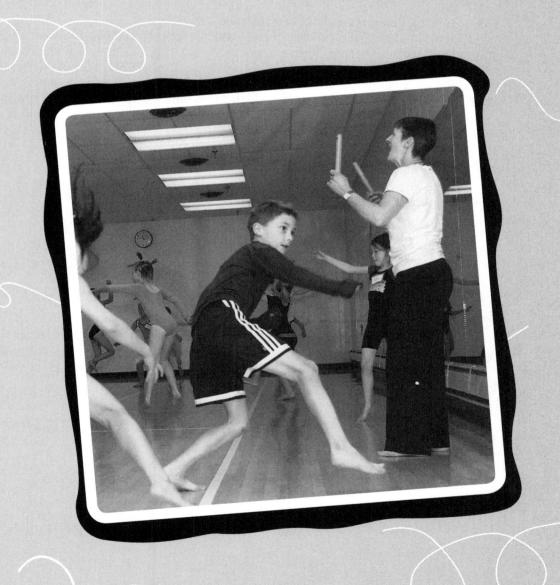

The expression "variety is the spice of life" holds true in some aspects of teaching and learning. Children need continuity in their work, but they also need fresh ways of approaching ideas. Working with rhyme is another way of exploring action words. Children like rhymes and learn the words very quickly. This seems to be reflected in the flow of their movement because knowing what comes next in the rhyme leaves them free to concentrate on how and where to do it.

To make the most of working with rhymes, children should explore rhymes in much the same way as they explored the action phrases in the previous chapter. That way, the children, having learned some new movement ideas with your guidance, can select from the material explored and create their own dances. You also have choices about concepts to explore in relation to a particular rhyme. Consider the following rhyme:

> Rising, rising
> Spin around
> Bounce, bounce, bounce
> Freeze upside down.

There are four action words to be explored in that rhyme.

Rise could start from a focus on body shapes (round, twisted, narrow, wide) or from body bases (standing, sitting, kneeling, lying). It is an action that changes from a lower to a higher level, and the action could be led by different body parts (e.g., hand, head, elbow, shoulder, knee). The rising action could take place on the spot or involve traveling. It could be very sudden or sustained, firm or fine. *Spin* has many possibilities too. *Bounce* has one limitation in the rhyme—there are three in a row. *Freeze* has the limitation of being upside down.

Here is an overview of the teaching progression:

- Lead the children through a guided exploration of the action word in the first line of the rhyme with a focus on one aspect of a dynamic concept and one aspect of a spatial concept (chosen by you).
- Similarly, explore the second action word.
- Link the first and second lines.
- Explore the third action word.
- Link the first three lines of the rhyme.
- Explore the final word.
- Link them all together.
- After a short practice, ask the children to show their dances, and replicate it: Do it the same way twice (for children 4 to 8 years). Or, ask the children to show you their finished product, followed by a variation (for those 9 to 12 years).

Action Rhymes for Younger Children (Ages 4 to 9)

Wibble wobble, wibble wobble

Wibble wobble, wibble wobble
Rush away
Sinking gently
Freeze and stay.

Jumping, Leaping

Jumping, leaping
Curl down low
Skip to a new place
Stop! Don't go!

Rising, Rising

Rising, rising
Spin around
Bounce, bounce, bounce
Freeze upside down.

TIP

From the possible ways in which an action can be explored, you select a main focus (though you may touch on other aspects). This may be a new concept for the children, or it could be one previously explored, but in this new context of the rhyme.

Example of Exploration (Space)

This in an exploration for the "Rising, Rising" rhyme with a focus on high and low.

1. Explore *rising, rising.*

The children find a space on the floor and make a small, low shape. Give these instructions:

Make your shape as close to the floor as you can. Are you curled up or folded up so that your shape is small? Can you make a different low shape, perhaps on your side, back, or knees? (Point out a few clear examples.) From your small, low shape, see if you can rise and continue to get higher very slowly until you are as high as you can get. Hold your high shape. Now start again. As you feel yourself getting higher, decide which part of you will finish highest. Could it be an arm, your head, a toe? Try it again, but choose a different part to finish high. Really stretch it as high as it can go.

2. Explore *spin around.*

Show me a shape that looks like it's going to spin (point out relevant features). Spin around, then stop. Try it again, but this time make sure that you are high on your toes and stretched through every bit of you—and again. Still on your feet, could you show me a spin that is very low? Now very high? What other parts of you could you spin on in a low shape? (Buttocks, belly?) Try them. Now do a low spin one way, then a high spin the other way.

3. Link *rising rising, spin around.*

Making sure that you are still in a space, start in a low shape. Then rise and rise until you are very high, then spin as low as you can. Have another go, but this time you decide whether the spin will be high or low.

4. Explore *bounce, bounce, bounce.*

Start standing with your feet close together and show three bounces in a row, landing lightly each time. Ready? (Work on the quality, and bend knees on landing.) This time, bounce as high as you can each time for the three bounces, but still land really softly. (At this point, use of directions could be added, or perhaps bouncing on the spot and then traveling.) Now try three really high bounces—and freeze—and three quick little bounces. And again.

5. Link *rising rising, spin around, bounce, bounce, bounce.*
Be ready to spin and let me see by your starting shape whether it will be a high spin or a low one, then right away do your three bounces. (Repeat, possibly showing a different answer or duplicating the first one.) Now go back to a small low shape, and start with the rising, then spin, then bounce. You choose whether to spin high or low and whether to do three high bounces or three quick little ones. And again.

6. Explore *freeze upside down.*
Be ready to do your bounces again, then very quickly show me an upside-down shape. And again, but make sure that you can freeze the upside-down shape very tight. Try some other ways of freezing upside down. What parts are touching the floor? (Two hands, one foot, shoulders, knee, elbow?) Stretch the other parts away from the floor; try another.

7. Link all the actions.
Come over quickly and see if you can tell me the whole rhyme. (Say it together a few times.) Now go and practice it on your own, but remember to decide which actions will be high and which actions will be low. Could anyone tell me an idea? (Listen to a couple of possibilities.) Good—off you go.

After some individual practice and feedback where required, the children should be ready to do their final sequences. They may be asked to find a partner and watch each other's sequence, telling the partner which actions were high and which were low.

Action Rhymes for Older Children (Ages 8 to 12)

Whirling, Twirling Up So High

Whirling, twirling up so high
Hanging gently in the sky
Shrinking, sinking to the ground
Quiver, shiver, not a sound.

A quietly held position for "not a sound."

Toss, Toss, Toss, Toss

Toss, toss, toss, toss
Whip around
Shrivel, shrink
Right through the ground.

Zigzag, Zigzag

Zigzag, zigzag
Whirling very low
Stretch like elastic
Snap! Oh, no!

There are a few subtleties to be explored in these word combinations. *Hanging* requires a combination of balance and fine tension that would be outside the physical and cognitive capabilities of a younger child. *Toss* is a jumping action that requires enough strength and time for a child to get into the air and add the sudden flick of the upper body before landing again.

Examples of Exploration for the Zigzag, Zigzag Rhyme

These explorations focus on firm and fine effort.

1. Explore *zigzag, zigzag.*
Decide on a way to travel on your feet (skip, run, gallop, bounce) and experiment with making a sharp zigzagging pathway (give a minute or so to try this out). Keep the action clear, and concentrate on making sharp corners as you go from a zig to a zag. How many steps (or bounces) do you make for each part of the zigzag? (Watch a few, noting the action, such as gallop, skip, run, leap, and the number of steps, such as four gallops for each of zig and zag; two and two or uneven patterns such as four for a zig, two for a zag.) Now decide which one you want to practice.

Keeping your own pattern, make the actions as light as you can—soft on the floor and a fine tension throughout your body. Now try the same pattern but with a very strong action—still light on your feet. Show the difference between the light and the strong by practicing, say, two patterns that are light, then two strong ones, then back to light.

How else could you alternate between light and strong in a zigzag? (zig strong, zag light).

Try it, keeping your feet light even when your body is firm.

2. Explore *whirling very low.*
Would *whirl* be a strong or a light action? (It could be either.) What about fast or slow? (Fast.) Experiment with strong whirls and then light ones, holding your ending each time. Be sure that your whole body is either firm or fine as you whirl.

Now, still using a whirl, decide whether you want to be strong or light and whirl from your starting shape, going as low as you can without losing the whirl. Now try the one you didn't do (fine or firm). (Watch a clear example of each, pointing out features.) What do you have to do with your body to whirl really low? (Bend hips and knees.) Can you transfer your weight to your buttocks or knees to finish even lower?

3. Link *zigzag, zigzag, whirling very low.*
Now, start with your zigzag pattern, then go into the whirl. Remember to show which parts are strong and which are light. If you wanted to do a light whirl, would it be better if it followed a strong zigzag or a light one? (Strong.) What about a strong whirl? (Light.) Go and decide how to do yours. Try it once more and hold the shape you are in at the end of your whirl.

4. Explore *stretch like elastic.*
From your finishing shape, choose two body parts that are fairly close together—like a knee and the opposite hand, or a foot and the opposite elbow. (Point out clear examples.) Now, slowly and with firm tension as if it is hard work, pull those two parts away from each other—keep pulling as far as they will go—and hold it there. Relax.

Try it again with two different parts, and think about where you want them to go. Could one part pull higher than the other, or could one go in front and one behind? Look at one of the parts as you work and pull them as far apart as you can, and hold. Some of you are close to the floor; others have parts of the body higher. Try it again and think about where you can stretch these parts.

Start again, and imagine that there is a strong piece of elastic attached to the two body parts and you have to work hard to stretch the elastic as much as it can be stretched. Ready? Hold your stretch.

5. Explore *snap, oh, no!*

Now, suddenly, you can't stretch it any more. Show me what would happen if it snapped back to short again. Try it again, but this time show me how your whole body is involved as the elastic snaps back to its original size. Do you end up where you began, or does it make you turn, or roll, or jump into a crunched shape? (Experiment.) Go from where you start to stretch the elastic, but make the snap so sudden that you surprise me.

6. Link the whole sequence.

Come over and look at the rhyme on the board. Which actions *have* to be strong? Why? Which actions *could* be strong? Which ones *could* be light? Now go and try from the beginning, but remember you have to show a contrast between strong and light in your sequence.

Moving into a full stretch during "stretch like elastic."

During the class, after the review, this could lead to partner work. You could set limitations for some parts of the sequence and let the children decide others: "You must meet at the end of the whirl and stretch one piece of elastic between you. Or, during your zigzags, while one of you is strong, the other must be light. Or decide whose elastic will snap first."

Regular practice with exploring action words either in phrase or in rhyme allows the children to explore a small area of movement in some depth. The depth will depend on the age and experience of the children. If you choose the main focus wisely (appropriate for the words and rhymes and the needs of the class), the children can do some valuable exploration with aspects of effort, space, and body awareness. For the children, the learning process is as much fun as having a finished product. The experimentation allows them to try things that may or may not work; they take chances knowing that if they fall, lose balance, or get in a muddle, they can safely have another go. They also discover to what extent they can play with a word and that some words can change weight or time while others cannot, or they become a different word. This kind of dancing shows you what the children know and how they are progressing over time in terms of awareness and movement vocabulary. The development of these dances will take less time than the dances with music, but they have equal value if the process is well taught.

Dances With Poetry

Working with poetry is similar to, yet different from, working with action rhymes. The process is similar because you need to decide the concepts to explore with the children, but it is also different because now an idea or a feeling or an image is being expressed. A wealth of material is available, such as nursery rhymes, short poems or excerpts of longer poems, and haiku, but the challenge is selecting poetry that has movement possibilities and then developing a framework for teaching and learning. Many poems, while excellent as reading material, do not translate easily into dance because now the body is being used instead of the words. Once you have selected a poem, you examine it for possibilities of actions, spatial concepts, effort concepts, and in some cases relationship concepts so that you can plan a lesson. The idea is for the children to be guided through an exploratory process that enables them to extend their ideas, improve the quality of their movement, and create a movement answer reflecting their choices. This is very different from learning a song or poem with actions. For example, preschoolers love "Itsy-Bitsy Spider" and learn both the words and accompanying actions by listening to and copying the teacher. The result after many repetitions is a group saying and doing the same thing, which is valuable memory and motor control work and very exciting for young children, but it should not be confused with creativity. The children have all learned to do what they were shown. In a poem for dance, there must be concepts that can be explored so that each child will eventually find a way of expressing the ideas in his or her own way.

For younger children, poetry that includes fairly concrete images works the best. It provides an opportunity to explore something within their tactile experience (such as the wind and bubbles) or within their story experience (such as witches and goblins). The words in the poetry conjure images for the children, and exploring these words through dance allows them to know about the images in a different way.

Four simple ideas for 4- to 6-year-olds follow, each with ideas for the teaching process:

Little Tiny Raindrops Drop to the Ground

Little tiny raindrops drop to the ground
Plip, plop, plip with a very soft sound
Great big raindrops splash into a puddle
Splish splash, splish splash, what a muddle!

Not exactly a masterpiece, but a good basis for exploring action, body shape, and effort contrast. First, raindrops can *plip, plop* by running. The initial rain is light (with a very soft sound), so the focus, once the children have run for a moment, is *how*: lightly and quickly with careful feet. Next, introduce where the rain goes, which allows exploration of on the spot (personal space) and all over the place (general space) as the rain tries to make all the earth or grass wet. The second raindrops are larger and splash (jump) into a puddle, which provides the opportunity to explore body shape: wide, curled, and long and deep puddles. Once children have practiced puddle shapes, they can play with big jumps that land them in their puddle shapes (landing on feet, then making the puddle shape).

After some guided exploration, each child can show the whole poem, consciously choosing where she or he is traveling during the running and what puddle shape to make. In this way, a simple poem provides material for exploration, experimentation and conscious choice by the children.

Toby the Goblin

Toby the goblin, a little tiny elf
Built a house for his very own self.
Wibble wobble, wibble wobble, the house fell down
So Toby skipped to another town.

This poem calls for exploration of balanced house shapes: balancing on four, three, or two body parts; creating spaces for the elf to live; part or whole-body vibratory action of wobbling and then tumbling down; skipping off to a new place and starting all over again.

There Was a Little Fellow Called Mr. Upside Down

There was a little fellow called Mr. Upside Down
He had a lot of trouble when he tried to go to town
Then early in the morning when the sun came up to play
Mr. Upside Down stretched up the other way
"This is so much better," he said, jumping up and down
"I'll skip and skip and skip and skip until I reach the town"
But later in the evening when the sun went back to bed
Mr. Upside Down tipped back upon his head.

This poem calls for exploration of upside-down balanced shapes, then traveling (forward, sideways) in those shapes; sustained, firm stretching to turn rightside up; jumping and skipping; sudden or sustained tipping back to upside down.

A Curly Yellow Leaf, Hanging on a Tree

A curly yellow leaf, hanging on a tree
A small puff of wind wiggles him, you see
A large puff of wind blows him all around
Then flittering and fluttering, he settles to the ground
Sweep, sweep the leaves on the ground
Sweep them into a great big mound.

This poem calls for exploration of crinkled leaf shapes suspended from various body parts, hanging on low or high trees; wiggles to change the way the leaf hangs; spins, runs, and jumps as the leaf blows away; gentle, sustained sinking to leaf shapes on the ground; tumbles along the ground into a pile of leaves where different body parts contact another leaf.

Exploring a crinkled leaf shape, thinking about pointed elbows and knees.

67

Poems for Ages 7 to 12

As the children grow and develop both physical and cognitive abilities, the range of possible material widens. I learned about a tool for developing rhymes with imagery from the late Virginia Tanner of the Children's Dance Theatre in Utah. Her poems were built around the following:

1. Action word, effort word
2. Spatial phrase
3. Finishing phrase

You may design these for various ages through careful choice of words and images and explore them much as you did the action rhymes.

Reaching Swiftly

Reaching swiftly

Follow a pathway

Discover a hedgehog, jump over it

Curl into a ball

Children enjoy these if they are challenged to explore lots of possibilities for how and where each action can be tried, and they develop very different interpretations of the images of the finishing phrases.

You can introduce older, more experienced children to haiku. Originating in Japan, a haiku is a word picture. Each has three lines: five syllables in the first line, seven in the second, and five in the third. These are more difficult to work with because they have fewer action words, but each word picture suggests something about effort.

When working with haiku (always after either an energetic introductory activity or after work on part of another dance idea so the children are physically and mentally awake), I tend to offer the class choices of two or three haiku because each one offers a different appeal. We might talk about them for a few minutes, then they go off and play with the ideas on their own, receiving help when it is needed. I find it as much of a learning experience as the children do, seeing how each of them interprets the idea—sometimes very differently from what I would have expected.

An abundance of haiku is available in poetry books and on the Internet. You can link work in dance and language arts when using haiku.

One of my grandchildren, while playing with a box of magnetized words intended to be stuck to a refrigerator, wrote a lovely word picture similar to a haiku:

The river is battling against the rocks

While fish jump into the air

Seabirds are circling, high above the ground

As leaves dance through the blue sky.

Used with permission of Ian Vickers.

Various anthologies of children's literature (such as those from Norton or Riverside) are good sources of material for use in dance, as are other collections in which the poems have been organized into topics such as magic, seeing, and hearing. From a good supply, you may select a poem that would appeal to the class, often in conjunction with another area of the curriculum.

The first verse of "Hallowe'en," by Leonard Clark (1905-1981), conjures up images of silhouettes:

This is the night when witches fly
On their whizzing broomsticks through the wintry sky;
Steering up the pathway where the stars are strewn,
They stretch skinny fingers to the waking moon.

Copyright © 1968 Leonard Clark from *Good Company*, published by Dobson Books Ltd.

The verse suggests traveling at high speed with an emphasis on pathways and level changes followed by exploring silhouette shapes on various body bases and levels and determining which body parts can help to create a focus on the distant moon. After your guided exploration, the children can develop a short individual or partner dance that reflects their own interpretation of the poem.

On a similar note, "Check" by James Stephens (1882-1950) may be used by 9- to 12-year-olds to develop a dance in small groups, each group taking several lines to develop its part of the whole:

The night was creeping on the ground!
She crept, and did not make a sound
Until she reached the tree: And then   } Group 1
She covered it, and stole again
Along the grass beside the wall!

I heard the rustling of her shawl
As she threw blackness everywhere   } Group 2
Along the sky, the ground, the air,
And in the room where I was hid!

But, no matter what she did
To everything that was without,   } Group 3
She could not put my candle out!

So I stared at the Night! And she   } Groups 1, 2, 3
Stared back solemnly at me!

Depending on the size of the class, one or two groups of four or five children could each take a portion of the poem and develop their own sequence of movement. Once they are satisfied with the result and it is fluent, the class can collaborate to find a way of using the space, each group ready in its starting shape so that the whole poem may be performed sequentially. Each group is just a part of the whole dance, but all are involved in the organization and timing of its performance. Aspects are suited to the abilities of the older children.

Experiences such as this are a valuable contribution to dance development. They allow the children to put their current movement knowledge to use while drawing on their imaginative powers to make the majority of the decisions. At the same time, you can watch their methods of working and evaluate their progress, noting aspects of their movement or of their ability to work in groups that may need to be developed in future classes.

A response to "The night was creeping on the ground" in the poem "Check."

Dances
With Rhythm

There are numerous methods of working with rhythm, and of course the dances with music (all the chapters in part III) do so in very many ways. What follows are some suggestions and processes for working with rhythm but without recorded music. You and the children will instead find the rhythm in a word, a phrase, a poem, or the sound of a moving object. A possible basis for exploration is suggested for each age group. The following ideas may be developed in several ways, and exploring a similar process with two separate classes of the same age can produce different results.

Rhythms for Ages 4 to 6

A good introduction to rhythm for 4- to 6-year-old children is for them to clap the syllables in their first names:

Mike	1 clap
Onsum	2 claps
Stephanie	3 claps
Alexandra	4 claps

Starting with the children sitting in a group, you can ask how many claps it would take to say each of their names. Some will be able to give an immediate response, so you can pick up from these children by listening to theirs, then clarify for the rest by saying and then clapping their names:

Teacher: Jer-e-my

Children: Jeremy (3 claps)

There are some tricky ones, such as Catherine, which the children tend to say in two syllables instead of three.

After this, you can ask the children to find a space and see how many bounces (for example) are needed for them to say their names. This sounds extremely simple, but it is quite a test of their motor control to *say* and *do* their names at the same time and also to stop effectively after the correct number of bounces. From here, two children could work together and bounce each of their names in turn. This could lead to exploring floor patterns: Mike does not have much choice, but partner Elizabeth does, so the two of them could explore what floor patterns they can make with one and then four bounces.

Alternatively, the focus could be on directions: Mike can take one bounce forward or sideways or backward. Elizabeth can change directions with each bounce or bounce twice in one direction if she wishes. If they work together, Mike has more syllables to play with. Adding a last name will increase the challenge for Mike!

After experimenting rhythmically with a single action, you can suggest using a combination. One idea is to work with jumps landing on one foot or two feet (hops, bounces, leaps). This requires thought and balance while each child devises a repeatable pattern with the syllables of his or her name.

Another day, after a quick review, you can revisit the use of directions so that forward, sideways, and backward are added to their one-foot or two-foot patterns. Once each child has a sequence, a partner relationship can be developed in which child 1 shows his or her sequence and freezes after the last syllable, then child 2 responds with her or his sequence. This can be further extended by putting *My name is* before the name itself.

Rhythms for Ages 5 to 7

Now, with improved coordination and memory, children can develop longer conversations. Still working through a clear process in which the syllables are translated into actions, then making it more challenging by adding floor patterns or direction changes, two children (or three where necessary) can "chat" by taking turns doing or listening and then adding a sentence together:

1   My name is _____ (child 2 watches)
2   My name is _____ (child 1 watches)
1, 2   We live in Edmonton
       or
       Our school is _____

Rhythms for Ages 6 to 9

As the children age, other actions may be substituted for words with one, two, three, or four syllables. Here is an example:

1: bounce

2: rise and sink

3: turn

4: foot patterns

A topic currently being examined in another subject area can be the material from which the words are drawn, such as insects, seasons, volcanoes, space, and place-names. Table 6.1 shows an example of the process, with the idea of baking a cake. Once the list of ingredients is complete and printed on the chalkboard (be prepared for later additions), you can work with the children to explore the actions using some of the suggested words.

Each child can choose one ingredient from the one-syllable list and practice saying it while doing one good (softly landed) bounce forward, backward, or to one side. Then, if three eggs are to be used, a sequence of three bounces can occur.

For two syllables, the children can work with two contrasting actions. For these ingredients, they could explore a sudden action that expands the whole body into the space around them (reaching limbs into different areas), then contract into various tucked shapes. This can be full of experimentation with appropriate challenges that you give the children so that they focus on where they expand in the space, their body shapes, and their use of levels and body bases. It is challenging for children in this age group to make two sudden, firm, opposite actions in a row (butter).

For contrast, a sustained turn has been selected for the words with three syllables (bananas). This may be low, medium, or high (or changing). The children's movement should be refined through encouragement of awareness of the whole body as they turn.

Words with four syllables are represented by a series of steps, with awareness of where the free foot is kicked high in front of the body, behind the body, or to the side.

TABLE 6.1 Baking a Cake

1	2	3	4
oats	butter	margarine	baking powder
salt	raisins	bananas	baking soda
eggs	cherries	chocolate	chocolate chips
nuts	almonds		
oil	cocoa		
	sugar		

Two dancers with their own ending for baking a cake.

Developing a clear sequence requires experimentation and practice, as does balancing at the end of the fourth syllable. The sequences can be quick as the children learn to transfer weight lightly from one foot to the other (baking powder).

Once the children have explored a few words from each list, several routes are possible:

- Each child could choose one ingredient from each group and develop an individual sequence.
- In pairs, children could develop a sequence, deciding on the order and whether they both move at the same time, or taking turns with some of the words. A similar idea could develop with groups of three or four children.
- You could divide the class into five or six groups, each group deciding which words to use, in which order, and how many times they are repeated (e.g., oats, baking powder, cocoa, cocoa, eggs, margarine).

When they have finished, with help from you circulating throughout the class, you (now the baker) can coordinate the baking of the cake by indicating to each group in turn to perform its sequence (sometimes possibly more than one group at a time!).

There has been little traveling in the recipe, so you and the children could decide on a finishing phrase, the rhythm of which would involve travelling, and perhaps bring all the children into a group:

/	/	/	/	/	/	/	
mix	them	up	to	bake	a	cake	
step	and	step	and	step	and	step	(slowly)
or							
skip	and	skip	and	skip	and	skip	(quickly)

As a finale, the children could add one word, such as *candles* or *icing*, and choose an action to go with it.

The development of a dance like this would take part of two or three classes, allowing for consolidation of ideas, refinement of the movement sequences, and coordination of the whole.

Rhythms for Ages 7 to 10

A dance that developed around Halloween was based on the rhythm of excerpts from Shakespeare (*Macbeth*, act 4, scene I) and the ingredients for a magic spell.

First of all, with the children in their own spaces, they explored light, careful, creeping steps to the following verse:

/	/	/	/
By the	pricking	of my	thumbs

/	/	/	/
Something	wicked	this way	comes.

With feedback, the children stepped purposefully, reaching each step into the space ahead, behind, or to one side, so that without traveling far they were balancing and adjusting their bodies for each step. (This may be explored to the accompaniment of voice or drum.)

To vary the pace and add a bit of excitement, we introduced a quick, small jump for *wicked*, and the phrase became this:

/	/	/	/
By the	pricking	of my	thumbs
(step and	step and	step and	step)

/	/ /	/	/
Something	wicked	this way	comes.
(step and	jump and	step and	freeze)

Then the children (who were, by this point, looking very much like witches and wizards) started at the edge of the space, gradually filling it as the phrase was repeated several times. We put that idea aside for a while and compiled a list of ingredients for the cauldron:

frog's legs	jumps
adder's fork	rise and sink
bat's wing	spin
lightning bolt	zaps (sudden reaches)

The children explored these actions, encouraging the use of whole-body involvement, changes in level, and contrasts in effort. Then, in small groups (three to five), the children decided on the order and number of ingredients desired for their spells—excluding the zaps, which would come later. They practiced their sequences, verbalizing as the actions took place.

Next, they gathered to learn the following:

> Double, double, toil and trouble
>
> Fire burn and cauldron bubble

Then they returned to their groups to develop a way of traveling around the cauldron while stirring the ingredients with a large imaginary paddle. One group, for example, made a circle facing each other and stepped to the rhythm of the couplet while grasping the handle of the paddle. Another group circled by traveling forward and backward around their cauldron. With a little help, the children are capable of developing clear, rhythmic sequences.

Now it was time to look at the transitions, so they practiced from the beginning, knowing that the *by the pricking* patterns needed to be used for locating their groups of fellow witches to make the spell. Following the spells, the children moved into their stirring of the cauldrons. As those phrases came to an end, we added a few lightning bolts—strong, direct, sudden extensions into space (zaps), working on where each zap was directed. Together we decided how many lightning bolts would be needed to complete the spell. Then with their wicked work finished, the witches repeated the *by the pricking* stepping to retreat into their lairs.

A sudden clap to illustrate a lightning bolt.

Rhythms for Ages 9 to 12

This dance idea is based on three rhythms:

1. Pendulum (even)
2. Steam engine (uneven)
3. Heartbeat (uneven)

It will develop differently with each group of children. In this case, I chose the rhythms and actions, but the children decided on the small- and large-group relationships and length of each section.

Pendulum

After a vigorous introductory activity, and with the children standing while spaced well apart, I asked them to extend one arm out to the side and raise it, well stretched, above shoulder level. Then they experimented with letting the arm swing down, across the front of the body, upward past the opposite shoulder, then back to the starting position. As they continued to swing, they were reminded about having a stable base so that the arm could swing freely without throwing them off balance. While they tried this, I encouraged them to let their weight transfer slightly from one foot to the other to extend the range of the swing, watching the pathway made by the hand. Then they tried with the other arm. Gradually they focused on increasing the involvement of the body by reaching up at the height of the swing and bending the knees and dropping the head as the arm swung downward, rising and extending again on the other side. Next we talked about the way a pendulum swings, then had another go, this time trying to show a slight pause at the top of the swing, then letting the weight of the arm fall, swing up to the other side, and pause slightly again. This is difficult because it requires just the right amount of tension, but the children can do it. They are often helped by watching a couple of others who have the right feeling.

Now the idea was opened up when I suggested that they explore swinging from other body bases and swinging both arms or a leg. This took trial and error as the children discovered what might work and what definitely did not! They tried from high kneeling bases or a knee and a foot, swinging one or both arms in front of or behind or across the body, and experimented with balancing on two hands and a knee while swinging a leg. We used a metronome for the rhythm, adjusting it until we found the right pace for the children to swing fully. In this way, their bodies worked so that the beats of the metronome occurred at each end of the swinging action.

The children divided into groups of four and decided among themselves at what level and at what angle each would be in relation to the others so that each could swing freely, close together, but not interfering with the action. At this point, with so much decided, we moved on to other dance ideas in progress. But during the next class, after a review of the swinging action and positions, the children returned to their groups to adjust and improve on their previous ideas.

Now a form for the relationship was given: Decide which person should start the pendulum swing; when 2,

Showing stillness after binding the flow of the swinging pendulum.

then 3, then 4 should join in; and when 1 should stop followed in turn by 2, 3, and 4. This was fun and quite challenging because, in some groups, one or more people were facing away, unable to see the rest of the group. Learning to stop effectively was a challenge too—being able to swing fully several times, then suddenly and surprisingly bind the flow. After much experimentation and help where needed, each group had an effective and workable sequence. Over time, again with feedback about tension, focus, and use of the whole body, the quality as well as the timing of the group work improved.

Steam Engine

First we established the rhythm for the action by sitting and clapping, noting that the emphasis is on the first beat followed by three shorter, even beats. Then I asked the children to develop stepping patterns that would reflect that. I gave feedback as they worked, and a variety of clear rhythmic patterns emerged, such as one long, strong (but light on the floor) step forward and three short, light steps back and a jump from one to two feet followed by three springy running steps. Then I asked them to increase the contrast between the first beat and the following three beats and to change direction or possibly the level as well as the effort.

The children returned to their pendulum groups and worked through that sequence. Then each child started the steam engine rhythm, using the pattern to travel away individually. Then they had a better idea. It was decided that everyone would learn one of the patterns that they had all particularly liked, which consisted of a strong forward step with the body dropping low over the foot and three tiny backward steps with the body extending to full height. It had clear contrast in weight, direction, and levels. They decided that once the pendulum sequences were complete, the originator of this steam engine pattern would start (all the rest holding their pendulum freezes), gradually "collecting" the others as she passed them. The result was a gradually lengthening line of children, in unison, weaving its way about the space.

Heartbeat

Once again, we used clapping to establish the regular but uneven beat with the emphasis on the second of each pair of beats. This idea was further enlivened the following week when somebody brought in a stethoscope. While the children were working, a few at a time went to listen to their hearts. I chose the action for the rhythm: close and open. To try this (within the limitation of the rhythm), the children stood, well balanced, and played with closing one shoulder (turning it toward the chest), then opening it (stretching it farther back than the normal stance). Gradually, they increased the range of movement so that the arm joined in, then that side of the body (head following the movement, hip and knee closing and opening). Because the second beat is dominant, we put the emphasis on *open* so the action became a sudden, short close and then a stronger, slightly longer open.

This was to be the third part of the whole, so the children decided that following the group pendulum rhythms, the steam engine rhythm would take them from the long, weaving line to a certain space, where each child would begin the heartbeat rhythm. They worked on this rhythm until the whole group was clustered fairly tightly together, all in time with each close and open action. A child whom everyone could see was chosen as the timer so that the pattern could come to a sudden, whole-group stop.

Work of this nature involves lots of exploration, and some ideas might be more successful than others! It helps to have one or two possible solutions to start the children off. Here's an example of two choices from the steam engine rhythm for 9- to 12-year-olds:

- The pattern must show one change of direction.
- The pattern must show both bounces and steps.

This helps the children who have more difficulty developing patterns because they have something to fall back on. Observation is key; watch for children who are developing something interesting and help them to clarify their ideas. Scan the class for patterns that everyone can watch and then try.

PART III

Dances With Music

Each chapter in part III is devoted to one age group and describes the movement content and teaching process for four dances. The complexity of the dances is appropriate for that particular age group, but you may decide that a dance for slightly older or younger children might be suitable too. Obviously, dances for children several years older or younger would not work because of the movement content and, in many cases, the story.

Now the dances are driven by the story and the selected music. (See appendix B for information about where to find the music referenced in these chapters.) It is important for the children to relate to the ideas; this is about the affective domain.

The stories for younger children are based on things in their experience, concrete ideas. They enjoy seasonal events such as snow and stories that capture their imagination, like rice krispies that refuse to behave. Some are my inventions, and others have a basis in existing literature.

As they get older, the children enjoy exploring characters and other times in history—archers, wizards, warriors, and the sheriff and cowboy, for example.

For the oldest groups, some abstract ideas (e.g., The Mirage, Changes in chapter 12) and some dances require the children to put themselves in another's shoes. Exploring working in a banana plantation, being a lowly jester, or living as a coal miner can be an immensely satisfying journey for both the children and you.

To get a handle on teaching any of the dances in part III, do the following:

Turn to the page showing the music visualization, actions, concepts to be explored, and story or idea for the dance. Listen to the piece of music while following the squiggles in the music visualization column. Listen again to become familiar with the tempo, phrases, repetitions, and overall pattern of the music. As you become familiar with the music, note which actions are suggested for which parts of the music. Read the images or sequences column to get an idea of what the dance is all about. Some dances tell a story or part of a story.

Next, read the dynamic emphasis column. The emphasis in each dance will depend on what is important for the children to explore and learn in order to better express the ideas in the story. These choices will be supported by the music. The selection of concepts is also dependent on the age of the children—what aspects of dynamics are appropriate for their exploration or comprehension as they learn to control their bodies.

The spatial emphasis column suggests one or two areas of focus for where the action takes place. The relationship emphasis describes whom the child is dancing with.

Once you have connected the various parts of the music with the actions, how (dynamics) and where (space) they are explored, and the relationships involved for the idea, the next stage is to read the suggested teaching progression. This divides the material into sections, or concepts to be explored and then linked. Read all of it for that particular dance and then decide what tasks to set, where your children will need help with refining their movement, and how far to progress during one class. Remember that at least a small part should be complete for a first time to the appropriate part of the music. From the first lesson comes a second: whether to review physically and develop a part of the dance that has been started, or begin with a new part and then review an old, gradually building a whole. Building a particular dance idea over time is important because it allows the children to absorb ideas, and their interpretation improves as this happens.

Dances
for Ages 4 to 6

SNOWDRIFTS

4 to 6 Years

The Little Musical Box: Samuel Maykapar

Music pattern	Music emphasis	Action emphasis	Dynamic emphasis	Spatial emphasis
A	*(rhythm notation)*	Run, run, run	Contrast is between fine and firm actions. The runs are light and quick, with a sudden strong jump into the snow. The pushes are strong with a degree of sustainment.	The runs weave all over general space as the elf looks for a deep snowdrift to jump into. The pushes take the elf from low to high in personal space as he struggles to get out of the drift.
	(rhythm notation)	Jump		
A	*(rhythm notation)*	Push, push, push, push	**Relationship emphasis**	**Image or sequence**
	(rhythm notation)	Push, push, push, rise	This is an individual dance.	A little elf woke up one morning to find that the field behind his house was all white with snow! In some places the snow wasn't very deep, but in other places the wind had blown it into big snowdrifts. The elf ran all over the field (leaving footprints) looking for a big snowdrift. When he found a good one, he jumped high into the air to land in it. Then he had to push very hard at the snow to make his way out. When he finally reached the surface, the elf decided that it had been so much fun, it was worth finding another snowdrift and doing it all over again!
A	*(rhythm notation)*	Run, run, run		
	(rhythm notation)	Jump		
A	*(rhythm notation)*	Push, push, push, push		
	(rhythm notation)	Push, push, push, rise		
A	*(rhythm notation)*	Run, run, run		
	(rhythm notation)	Jump		
A	*(rhythm notation)*	Push, push, push, push		
	(rhythm notation)	Push, push, push, rise		

From S. Carline, 2011, *Lesson plans for creative dance* (Champaign, IL: Human Kinetics).

SNOWDRIFTS

The Little Musical Box: Samuel Maykapar

TEACHING PROGRESSION

You can build lesson plans based on this suggested progression:

1. Run and jump (first and alternating phrases)
2. Push and rise (second and alternating phrases)

DANCE SEQUENCE

1. Run and Jump (First and Alternating Phrases)

Starting in their own spaces, ask the children to run very lightly all over the space and then stop. Ask them to run again, but this time they imagine that they have very pointy knees, which you want to see as they run. Encourage the children to lift their knees up a little as they run and to keep their feet very soft as they touch the floor. Now tell them that you are going to give them a rhythm (with drum or claves) and that they can run in and out of each other, seeing how many areas of the space they can visit (see figure 7.1).

Try it again, encouraging them to run into empty spaces and keep their feet really light. Several practices are in order—the children enjoy the fast pace and need lots of reminders about traveling where there isn't

Listening to the music and "dancing with hands," which helps the children to hear the form of the music.

FIGURE 7.1 The rhythm and length of the phrase for run and jump.

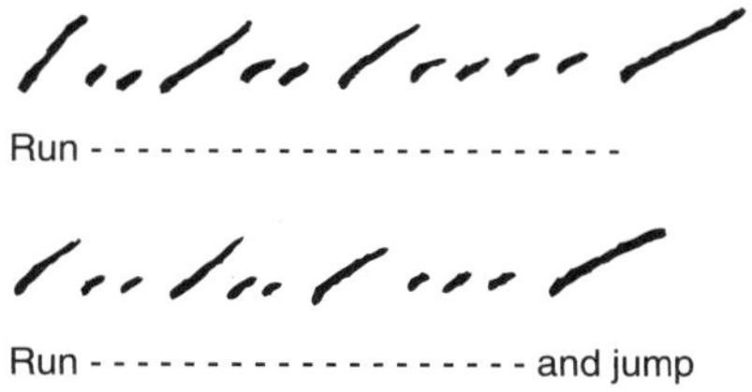

FIGURE 7.2 Adding the jump.

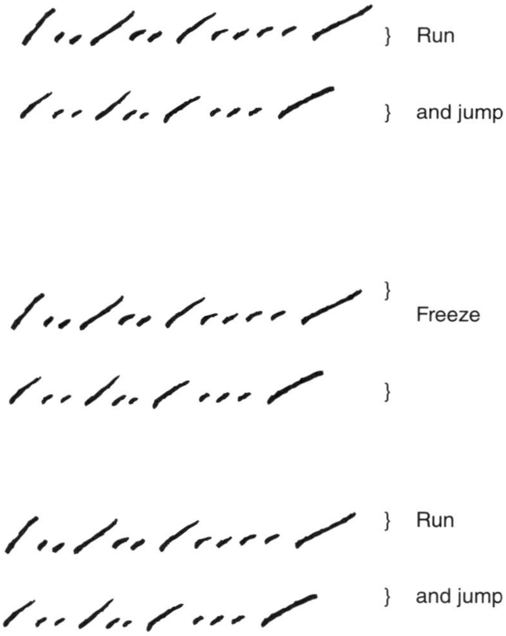

FIGURE 7.3 Dancing with hands: run and jump on alternating phrases.

anyone else so that they learn to use the space well. Each time, be sure to cue the "and freeze" so that they become accustomed to the length of the music phrase and learn to prepare to stop.

Gather to listen to the first A of the music, and introduce the idea of an elf waking up to find that it has snowed all over his field. Let them run "with their hands" as they listen to the music. Now let them start back in the space and see if the elves can make footprints (light ones) all over the field.

In their own spaces, ask the children to show you what kind of a big jump the elves could do to land in a deep snowdrift. Give them a jumping sound (three beats, with the emphasis on the middle beat) with drum or claves. Try it again, encouraging them to swing their arms so that they can jump high, and tell them that they *must* land on their feet first, even if they transfer weight down onto other parts after they land. At this point, look for clear jumpers who perhaps tuck their legs up, or turn as they jump, or show good effort in getting high, or land softly. Ask the children to watch a couple of jumps, pointing out the qualities as they do so. Let the children practice a few more times—they love to jump.

Now tell them that as the elves run making footprints, they are looking for a big snowdrift to jump into. They are going to run again—but this time jump into a snowdrift and then freeze tight. Make sure that the elves are spread out and ready to run with their pointy knees; give the phrase "And freeze" again (see figure 7.2).

Now they can do this to the first A of the music. To get the children accustomed to running and jumping during alternating A phrases of the music, gather them together and listen to the whole piece. Let them run and jump with their hands as they listen to the first A, then hold very still for the second A, then run and jump for the third A, and so on. As soon as they have done this, back out into the snowy field to try it (see figure 7.3).

2. Push and Rise (Second and Alternating Phrases)

In their own spaces, ask the children to do one more really big jump into a snowdrift and freeze at the bottom of it. Take a moment to point out some of the frozen shapes so that the children become aware of their own. Now

(continued)

the elves have to get out of the snow, so ask the children to stretch their hands (flat) and push into the space above their heads. They push again, looking up at where they are pushing, remembering to push very hard at all the snow. Some of the children will exhibit strong body tension, but to help the others, travel around and test their tension by pushing against their hands so that they can show you how strong they are. Ask the children which other body parts they can use to push (shoulder, back, head, foot), and try those. Explain to the children that the elf might get tired if he pushes with one part all the time, so he needs to change to a new part as he gets nearer the top of the snowdrift. Ask them to be ready to start pushing again, and give them the rhythm of the music (see figure 7.4).

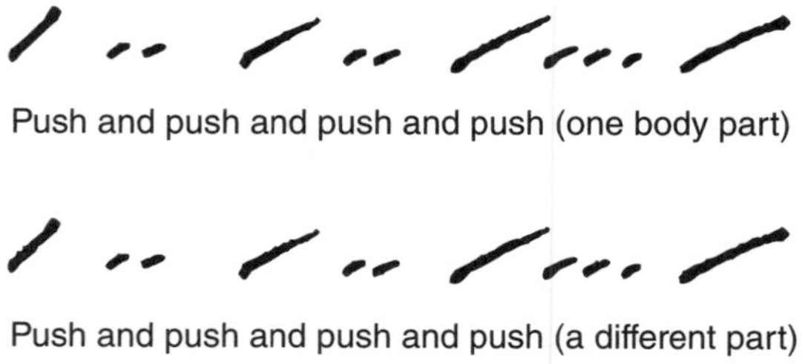

Push and push and push and push (one body part)

Push and push and push and push (a different part)

FIGURE 7.4 The timing of pushing out of a snowdrift.

The children will tend to make a series of short, firm pushes with the rhythm of the music rather than a couple of more sustained ones that an older person might do, and that is fine. Firm, sustained movement is tiring for young muscles.

Try it once more from the bottom of the drift, this time with a different starting shape, encouraging the children to get a little higher with each push so that by the end of the phrase, they are suddenly out of the snowdrift and can rise onto their toes.

After all this pushing, it is better to put this part into the context of the dance and the music. So ask the elves to be ready to run; then practice the run, jump and the push, rise during alternating phrases. As the children rise out of the first snowdrift, cue them to run again to find an even bigger snowdrift to jump into next time!

THE QUEEN'S GUARDS
4 to 6 Years

March from the Nutcracker Suite: *Tchaikovsky*

Music pattern	Music emphasis	Action emphasis	Dynamic emphasis	Spatial emphasis
A	(notation)	One knee high	The one knee high where the guards raise each knee preparing to skip is sudden and firm. The skips are quick and lively as they circle the palace on guard duty. The runs are quick and excited—the queen is coming!	The guards skip in a large circular route from and to their sentry boxes for the majority of the dance, but they skip in tiny circles inside the sentry box during section C of the music. For the last 2 A and B sections of the music, they skip following the queen on whatever pathway she chooses.
	(notation)	Other knee high		
B	(notation)	Skip, freeze		
A	(notation)	One knee high		
	(notation)	Other knee high		
B	(notation)	Skip, freeze		

Music pattern	Music emphasis	Action emphasis	Relationship emphasis	Image or sequence
C	(notation)	One knee high	This dance is about learning a turn-taking relationship where two guards stand side by side in their sentry boxes. One guard wakes up, lifts one knee high and then the other knee, skips off on guard duty and back to the sentry box, where he wakes guard 2 before falling back to sleep (sections A, B). For section C they both wake and practice guard duty at the same time inside the sentry box. During section D, both guards run, looking for the queen who is apparently on her way. For the last 2 A and B sections of the music, all the guards follow the queen.	Pairs of the queen's guards stand asleep on their feet in their sentry boxes outside the palace. Suddenly one of each pair awakens, does sentry duty, then returns to wake his partner. At one point (section D) they hear that the queen is coming, so panic ensues! They return to their duty until section C of the music, then all fall in behind the queen in a long procession.
	(notation)	Skip		
	(notation)	Other knee high		
	(notation)	Skip		
A	(notation)	One knee high		
	(notation)	Other knee high		
B	(notation)	Skip, freeze		
A	(notation)	One knee high		
	(notation)	Other knee high		
B	(notation)	Skip, freeze		
D	(notation)	Run, look		
	(notation)	Run, look		
	(notation)	Run, look		
	(notation)	Run, look		
A, B, A, B, C, A, B, A, B repeat				

From S. Carline, 2011, *Lesson plans for creative dance* (Champaign, IL: Human Kinetics).

THE QUEEN'S GUARDS

March From the Nutcracker Suite: *Tchaikovsky*

TEACHING PROGRESSION

You can build lesson plans based on this suggested progression:

1. One knee high, other knee high, skip, freeze (sections A and B)
2. One knee high, skip (section C)

   Link 1, 2
3. Run, look! (section D)

   Link 1, 2, 3
4. Procession

   Link 1, 2, 3, 4

DANCE SEQUENCE

1. One Knee High, Other Knee High, Skip, Freeze (Sections A and B)

Starting in their own spaces, experiment with skipping away from that space in a big circle, which will bring them back to their starting place. With a drum or claves, give a skipping rhythm of 15 beats with a strong beat for freeze at the end so that the children get used to the length of time they have to travel. Try it again a few times, encouraging them to make as big a circle as possible and still be able to return to their places. (The route is circular, but the circles don't need to be perfectly round!) Now, starting in their own spaces, ask them to stand very straight and tall, then to raise one knee sharply in front, balance for a moment, put it down, then raise the other knee, all the while keeping as straight as they can. After practicing this, give a phrase on drum or claves that matches section A (see figure 7.5).

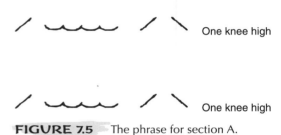

FIGURE 7.5 The phrase for section A.

Then they skip energetically off on the large circular route, returning to their starting places (section B of music) (see figure 7.6).

FIGURE 7.6 The skipping in a circle phrase.

Starting again, straight and tall in their spaces, ask the children to let their heads flop over to the side, or forward as if they have fallen asleep standing up. This time, as they lift one knee high, they suddenly wake up, bringing their heads upright again too. This may take a few tries—it's fun because the movement is so sudden, but it's not easy to coordinate the head movement with bringing one knee up sharply in front! From here, they need to start "sleeping," wake up with one knee high, other knee high, skip away and back, and immediately fall asleep again.

At this point, the children can gather to listen to the first two A and B sections of the music as you talk them through it and they dance with their hands. This is a good place to introduce the idea of the soldiers who stand guard outside the queen's (or king's if you prefer) palace, and that they have a little house to stand in, which is called a sentry box. I show the children a picture of this. At this age, they love the idea of standing very straight like a soldier and of being a guard for the queen or king. Next, they need to run out to stand in their own spots (sentry box) and let their heads fall asleep, ready to try it to the music.

When they have a grasp of the phrasing—usually during the next lesson after a quick review—it is time to put two guards in one sentry box side by side. Now one guard wakes up and eventually skips back to the partner. As guard 1 returns, he or she falls asleep while guard 2 wakes up and takes his or her turn (see figure 7.7). This can be practiced with the rhythm given on a drum or claves and then with the music.

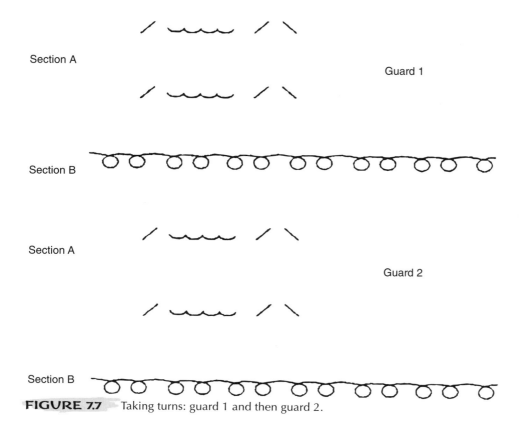

FIGURE 7.7 Taking turns: guard 1 and then guard 2.

2. One Knee High, Skip (Section C)

Section C of the music is slightly different, so it needs its own part in the story. Now the guards decide to change places in their sentry boxes, so they both lift one knee high at the same time, then skip in a tiny circle to change places, decide they don't like it, lift one knee high, and skip in another tiny circle back to their original places. The emphasis needs to be on keeping high knees and a skipping rhythm as they do this. Once the children have explored this, they can listen to the music from the beginning, dancing with their hands as they do so, hear where the place changing comes in, and hear that the A to B sections return right afterward. As we sit and listen I often ask them, "Which part is this?" or "What's happening now?" and they are quick to respond. Now, having practiced back from the beginning, they know all the music except part D.

3. Run, Look! (Section D)

At this point the soldiers lose their orderly behavior because they hear that the queen is coming, and all of them run all over the place looking for her in a bit of a panic.

To a rhythm, they need to try quick light runs, stop suddenly, then quick light runs somewhere else (4 times altogether). This is very enjoyable, but they need to be reminded to run into open spaces quickly and still be able to stop.

The look is just the brief freeze at the end of each phrase (not much more than a pause) where the soldiers can look behind (a slightly twisted shape), or look in front, or look to the side, and so on. They need to experiment with all shapes. For example, they should show a shape where the whole body indicates that they are looking to one side—in other words, display clear, focused shaping. Then they put these ideas into the whole piece: run, look! They listen to the music and try it in the space, then start from the beginning and link everything together.

4. The Procession

Once the soldiers have recovered from their running frenzy, they resume orderly guard duty once more. Then, during the next C section of music, the queen does arrive, and the soldiers use C to join in behind her (she may be imaginary or she may be the teacher!). From then on, for the last two A and B sections, the whole class does one knee high, other knee high, and skips following the queen in a grand procession. Great excitement!

RICE KRISPIES
4 to 6 Years
Pop Goes the Weasel: Vera Lyn

Music pattern	Music emphasis	Action emphasis	Dynamic emphasis	Spatial emphasis
	⌒⌒ ⌒ ⌒	Introduction	The snaps are firm, sudden changes of shape, and the pop a firm, sudden jump either out of or back into the cereal bowl. The skips are quick and light and hurried as the rice krispies travel about the kitchen and then hurry back to their cereal bowls.	The dance focuses on level changes. Each cereal bowl contains 3 rice krispies (one low, one high, one at medium level), each in a holey rice krispie shape. With each snap, the 3 change shapes and levels before popping up and over the rim of the cereal bowl. The skips weave the individual rice krispies in and out of the space in the kitchen before they return to leap back into their bowls.
A		Snap and freeze		
		Snap and freeze		
		Snap and freeze		
		Pop		
A¹		Skip and freeze		
		Skip and freeze		

			Relationship emphasis	Image or sequence
		Skip and freeze	The children, each as a rice krispie with curled body shape with holes (air) in them, are in groups of 3, with body parts in contact with one another in their cereal bowls. With each snap, they change shape, level, and body parts in contact. They scatter during the skip and reform their groups as they pop back into the cereal bowl.	The story is about troublesome rice krispies. Rice krispies are clustered together in their cereal bowls, silent and still until they feel a drop of milk, which makes them snap and suddenly change their positions. Three drops of milk hit them, but when the fourth drop comes, they pop, leaping and turning up out of their bowls to escape all over the kitchen table! When they have dried off, they leap back into their bowls, only to feel more milk descending on them. Imagine the surprise of the person who is trying to have breakfast!
		Pop		
	A repeats			
	A¹ repeats			
	A repeats			

From S. Carline, 2011, *Lesson plans for creative dance* (Champaign, IL: Human Kinetics).

RICE KRISPIES

Pop Goes the Weasel: Vera Lyn

TEACHING PROGRESSION

You can build lesson plans based on this suggested progression:

1. Skip, pop (section A^1)
2. Snap and freeze 3 times, pop (section A)

   Link 2, 1

DANCE SEQUENCE

1. Skip, Pop (Section A^1)

Starting in their own spaces, the children can skip to a rhythm on the claves or drum, weaving in and out of the space. Let them practice this in several short attempts, encouraging lively, light, and quick use of feet (pulling the knees high) as if they are in a hurry. The next time, instead of just freezing at the end of the skipping, ask them to leap high into the air, landing on their feet first, and freeze tight. Now isolate the leaping part, and let them try ways of jumping up and over, encouraging them to swing their arms high, tuck their legs up (as if going *over*), and land lightly but hold a strong finishing shape. After a little exploration on their own, ask them to make a ready-to-jump shape and give 3 beats on the claves or drum so that the emphasis is on the airborne part of the jump and they will hold the landing still.

Now link the skipping phrase with the concluding jump. It will help if they are allowed to skip (from a ready position) for the length of the intended music phrase (see figure 7.8).

The children can gather to listen to the music (section A^1, the second phrase) while they "skip" with their hands to feel the rhythm and imagine weaving in and out of the space. You can warn them to be ready to jump at the appropriate time and introduce this part of the story. Then, they should go back out into their starting shapes, ready to try this to the music.

2. Snap and Freeze 3 Times, Pop (Section A)

Ask the children to make a shape with holes in it and lots of knobby bits sticking out. The first attempts might all look similar, but with guidance their vocabulary will expand. The first focus is on body parts: What parts can make knobby angular shapes (elbows, knees, and so on)? Try a shape with a pointed elbow or knee (give a sudden tap, tap beat so that they make a shape quickly and hold it). Where are these parts sticking out (to the side, in front, behind)? Try again. Do the shapes have holes in them, little pockets of air?

It is good to take cues from the children, and at some points, drawing the group's attention to a feature of one child's shape can help them to clarify their own ideas.

During the exploration, some children will have made a shape close to or on the floor, and this makes a good cue for you to introduce rice krispie shapes that are at the bottom of a cereal bowl or on top. They can try several low and holey shapes, then high and holey shapes, then medium ones. Next, to reinforce this, ask for several in a row, quickly changing from one level to another. Give a series of clear, sharp beats to encourage sudden changes of shape (see figure 7.9).

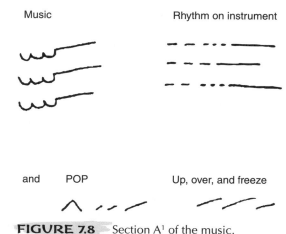

Music | Rhythm on instrument

and POP | Up, over, and freeze

FIGURE 7.8 Section A^1 of the music.

Exploring rice krispie shapes with "holes"— little pockets of air.

(continued)

This might seem long winded, but in fact it takes only a couple of minutes, during which time the children have lots of goes at quickly getting into and holding a variety of rice krispie body shapes.

The children can gather to listen to the music while you help them to hear the cues. The snap happens right at the start of each music phrase (see figure 7.10). Young children tend to take longer to make a complete shape and level change, so they need to start immediately.

At this point the children can go and start in their individual cereal dishes, ready for the first drop of milk to make them *snap* and dance both that section and the skipping one. They will readily pick up the idea that they now *pop* out of the cereal bowl at the end of the snapping phrase, just as they pop into it after skipping.

FIGURE 7.9 Sudden double taps on drum or claves.

FIGURE 7.10 Snap.

Another day, the relationship aspect can be developed. After a quick review of rice krispie shapes and pops, rice krispie skips and pops, you can put three rice krispies into each cereal bowl. Within each group of three, there must be a high one, a low one, and a middle one *and* the rice krispies are joined together. This requires exploring body parts in contact, a concept that young children readily understand. If you point out some possibilities, such as "Look, this rice krispie's elbow is joined to this rice krispie's ankle," the children are quick to pick up and invent ideas of their own. Now they need to practice changing shapes, levels, and parts in contact for each snap and to pop away from each other as they leave the cereal bowl. For the youngest ones, remembering where their cereal bowl was after the skipping can be a problem! It doesn't really matter. It's more important that the children enjoy playing with the body shapes and the excitement of the story than find the correct cereal bowl right away—it will come in time!

THE GHOST
4 to 6 Years
Skin and Bones: Raffi

Music pattern	Music emphasis	Action emphasis	Dynamic emphasis	Spatial emphasis
Intro		Ready	The contrast is between the light, cautious creeping of the old person and the firm, sudden hiding shapes. The light, airy spin contrasts with the ghost's firm, sudden hiding shapes.	The focus is on hiding behind imaginary objects encountered on the walk. The old person takes the shape of a tree trunk (tall and thin), a gate (wide), a rock or bush (curled), and so on. The child explores body shapes at different levels.
A		Creep, creep, creep, hide		
B		Spin, hide		
A		Creep, creep, creep, hide		
B		Spin, hide		
	A and B repeat 4 times		**Relationship emphasis**	**Image or sequence**
C		Jump	This is a leading-and-following partner dance involving matching hiding shapes. The old person, during a walk in the dark, hears a sound and hides, taking on the shape of the object she or he hides behind. The ghost spins to catch up and matches the hiding shape of the old person so that she or he doesn't know it's there! This A and B pattern continues until the end when the two meet face to face.	(Loosely based on the lyrics.) One dark evening, a bony old woman went for a walk to the graveyard near her home. As she traveled along, she felt as if she was being followed, so she hid behind a tall tree. Nobody was there! Each time she continued her soft creeping journey, she could sense that something was behind her. Each time she hid (behind a rock, a gate, a bush), nobody came. Eventually the old woman went home to fetch a broom to sweep up the old bones that she had noticed lying around. But, when she opened the closet, a ghost jumped out!

From S. Carline, 2011, *Lesson plans for creative dance* (Champaign, IL: Human Kinetics).

THE GHOST

Skin and Bones: Raffi

TEACHING PROGRESSION

You can build lesson plans based on this suggested progression:

1. Creep, creep, creep, hide (section A)
2. Spin, hide (section B)

   Develop partner relationship between 1 and 2

3. Jump (section C)

DANCE SEQUENCE

1. Creep, Creep, Creep, Hide (Section A)

Starting in their own spaces, the children can explore creeping by working on lifting their knees high and reaching to place each foot down on the floor quietly and softly. You can suggest that they creep to the side or diagonally rather than always travel forward. Now they can build a sequence of creep, creep, creep and freeze suddenly. This will establish the contrast between the light, ongoing feeling of the creeping and a strong, sudden freezing action. Once they have practiced that a few times, the freeze can be developed into hiding.

Ask the children to show you the shape they might make if they were hiding behind the trunk of a tree (give a beat on drum or claves). Most of them will probably stand very straight, either with arms at their sides or above their heads. Point out a clear, firm shape that looks as if it's trying to be long and thin and very still. If the children are asked to observe some of these features, it might help them to clarify their own shape, tension, and focus. Now they can link the shaping with the creeping phrase (so they have creep, creep, creep, hide), working on the suddenness of the hiding action. Next, you can explore various hiding shapes with the class. The children can show what shape their bodies would make if they were hiding behind a bush. This will likely produce varied semicurled shapes, either at a low or a medium level. Again, point out qualities, such as tension in every part of the body and clear and interesting shaping. From this point you can ask the children what other objects they could hide behind if they were going for a walk in the woods or a park or down a country road. The point is to establish conscious use of body shapes and levels, so various wide hiding shapes as well as long ones and curled ones are developed. Let them practice the creeping and hiding again, but this time they should show you, with their hiding shapes, what they are hiding behind.

Now they can gather to listen to the music while you introduce the story (don't mention the ghost yet, just the old person going for a walk). Listen to section A; with their hands, they practice creep, creep, creep, hide. Keep still for section B, then creep again. Listen to a few repetitions of A and B in the music, then they can go out into the space, ready to creep, and dance three or four of the creep-and-hide sequences, changing their hiding shapes each time (see figure 7.11).

Creeping, working on lifting the knees high and placing each foot carefully and softly.

Creep, creep, creep, hide

Remain hidden

FIGURE 7.11 Actions of the old person (child 1).

2. Spin, Hide (Section B)

Starting in their own spaces, explore a light, fast spin, holding their finishing shapes. You can give a sound on the drum or claves that is approximately the length of section B. Try again, encouraging the children to spin lightly, quickly, and high on their toes and then to freeze tight. Now ask them to travel as they spin, and then add the idea of changing level as they go. Have them show a spin where they start high and get lower as they travel, then try a spin where they start low and get higher as they travel.

As with the creeping, hiding phrase, the spinning can be linked with their already-practiced store of hiding shapes. Listen to the music again, this time freezing through the creeping part, but they should be ready to spin and hide to section B. They should go back into the space and try this for three or four repetitions (see figure 7.12).

Now that they have explored the vocabulary, the children can find a partner, and each pair will get into a starting shape showing who is the old person (ready to creep) and who is the ghost (behind the old person but ready to spin). Giving them the appropriate rhythm, let them practice the lead–follow relationship where the old person creeps and hides, then the ghost spins and hides, matching the old person's shape (so that the old person doesn't know that the ghost is there). Sometimes letting the children watch a pair who have been quick to pick up the lead–follow idea and who show clear matching can clarify the whole partner relationship.

Sometimes, when a new degree of difficulty has been introduced (in this case the relationship), the children might lose some of the clarity that they had shown earlier in the hiding shapes or the creeping and spinning. But with reminders and repetition over time, they will be able to think of it all.

The next step is to listen to the music knowing who is 1 and 2, and try the dance. It is important that on a second attempt, the children switch roles.

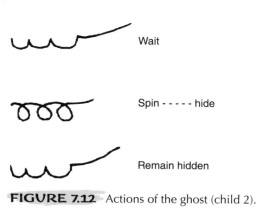

Wait

Spin - - - - - hide

Remain hidden

FIGURE 7.12 Actions of the ghost (child 2).

Stillness   Jump

FIGURE 7.13 The old person and the ghost jump.

3. Jump (Section C)

During the previous teaching process, I keep the end as a surprise by turning the music off before the children hear the C part. The idea of the story is that at the last minute, the ghost, who of course has remained a mystery to the old person, turns and jumps, causing the old person to jump too! The children can all practice the moment of stillness and sudden jump into the air (see figure 7.13). They enjoy saying, "Boo!" as they jump. Finally, the children can show the whole dance, including the scary ending.

Dances
for Ages 5 to 7

WHEN I GET TO THE FAIRGROUND

5 to 7 Years

Theme I, Upstairs, Downstairs: Alexander Faris

Music pattern	Music emphasis	Action emphasis	Dynamic emphasis	Spatial emphasis
Intro	～～ ——	Ready	The skips are quick and lively with an upward feel. The bounces are controlled and rhythmic. The spins are strong and wild.	The focus of the skips is on randomly zigzagging pathways with changes in direction. The bounces travel far in a long line. The spins change level—up to the sky and back down to earth.
A	～～～	Skip		
B	∩ ∩ ∩ ∩ ∩ ∩ ∩ ∩ ∩ ∩	Bounce, bounce, bounce–bounce–bounce Bounce, bounce, bounce–bounce–bounce	**Relationship emphasis**	**Image or sequence**
A	～～～	Skip	This is a partner dance, where A and B meet at the end of the first part of the bounce pattern and part during the second.	A journey to the annual visit of a fair to a neighboring community, anticipating the joys of bumper car rides and the ferris wheel.
C	ටටටට	Spin		
	ටටටට	Spin		
	ටටටටට	Spin		
A	～～～	Skip		
B	∩ ∩ ∩ ∩ ∩ ∩ ∩ ∩ ∩ ∩	Bounce, bounce, bounce–bounce–bounce Bounce, bounce, bounce–bounce–bounce		
A	～～～	Skip		
C	ටටටට	Spin		
	ටටටට	Spin		
	ටටටටට	Spin		
	～～——	Collapse		

From S. Carline, 2011, *Lesson plans for creative dance* (Champaign, IL: Human Kinetics).

WHEN I GET TO THE FAIRGROUND

Theme I, Upstairs, Downstairs: Alexander Faris

TEACHING PROGRESSION

You can build lesson plans based on this suggested progression:

1. Skip (section A)
2. Bounce, bounce, bounce–bounce–bounce (section B)
   Link 1, 2
3. Spin (section C)
   Link 1, 2, 3

DANCE SEQUENCE

1. Skip (Section A)

Starting in their own spaces, while you give a rhythm on drum or claves, the children can practice a vigorous, light skipping throughout the space. The focus should be on pulling the knees and feet away from the floor as quickly as possible. With this skip, introduce the idea of rapidly changing pathways—zigzags, curves—as if skipping up a hillside from rock to rock. When the children show some competence at this, perhaps during another lesson, introduce changing direction also so that sometimes the skipper is moving forward and at other times sideways or backward. Practice to the length of the music phrase, then listen to the music (see figure 8.1). Now the children can go back into the space, show a ready-to-skip shape, and try it.

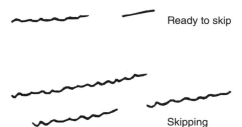

FIGURE 8.1 The skipping phrase, section A of music.

2. Bounce, Bounce, Bounce–Bounce–Bounce (Section B)

Practice bouncing (two feet to two feet), reminding the children to spring high but bend their knees and ankles so that they land softly. Next, clap a rhythm of 1, 2, 123 (big, big, small-small-small) and let them try bouncing to this rhythm. Try again, but traveling sideways (one hip leading) as they bounce. From a starting point in the space, try traveling sideways to a different point with the bounce pattern, then bounce back to the original spot. With a partner, let them experiment to see how far apart a pair needs to start in order to bounce (with the pattern) together, then away. Then introduce the idea of bouncing toward each other so that the pair finish with hips (only) in contact—like bumpers on a car. Gently! Listen to the music from the start through to the end of the bounce pattern so that they are ready for the change of action (see figure 8.2).

Back in the space, they need to start alone but keep an eye on their partner's whereabouts so that they are ready to meet (it doesn't matter if they miss a few times). Try from the beginning through the bouncing, and then leave the music on as the skipping section repeats. At some appropriate moment, discuss the idea of visiting a fairground. In this story the fair has arrived in a neighboring community (over the hill), and comes only once a year, so the people save their money for the best rides. Most children connect bumper cars to the bouncing section previously explored.

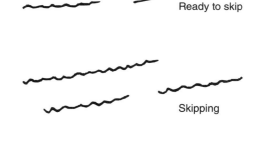

BOUNCE BOUNCE bounce bounce bounce

BOUNCE BOUNCE bounce bounce bounce

FIGURE 8.2 Section A of music (skips) and section B (bounces).

(continued)

3. Spin (Section C)

Explore shapes that look like they're about to spin (ready stance with a slight twist, evident direction of spin, and so on). Go into a fast spin, and freeze tight. Repeat this, thinking about levels. Try going low to high or high to low, freezing the end shape each time. Now try changing levels *and* traveling a short distance with each spin. When the children have a good idea of what they are doing, they can try passing a spin to a partner: One partner starts (the other is a few feet away, ready to spin) and spins to the partner, who continues the spin. A stops as B starts. Try going ABA, focusing on level changes. Listen to section C of the music (see figure 8.3).

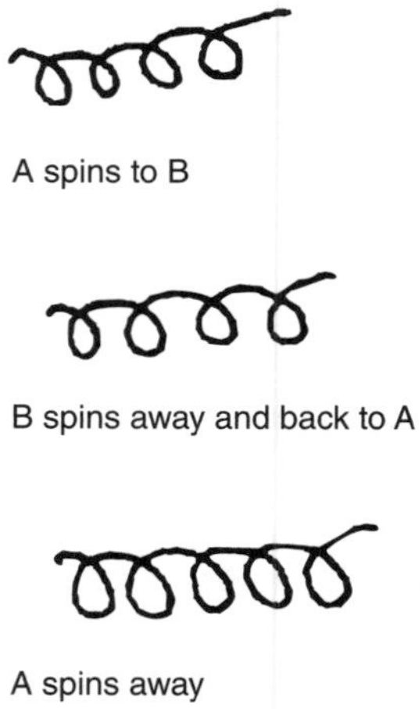

Go back into the space and try the movement to the music. At this point, the children can add to the story by discussing carnival rides that spin. In modern amusement parks, such rides have fancy titles, but most children suggest carousels and ferris wheels.

Listen to all the music and elaborate on the story. The idea is that the children skip up the hillside thinking about what ride to go on first (bumper cars), so they bounce to meet and part with a partner. They continue, then think of the ferris wheel, so the spin occurs. The idea was so exciting that they decide to have another go on the bumper cars, then the ferris wheel. By the time they reach the gates of the fairground, they are so exhausted that they collapse in little piles. (See figure 8.4.) They have had so much fun *thinking* about the rides that they don't have enough energy to actually go to the fair!

At this age, the children understand the idea of anticipation: All these rides happen in their heads before they have reached the fairground. The development of this dance should take part over several classes. It is important that the children feel a sense of completion each day. This may, for example, mean exploring the skip section and the bounce pattern on the first day, possibly without working with a partner, but definitely working with those parts of the music. They can review and improve on this next time, add the partner relationship, and introduce exploration of the spin section.

A spins to B

B spins away and back to A

A spins away

FIGURE 8.3 Passing a spin to a partner.

Collapse

FIGURE 8.4 Collapse!

THE SNOWSTORM
5 to 7 Years
The Boy Who Could Fly: Bruce Broughton

Music pattern	Music emphasis	Action emphasis	Dynamic emphasis	Spatial emphasis
Intro		Ready	The turning, drifting, and settling are fine, gentle, sustained actions (section A). The whirl and twirl of section B and the tumble, leap, fly, and freeze of section A^1 are powerful and as wild as possible. The energy fades gradually as the snowstorm comes to an end, so the final drift and settle are soft and gentle.	The dance is based on changing levels and pathways among other snowflakes. The gentle snowflakes of section A enter in curved pathways to fill the space at a variety of levels, settling on different points of the snowflakes (body parts). The whirling and twirling of the approaching storm change level rapidly, and the tumbling, leaping, flying, and freezing during the storm use all levels as the snowflakes are blown through the air and over the ground.
A		Turn Drift Settle		
A		Turn Drift Settle		

			Relationship emphasis	**Image or sequence**
	A repeats		In section A, the snowflakes drift into the space a few at a time to settle alone. As new snowflakes enter and move among those already settled, they cause them to change shape or level. There is no set order to the entry, so the group relationships will vary each time the story is danced. During the storm (section A^1), the snowflakes work individually, using all the storm action words, but each child develops an awareness of what is going on within the group and reacts accordingly, so at all times, all actions are taking place.	This is a story of the first true snowstorm of the season. As so often happens, a few snowflakes fall gently, settling on the ground, followed by a few more. Then, almost without warning, the wind gathers strength and the snow falls thick and fast, blowing in all directions, filling the air and tumbling over the ground. Just as suddenly as the storm started, it dies down, leaving a gentle snowfall once more.
B		Whirl Twirl		
A^1		Tumble Leap		
A^1		Freeze		
End		Drift Settle		

From S. Carline, 2011, *Lesson plans for creative dance* (Champaign, IL: Human Kinetics).

THE SNOWSTORM

The Boy Who Could Fly: Bruce Broughton

TEACHING PROGRESSION

You can build lesson plans based on this suggested progression:

1. Turn, drift, settle (section A)
2. Whirl, twirl (section B)
   Link 1, 2
3. Tumble, leap, fly, freeze (section A[1])
   Link 1, 2, 3
4. Drift, settle (end)

DANCE SEQUENCE

1. Turn, Drift, Settle (Section A)

The first requirement is to establish some shaping to be used for the moments of stillness in the dance. With the children in their open spaces, ask them to make a shape that has several points. Then ask them to make a different one (to start them thinking). Try to take cues from the response of the class; for example, if one child has sharply bent an arm so that the elbow makes a point, comment on it. This will stimulate an awareness of which body parts can become points (in addition to the obvious fingers and toes). If a child has placed a limb in a different area of space (e.g., an arm above and behind the body), notice it. Follow up by asking the chil-

dren where the points are in the space around them, always giving them the opportunity to try a few more shapes. In addition to these ideas, the aim is to work on levels of snowflakes, so ask them to make a pointed shape that is low (this may cause kneeling, sitting, lying, or low standing shapes to occur). Each time, give a sharp cue with the drum or claves so that the children have to think quickly; by using appropriate body tension, control the result. Do the same with high pointed shapes (possibly semi-upside-down ones) and medium ones. Next, tell them that every snowflake is slightly different and that they are going to show you four or five in a sequence.

Now the exploration can focus on ways of getting into the snowflake shapes. Ask the children to make a shape that is going to turn, and say that the wind is going to blow them gently into a new space and that when it dies down, they will freeze in a snowflake shape. Try this several times, encouraging soft, gentle

Developing awareness of body parts that can make points for snowflake shapes.

turning (light on their toes) and with a different resulting snowflake shape each time. Now instead of turning the snowflakes, the wind is going to make them drift gently to a new spot (light, sustained traveling). Explore this idea several times. The third way of moving into stillness for this section is settling. Each snowflake can start fairly high, then bit by bit, with a slight side-to-side movement, lower into the shape. Start the children in spaces, each in a snowflake shape of choice, and play the first part of the music. Verbally (softly) cue them to turn and freeze, drift and freeze, turn and settle, and so on, continuing to encourage good-quality movement and interesting snowflake shapes.

At this point, gather the children together and talk about the way in which a snowfall sometimes begins, with one flake all alone, then a few more, so that the ground gradually turns white. To introduce a relationship idea, ask one child to turn into the space and freeze in a snowflake shape, then ask a second child to turn or drift gently into the space, passing close to the first snowflake. Explain that as this second snowflake passes the frozen one, it will cause it to gently change to a new shape. Try it again with a couple more children, so those watching can both hear and see what will happen.

Now the exciting part. Ask the children to spread out along one wall (in snowflake shapes) so that the space is empty (no snow yet). Send one child gently out into the space to freeze and settle, then a couple more, then two or three more, then another one, and so on. Cue them to pass snowflakes on their journey into the space so that the ones who got there earlier can change shape. Ask them to look for an empty space to travel into. Gradually all the snowflakes will be in the space.

Gather again to listen to the introduction (which is when the children will be in snowflake shapes, spread out along the wall), and the three A sections of the music, and let them travel and freeze with their hands as you talk about the snowflakes filling the space. Then, back to the side, try it to the music, again helping the children to enter in ones, twos, and threes but in a different order than in the previous attempt.

A snowflake landing from a leap during the blizzard.

2. Whirl, Twirl (Section B)

This part is about the approaching blizzard. With the children in spaces (possibly after a practice of the previous section), ask them to whirl to a new space, really quickly, but lightly on their feet. Now explore, in short doses, the possibility of whirling from low to high and back to low as the wind picks up the snowflakes. They can whirl and twirl on the spot, then whirl and twirl into new spaces. Encourage awareness of not just feet, which must be light, but the full stretching of their arms and fingers and full opening across the shoulders.

Ask them to make a snowflake shape but to be ready for a strong wind, and let them try this to part B of the music. Next, possibly immediately, or after a review during another lesson, link this to the gentle section A of the music.

3. Tumble, Leap, Fly, Freeze (Section A¹)

The melody of section A¹ is a repetition of section A but with the addition of new instruments and much speed and excitement. During this storm, the children work individually and have a choice of when and for how long they want to use the vocabulary of tumble, leap, fly, and freeze. They need to explore each of these words so that they expand their ideas.

Ask the children to start in a snowflake shape, and then tell them that the wind is going to blow them along the ground so that they tumble over the floor. This can happen in many ways, transferring weight over areas of the spine, arms, legs, and buttocks. It helps if you ask the children to make sure that they have holes in their bodies as they tumble. This will cause them to keep an awareness of where their body parts are and to maintain appropriate body tension as they tumble. Encourage changing direction so that they can avoid other snowflakes. Again, use good examples of tumbling snowflakes, pointing out clear features so that the watching children are aware of what they are observing.

Explore leaping (airborne snowflakes) in much the same way, helping with using points (arms) to help with height and soft landings. Children at this age enjoy running and leaping all over the space. Next, try flying snowflakes, which can be fast, light running over the floor, weaving in and out of others.

The freeze is included in this set of words so that when a child needs a brief rest during this fast-paced storm, he or she has a way of taking one! Of course, they will always freeze in snowflake shapes. Now, review this explored vocabulary by questioning the children. What can the snowflakes do during the storm? Then tell them that each snowflake can choose which word to do first, what to do next, and so on. Listen to the section A¹. Some children may suggest an order. Ask them if they all know what they are going to do (it will change, but

(continued)

it doesn't matter) and to take a snowflake starting shape. Practice this to the music, giving verbal help (e.g., "I see a flying snowflake") to remind the children of actions they might have forgotten.

Over time, introduce the notion that lots of different things are happening to the snowflakes at the same time so that while some are tumbling, others may be leaping, others freezing. This just plants the seed for group awareness (whoops, too many tumbles, I'll freeze now) that will develop as the children grow and be stored for future use in similar situations. The next step is to dance all the story so far.

4. Drift, Settle (End)

This vocabulary has been explored in the context of snow. The children might like to decide how the story should end: Would they like to drift and settle in the space as this short section of gentle music occurs, or to exit softly, leaving bare ground? They will need to be encouraged to change the pace from the highly charged storm back to the sustained, fine movement that started the whole dance.

This dance provides many choices for the children: They choose the order of their sequences, when and where to go, and how. If they explore the vocabulary thoroughly and develop it over time, they will have the confidence and knowledge to make good choices.

PATTERN TO CURE A HEADACHE

5 to 7 Years

Minuet: Paderewski

Music pattern	Music emphasis	Action emphasis	Dynamic emphasis	Spatial emphasis
A	*(music notation)*	Step, step, step, step	The sequence of 4 steps backward is light and controlled, contrasting with the spin, which is wild and free flowing. The bounce, bounce, bounce, rise pattern has a clear rhythm and is light and sudden.	The focus of the dance is on doing things backward. The steps are backward and far reaching and the spins are backward as if chasing one's tail. This causes an off-balance sensation, so the bounce, bounce, bounce pattern travels in every direction as if being bounced off objects, with a slight rise between each pattern to regain balance. The rushes cover as much space as possible to determine if the headache has been cured.
B	*(music notation)*	Spin		
C	*(music notation)*	Bounce, bounce, bounce, rise Bounce, bounce, bounce, rise 2 times		
A	*(music notation)*	Step, step, step, step		
B	*(music notation)*	Spin		
C	*(music notation)*	Bounce, bounce, bounce, rise Bounce, bounce, bounce, rise 2 times		

			Relationship emphasis	**Image or sequence**
D	*(music notation)*	Rush	This is an individual dance but with an imaginary relationship to objects in the garden, such as a birdbath, a clothesline, rosebushes, and trees, all of which Prince-What-a-Mess bumps into.	In the story Prince What-a-Mess by Frank Muir, the Afghan puppy gives himself a headache (by too much thinking) and luckily remembers a pattern to cure a headache that he had recently invented: Do everything backward. He steps backward, then chases his tail, which of course makes him fairly dizzy and causes him to bump into the birdbath, the clothesline, and several other objects in the garden. Occasionally Prince What-a-Mess rushes forward to see if his headache is cured, and when it isn't, he does his pattern to cure a headache all over again!
A	*(music notation)*	Step, step, step, step		
B	*(music notation)*	Spin		
C	*(music notation)*	Bounce, bounce, bounce, rise Bounce, bounce, bounce, rise 2 times		
D	*(music notation)*	Rush		
A	*(music notation)*	Step, step, step, step		
B	*(music notation)*	Spin		
C	*(music notation)*	Bounce, bounce, bounce, rise Bounce, bounce, bounce, rise 2 times		

From S. Carline, 2011, *Lesson plans for creative dance* (Champaign, IL: Human Kinetics).

PATTERN TO CURE A HEADACHE

Minuet: Paderewski

TEACHING PROGRESSION

You can build lesson plans based on this suggested progression:

1. Step backward (section A)
2. Spin to chase one's tail (section B)
3. Bounce, bounce, bounce, rise (section C)

    Link 1, 2, 3

4. Rush (section D)

    Link 1, 2, 3, 4

DANCE SEQUENCE

1. Step Backward (Section A)

Starting in their own spaces, the children can experiment with walking backward but with the emphasis on lifting each knee and reaching carefully backward with each foot. They need to imagine that they have very long legs. Walking backward isn't too difficult, but taking large, clear steps backward takes practice, and the children need a little time to try lifting, reaching the foot back, and placing it gently on the floor because it requires balance. As the class catches on to this method of walking, ask them to be aware of which foot will step first, and give them a rhythm with a drum or claves similar to section A (see figure 8.5) so that they get used to taking

four backward steps in a row. They will need reminders to find a space to step into since they are traveling backward. Sections A and B of the music are very short, so it makes sense to explore the spinning of section B before using the music.

Step   and   step   and   step   and   step

FIGURE 8.5   Four big steps backward.

2. Spin to Chase One's Tail (Section B)

Originally I had wondered how a person could spin backward because a spin is either led with the right or the left side of the body. To my delight, the children were able to give the distinct impression that they were spinning backward by the position of their heads and shoulders!

Starting in their own spaces, the children can try a spin where they fling out one arm and follow it around (an open spin). Then, of course, they need to try this to the opposite side. You can give them a series of taps on the drum or claves, during which they spin and then freeze tight. Next, they can imagine that they have a tail and when they spin, they are chasing it. The children should be allowed to experiment here but in short bursts so that they don't get too dizzy! Watching a couple of children whose focus is over a shoulder as they spin chasing their tails will help others to get the idea.

Now they can link together the four backward steps with the spinning to chase their tails.

At this point it is a good idea to gather to listen to the music and talk about the story of the scruffy Afghan puppy (see figure 8.6). Everything has to be done backward for Prince What-a-Mess to cure his headache!

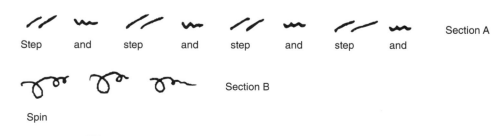

Step   and   step   and   step   and   step   and   Section A

Spin   Section B

FIGURE 8.6   Linking the stepping and spinning phrases.

Children ages 5 and 6 enjoy moving backward—something that they would have had a great deal of difficulty doing when they were younger.

As they listen, they can, with your guidance, dance it with their hands. This is something that they enjoy doing, and it helps you to see if they can hear the rhythm and anticipate the sequencing of events. After listening to the first two phrases a couple of times, the children should hurry back into the space (with a *terrible* headache) ready to try it out.

3. Bounce, Bounce, Bounce, Rise (4 Counts) (Section C)

This part of the dance is a great deal of fun because Prince What-a-Mess has made himself so dizzy by chasing his tail that he bumps into everything in sight! However, for 5- to 7-year-olds, being *in* control while appearing to be *out* of control takes a little time and practice.

First ask the children to stand with their long Afghan legs together and practice bouncing (two feet to two feet). Encourage springing high, using their arms to help, but landing softly, bending their knees. Then focus on where they are bouncing so that they practice bouncing forward, to either side, and even backward, keeping light and springy all the while. Next tell them that they can bounce three times only and that you would like to see a change of direction with each bounce—for example, sideways, backward, forward. Give a beat of 1-2-3, 1-2-3, let them try this, and perhaps watch one or two springy ones who are also changing direction clearly. The children can tell you what order of directions each is using, which may cause some others to be more conscious of their actions when they try it again. As the children practice again to your rhythm, remind them that on each bounce, they bump into something—a rosebush, a birdbath, a wheelbarrow (they will have ideas of their own).

The important thing now is the rise between each set of three bounces. This is where Prince What-a-Mess tries to regain his balance and briefly pulls himself up onto his toes. It will help the children if they take a deep breath and, from a slightly bent position, pull themselves up from their toes, through their bodies, up to their heads. Ask them to pull up and then hold it there so that you and they can check whether they are really stretched. Now they can put the rise onto the end of the three bounces, taking a deep breath for the rise (see figure 8.7). The next step is to try several of these patterns in a row, so give them a rhythm (see figure 8.8).

This is fun, and the children enjoy bouncing all over the garden bumping into everything possible.

Next, they should gather to listen to the music from the beginning so that they hear the stepping, spinning, and now the bouncing, then right back into the stepping, spinning, and bouncing again. Then they can go back into the space and try it with the music.

4. Rush (Section D)

From their own spaces, the children take a deep breath and rush quickly and lightly all through the space, but forward for a change. They enjoy going fast and will become adept at weaving in and out of each other. This is where Prince What-a-Mess experiments to see if his headache has gone. From a ready-to-rush shape, try again but warn them that after the rushing, they must come to a complete halt, ready to step backward once more (he *still* has a headache).

Bounce 3 times   Rise

FIGURE 8.7 Part of section C of the music.

and   bounce 3 times   rise   bounce 3 times   rise   bounce 3 times   rise   bounce 3 times   rise

FIGURE 8.8 Section C of the music.

(continued)

The class can either gather again to listen to the new section of music or stay out in the space and practice from the beginning with your cue to rush at the start of section D.

After this, the children have explored the whole idea and the movement concepts. Now it is a matter of becoming accustomed to the sequencing. As this occurs, they will make better transitions from one action sequence to the next.

They can decide what happens at the end after the last bounce sequence. Does Prince What-a-Mess cure his headache or does he collapse in a tangle of long Afghan legs?

PETER PAN AND HIS SHADOW
5 to 7 Years

Children's March: Percy Grainger (first 1 minute 24 seconds)

Music pattern	Music emphasis	Action emphasis	Dynamic emphasis	Spatial emphasis
Intro		Reach Extend Narrow 1 + 2 Reach	There is a contrast between the sustained, fine changing of shadow shapes during the introduction and the sudden movement of the rest of the dance. The skips are sudden and fine, the freezes sudden and firm. The bounces are sudden and firm but light on feet, and the spins are sudden and firm.	During the introduction, the focus is on the matching of stretched and curled shadow shapes at different levels. The shapes and levels contrast as Peter catches the shadow after his skipping in section A, as they do during the argument in section B.
A		Skip, freeze 1 Skip, freeze 2		

			Relationship emphasis	Image or sequence
B		Bounce, bounce Spin 2 Bounce, bounce Spin, freeze Bounce, bounce Spin 1 Bounce, bounce Spin, freeze	First, Peter and his shadow work together to match shapes or levels before 1 (shadow) breaks away to skip on his own. Peter (2) takes the second phrase of A to catch up. They take turns during the argument in section B, but this time Peter is first as he tries to convince his shadow to cooperate.	Peter Pan's shadow is full of mischief. At first it behaves and copies Peter's every move, but suddenly pulls away from its attachment to Peter's ankle and skips away! Peter has to follow and try to match his own shadow. After a brief argument, the shadow leaves again, leaving Peter no choice but to catch up. They cannot seem to agree at all.
A		Skip, freeze 1 Skip, freeze 2		
B		Bounce, bounce Spin 2 Bounce, bounce Spin, freeze Bounce, bounce Spin 1 Bounce, bounce Spin, freeze		

From S. Carline, 2011, *Lesson plans for creative dance* (Champaign, IL: Human Kinetics).

PETER PAN AND HIS SHADOW

Children's March: Percy Grainger (first 1 minute 24 seconds)

TEACHING PROGRESSION

You can build lesson plans based on this suggested progression:

1. Stretched and curled shadow shapes (introduction)
2. Skip and freeze in a shadow shape (section A)
   Link 1, 2
3. Bounce, spin, freeze argument (section B)
   Link 1, 2, 3

DANCE SEQUENCE

1. Stretched and Curled Shadow Shapes (Introduction)

If you choose to start with this sustained and controlled part, it should follow a vigorous introductory activity; otherwise the children may have difficulty concentrating.

Ask the children to find a space of their own and show you a curled shape. Try several more, giving a quick double click or beat with the claves or drum so that they change shape suddenly. Each time add suggestions: The shape could be on feet, side, or back; it is likely that many will curl in a kneeling position. Ask for one more, and giving a gentle accompaniment with a drum or claves, ask them to see if they can stretch very slowly until fully extended (including fingers and toes). Point out shapes of children who reach interesting positions, preferably those who are asymmetrical. Let them try again, thinking about where their arms and legs are stretching in the space around the body.

Back into a new curled shape, ready to stretch again, but this time introduce levels. Ask if they can stretch parts of the body into a high shape, then from another curled start into a lower stretch. If you let them have several goes, the children will begin to see their choices for high and low stretched shapes.

So far they have practiced curled to stretched shapes. Now they are ready to start curled, slowly stretch to high or low, then slowly curl again into a new shape, stretch slowly to the opposite level, and so on, in a continuous manner.

Gather the children together and introduce the story of Peter Pan and His Shadow. The shadow, of course, copies exactly the shapes that Peter makes (for now). Ask them to find a partner, quickly go to a space together, and decide who will be Peter and who will be the shadow. Peter chooses the starting shape (again point out clear high stretched and low stretched or curled ones). The shadow matches. Now they are ready to begin. Still giving a soft accompaniment and verbalizing, ask Peter to move slowly into his next shape (curled or stretched high and low) and ask the shadows to see if they can match the movements. Bring the children together to listen to the introduction. They could each use their hands (one hand Peter, other hand the shadow) and slowly make them match as they listen. Add a little more to the story as this is going on—the shadow is very well behaved and copying (as shadows do) Peter's every move. Get back into the space in starting shapes. The children may wish to switch roles now as they try the first part of the story to the music.

2. Skip and Freeze in a Shadow Shape (Section A)

Now it will be time to change the pace! Starting in their own spaces, give a skipping rhythm and ask the children to skip throughout the space, looking for empty spaces to go to. Encourage a lively skip by saying that the shadow is going to escape from Peter. Once you are satisfied with the quality of the skipping, ask them to stop and listen to the amount of time they will have for their skipping and to freeze at the end. Give a phrase the same length as the first half of section A of the music (I always sing it in my head as I use the drum or claves) (see figure 8.9).

Try this a couple of times and then tell the children that next time, instead of just a freeze, you want to see them very quickly make a shadow shape (ask for the choices they can make).

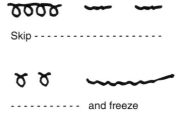

FIGURE 8.9 The first half of section A of the music.

108

Back to partners! They might need to remind each other who Peter will be and who the shadow will be. Now, the shadow (being naughty) skips away from Peter and decides what shape to freeze in at the end of the phrase. Immediately, Peter (second half of section A) skips over to his shadow—but when he freezes, he makes the opposite shape! Peter is trying to tell the shadow that he is in charge.

Try the 1 goes, 2 goes relationship again. If you think the children are ready to handle more information, suggest a weaving pathway as they skip. If not, you can introduce this at a later date. Gather once more to listen to the music from the beginning. This will remind them about the movement context and story of the introduction and the moment at the start of section A when the shadow skips away, leaving Peter to hold the shape he was in. Get back into the space and try from the start.

3. Bounce, Spin, Freeze Argument (Section B)

You could begin with this during the next class (after an introductory activity) or review the previous material first.

Ask the children to stand in spaces alone and to show bouncing, keeping their feet together and bending knees when they land. Suggest that they try "angry" bounces—strong in the body but still with light landings. Doing several bounces one after another is one thing, but Peter and the shadow have to make only two and on beat (see figure 8.10), and they have to be absolutely still after the second one. When they have tried this a few times with your voice, drum, or claves, you can add the spin (also angry). Ask for a quick, wide, strong spin and freeze. Add the spin with the bounces (see figure 8.11).

Good! But it happens twice (figure 8.12). This part of the music has a catchy tune and I tend to sing the action words to the melody: "And bounce, and bounce, and sp i i i i i n, and bounce, and bounce, and spin and freeze." Soon I see mouths moving as the children sing it too.

Try it again, but warn the children that after the second spin, you want to see them freeze in a shadow shape (ask for input: curled or stretched, either high or low). Have a few practices.

The children can find their partners again and switch roles. Explain that Peter is irritated because he wants to tell the shadow to copy his shape (figure 8.13). But the shadow argues (figure 8.14) and freezes in the opposite shape or level from Peter! It's time to gather to listen to the music from the beginning. This will help with transitions and remind them who skips first (shadow) and who bounces first (Peter). Again the children can dance with their hands as you say, "Off goes the shadow," "Off goes Peter," and so on. Then, back into the space quickly to try it from the start.

By this point, you've explored all the movement ideas and relationships (the trickiest part), and it is a matter of listening and doing to realize that after the first argument, the shadow escapes once more. For the second argument, each pair could decide *if* the shadow decides to match Peter or not.

This dance is a good one for letting half the class watch the other half, then vice versa. You can ask the children to look for content that has been explored: curled and stretched high and low shapes, matching partners; mischievous skips, contrasting shapes as Peter catches up; precise and cross arguments; and of course how the pairs decide to end the dance.

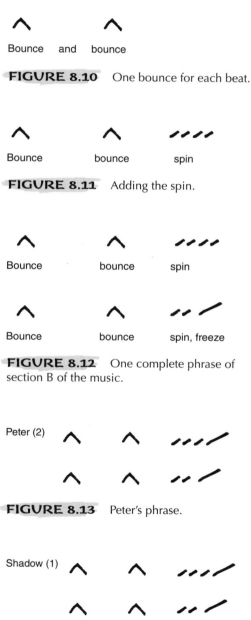

Bounce   and   bounce

FIGURE 8.10   One bounce for each beat.

Bounce   bounce   spin

FIGURE 8.11   Adding the spin.

Bounce   bounce   spin

Bounce   bounce   spin, freeze

FIGURE 8.12   One complete phrase of section B of the music.

Peter (2)

FIGURE 8.13   Peter's phrase.

Shadow (1)

FIGURE 8.14   The shadow's phrase.

9

Dances
for Ages 6 to 8

THE SNOWCHILDREN

6 to 8 Years

The Snowmaiden from Season Fantasies: *Herbert Donaldson*

Music pattern	Music emphasis	Action emphasis	Dynamic emphasis	Spatial emphasis
A	*[musical notation]*	Tumble, rise	This has many dynamic changes. The tumble and rise are very sustained as the snowchildren emerge from the snow.	The children tumble within their own spaces and rise from this low level to an extended standing. The skipping sections focus on making pathways (footprints in the snow). The leaping and freezing are in random pathways with a focus on the real children. The running and hiding travel anywhere in the space, using different levels to hide, still focusing on the real children.
B	*[musical notation]*	Skip, skip, pause	The skipping is light and lively (happy) with sudden pauses to brush off the snow.	
		Skip, skip, pause	The leaping and freezing are strong and sudden (angry) while the running and hiding are more tentative (afraid).	
	B repeats		The sinking and tumbling are as sustained as the start of the story.	
C	*[musical notation]*	Leap, freeze		
		Leap, freeze	**Relationship emphasis**	**Image or sequence**
		Leap, freeze	Most of the dance is individual as the children move among the group in the space. The D section of the music is with a partner as 1 runs to make a wide shape, and 2 then runs to hide behind 1. This may repeat, depending on how far and fast they move.	The snowchildren: One winter's evening, an elderly couple sit looking out of their window at their snow-covered garden. They remember their own children who used to play in the snow and wish that their children might be out there again. As they remember, the smooth snow starts to change shape, and children come to life from beneath it! These snowchildren, delighted to be in such a garden, play, making footprints and watching the snow brushed from their bodies sparkle in the moonlight. Suddenly, some real children come along and threaten the snowchildren. This makes the snowchildren angry, but their anger turns to fear as the real children produce sticks! Eventually the aggressors leave and the snowchildren play once more. But, as the moonlight fades, the snowchildren sadly sink back into the snow and disappear, leaving only a snowy garden, but one covered with small footprints.
		Leap, freeze		
	C repeats			
D	*[musical notation]*	Run, freeze　1		
		Run, hide　2		
	C repeats twice			
	B repeats			
A¹	*[musical notation]*	Sink, tumble		

From S. Carline, 2011, *Lesson plans for creative dance* (Champaign, IL: Human Kinetics).

THE SNOWCHILDREN

The Snowmaiden from Season Fantasies: *Herbert Donaldson*

TEACHING PROGRESSION

You can build lesson plans based on this suggested progression:

1. Skip, pause (section B)
2. Tumble, rise (section A)
   Link 2, 1
3. Leap, freeze (section C)
   Link 2, 1, 3
4. Run, freeze, run, hide (section D)
   Link 1, 2, 3, 4
5. Sink, tumble (section A[1])
   Whole dance

DANCE SEQUENCE

1. Skip, Pause (Section B)

Starting in their own spaces, the children need to explore a lively, light, quick skipping action where they concentrate on pulling their feet quickly away from the floor. Encourage and remind them to weave in and out of each other as they do this. Now introduce the idea of making footprints in snow—this might reinforce the idea of pathways as they want to make patterns all over the snow-covered garden. Another day, after a review of this part, you could suggest a little sideways and backward skipping to vary the pathways even more.

Listen to this section of the music, which occurs twice in a row near the beginning, then go back into the space and try it. Next explore the idea of gently—and with an upward motion—brushing snow off an arm, then watching as the snow sparkles in the moonlight. The action will be a sudden, light flick to brush the snow, letting the eyes follow the snow upward, and pausing briefly to watch it. Suggest brushing snow from the back of the wrist, a shoulder, the thigh, each time letting the focus travel upward. Put this idea into the skipping section—at first cueing the children to pause (brush) with claves or drum, but eventually letting each of them choose *when* to do this, *which* part to brush, and *how* long to pause. Try it with the music.

2. Tumble, Rise (Section A)

From shapes on the floor, explore a very slow, controlled tumble. It helps to suggest that their body shapes always have holes (this prevents them from turning into flat pancakes). They can tumble sideways and even backward. Occasionally you can say, "Freeze," so that they can check that whatever position they are in, they are *aware* of all body parts and that they are in control, using an appropriate amount of tension in the body. Now try rising *very* slowly from the floor (no jerky movements), becoming aware of their arms and legs as they turn into snowchildren.

Listen to the start of the music (section A) and introduce the story—the smooth snow where no children have played for years—and let the children hear the length of this section as the snowchildren slowly tumble and

Light, quick skipping to make footprints in the snow.

(continued)

rise to life. Now, they can practice this part to the music and be ready to move straight into making footprints and watching the snow sparkles in the two B sections that follow.

3. Leap, Freeze (Section C)

The children can practice large leaps and jumps, getting as high as they can but landing softly. Encourage variety here: upward jumps, turning leaps, as long as they really involve the whole body. Now introduce the idea of angry jumps with angular shapes and firm tension. Some children will be able to think of these features for the brief time they are airborne, but all can work on strong angular shapes upon landing, though the landing itself is always soft. Reminders of body parts such as elbows, fists, and knees should aid in this process. Giving a 3-beat sound on a drum or claves helps the children to prepare, leap, and land (note the accent is on the middle beat).

The next step is to tie the jumps firmly into the story idea. Each of the snowchildren can imagine the "real" children who are coming to threaten them in the garden. As they land from their jumps, they focus their eyes and whole bodies toward the aggressor. They should use the whole space, as if real children are approaching from many directions.

Listen to the C section of the music, noting that the snowchildren may choose when to jump (see figure 9.1). At this point, the children can start from the beginning and work through ABBCC, learning to anticipate the sequencing of the story and their movements to the music.

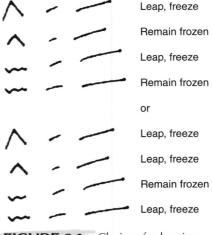

	Leap, freeze
	Remain frozen
	Leap, freeze
	Remain frozen
	or
	Leap, freeze
	Leap, freeze
	Remain frozen
	Leap, freeze

FIGURE 9.1 Choices for leaping and freezing in section C.

4. Run, Freeze, Run, Hide (Section D)

This part occurs once only in the music: when the snowchildren are afraid of the real children, because they see that they are carrying sticks. With the whole group, explore running quickly, but lightly, and freezing in a strong, wide shape. You can extend the children's responses by drawing their attention to the various kinds of wide shapes that occur and by having them experiment with levels, parts of the body that can make a shape wide, and so on. Link this with the run again, freezing suddenly in a wide shape that could be a barrier behind which a friend could hide.

Now the children need a partner so that one can run and make a barrier. As soon as the barrier freezes, the partner can run to hide behind it. Explore hiding shapes here: The hider peeps over, to the side of, or through a hole in the barrier.

After listening to that section of the music, the children can practice their partner work a couple of times so that each has a turn at being both the barrier and the hider. At this point, the children have explored all the movement concepts and linked them with the music and the story.

Now it is a matter of practice over time so that they can internalize the ideas. You can discuss the story, listening to the music so that they develop the sequence of events. After the partner work section when the snowchildren are afraid, section C of the music recurs (the children may have ideas about *why* they cease to be afraid), then section B, when they have one last go at making footprints.

5. Sink, Tumble (Section A¹)

The last part of the music is another A section, so to complete the story logically, the snowchildren reverse the actions from the beginning and sadly sink very slowly and tumble back to being part of the snowy landscape.

As a child once pointed out to me, "I get to do everything in this dance. First I'm happy, then mad (angry), then scared, then sad." The story, which is loosely based on the composer's snowmaiden, is a powerful one and should be developed over time.

THE FULL MOON

6 to 8 Years

Fireworks and Jig from The Little Mermaid: *Alan Menken*

Music pattern	Music emphasis	Action emphasis	Dynamic emphasis	Spatial emphasis
Intro		Wake Stretch	The skips and bounce, hop sequences of section A and the circle skips of section B are quick, light, bouncy, and lively. The waking and stretching during the introduction are sustained and somewhat furtive. The look and listen changes of shape of section C are firm and sudden, as is the hide at the end.	The patterns of section A focus on curved pathways. The introduction and the look and listen of section C focus on body bases.
A		Skip, bounce, hop 4 times 1 Skip, bounce, hop 4 times 2		
A		Skip, bounce, hop 4 times 1 Skip, bounce, hop 4 times 2	**Relationship emphasis**	**Image or sequence**
B		Circle skips 1 and 2	The A sections of the music are lead and follow as 1 creates a pathway and 2 catches up. In section B, the partners link hands and skip in circles, first one way, then the other. The rest of the dance is individual.	Every young elf looks forward to the time when he or she is old enough to join the secret outings that happen during the night when there is a full moon. On those nights, the elves wake from their pre-party sleep and enjoy themselves outside in the ghostly, shadowy moonlight. They have to be quiet and watchful because human beings have been known to be up during the night, and the elves mustn't be seen!
A		Skip, bounce, hop 4 times 1 Skip, bounce, hop 4 times 2		
C		Look, listen		
A		Skip, bounce, hop 4 times 1 Skip, bounce, hop 4 times 2		
End		Hide		

From S. Carline, 2011, *Lesson plans for creative dance* (Champaign, IL: Human Kinetics). Used with permission of Jackie Best-Walushka.

THE FULL MOON

Fireworks and Jig from The Little Mermaid: *Alan Menken*

TEACHING PROGRESSION

You can build the lessons based on this suggested progression:

1. Skip, bounce, hop (section A)
2. Circle skips (section B)
   Link 1, 2
3. Wake, stretch (introduction)
   Link 3, 1, 2
4. Look, listen (section C)
   Link 3, 1, 2, 4
5. Hide (end)
   Link 3, 1, 2, 4, 5

DANCE SEQUENCE

1. Skip, Bounce, Hop (Section A)

Starting in spaces, ask the children to skip quickly and lightly all over the space to a rhythm on drum or claves. Do it again, this time pulling their feet away from the floor very quickly and making sure that their knees lift high, being sharp and pointy. Once the children can do this, ask them to think about where they are going by trying to make curved pathways as they weave in and out of each other (see figure 9.2).

Let them listen to a skipping phrase the length of that part of section A (see figure 9.3). Ask them how many skips this is (eight). Ask them to listen again, then to do eight skips making a really curved path, then freeze. Let them try this a few times, continuing to remind the children about light feet and pointed knees. If two or three children show all this clearly, ask the rest of the class to watch as you point out the qualities of their movement. Then all try again.

Now ask them to try a pattern that starts with a bounce (2 feet), then into a hop (1 foot), bounce, hop, and so on (2–1–2–1–2–1–2). Try it again, but make each part springy and light, keep on their toes, and bend at the knees. Have another go, deciding which foot to hop on, or if it is possible, hop on one foot the first time and the other foot the next. This time, ask them to make this pattern travel in a long straight line and freeze at the end. Now give them a rhythm the length of this part of the music (see figure 9.4), making sure that they can freeze tight at the end of the phrase.

The next step is to join the skipping phrase to the bounce, hop phrase, remembering that the skipping is along a curved path and the bounce, hop is along a straight one (see figure 9.5).

Let the children practice this several times to the rhythm so that they learn to anticipate the change in both footwork

FIGURE 9.2 A curved pathway.

Musical phrase

Rhythm given

FIGURE 9.3 A phrase of eight skips.

FIGURE 9.4 The bounce, hop phrase.

Music

Skip - - - - - - - b h b h b h b   Action

Pathway

FIGURE 9.5 The actions and corresponding pathways for section A.

and pathway. Next, the children should find partners (if there is a group of three, it should have one 1 and two 2s), and decide who will be 1 and 2. Starting one behind the other in a space, give the rhythm so that 1 travels first and then freezes, then 2 takes the second phrase (see figure 9.6).

Repeat this several times, verbally cueing at first so that they learn to pick up immediately as their phrase occurs. When this is clear, focus again on the pathways so that whatever curved path 1 skips, 2 can follow it when his or her turn arrives.

Gather to listen to section A of the music, which happens twice in a row near the start of the dance. Let the children be ready with their fingers to skip, bounce, and hop to their individual phrases and freeze during their partner's phrases. Discuss nights when the moon is full, and how the creatures and the elves of the woods go out to party while the light is brighter than other nights. Remind them that all elves are light, with pointed elbows and knees, then send the children out to take a starting shape (ready to skip) with their partners. Sometimes two children may decide to switch. This is a good idea because now there is a new leader. If they don't initiate this, you may wish to suggest it. Try their patterns to the music a couple of times.

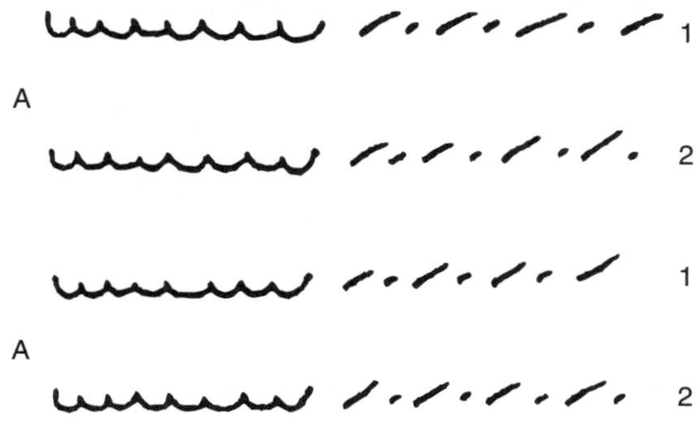

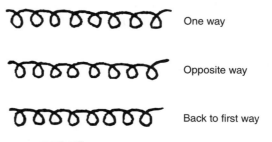

FIGURE 9.6 Partners dancing alternating phrases.

FIGURE 9.7 Skipping circles.

2. Circle Skips (Section B)

Now the elves join hands and skip in a circle, first one way, then the other, then the first way again. The children need to practice this so that they learn to change from skipping clockwise to counterclockwise (or vice versa) without missing a beat. After a little practice, listen to section B, and try it out (see figure 9.7).

I usually do this part with the partners joining both hands, and they are quite happy to do so (the movement is fun and the context is fun). At this age, boys and girls usually work together. An alternative is to link elbows.

Now the children can practice sections A, A, B, and then into the next A so that they develop an idea of the sequencing.

3. Wake, Stretch (Introduction)

Start the children in their own spaces, and ask them to curl up and go to sleep (possibly under a blanket of leaves). Notice the responses, and comment on interesting sleeping shapes. In this way, the children will think about it and not just plop down the next time! Giving slow, gentle sounds on a drum or claves, verbally guide them to wake up quite slowly, stretching each body part as they get up to their feet. This should be fairly easy to do, but draw their attention to full extension of parts, including fingers and toes. Once they are on their feet, ask them to keep their feet on the floor but rapidly bend and straighten their knees in a bouncing action that doesn't leave the floor. This is fun—the elves are eager to get going!

Listen to the introduction to the music and discuss where elves might sleep and possibly how old they need to be before they are allowed to go to full-moon parties, and verbalize the actions of waking, stretching, and bending the knees.

Now, back into the space to dance the story so far.

4. Look, Listen (Section C)

Suddenly, in the middle of their party, the elves hear a noise and fear that a human might be out and about—and elves *mustn't* be seen by humans!

While the children are in spaces, give them a sound to make a shape (and hold it tight) as if they have heard a noise. At first they may do this in standing shapes and need to explore other possibilities. Ask them to try again, this time showing that all parts of their bodies are helping the shape (awareness of all parts) and that they can show you by the angle of their heads where the noise came from. Look for children who show good

(continued)

body tension and are perhaps tensed and leaning toward the noise. Now ask them to make a kneeling shape that indicates listening, and look at some clear examples as they occur. Try one knee, two knees, stretched high, curled lower, and so on. Each new suggestion opens up lots of possibilities for the children. In a similar manner, explore sitting and lying listening shapes. Suggest that the elves hear four separate noises, each coming from a different area of the woods. Now they are going to make a series of four listening shapes, using different body bases, moving suddenly into each shape, and freezing there for a few seconds. Practice this several times.

Gather to listen to section C (see figure 9.8). Ask the children if they have each decided which type of listening shape to make first, second, third, and fourth; then send them back into the space to practice their sequences with the music.

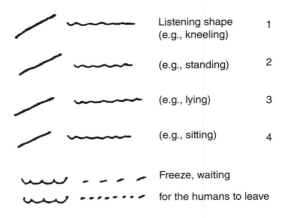

FIGURE 9.8 Music cues for the four listening shapes.

At this point the children could practice from the A section preceding the listening shapes so that they learn the order of events and make a good transition from the skip, bounce, hop into listening—continuing into the following A section when the humans have gone away and the elves continue to have fun.

5. Hide (End)

This part is brief—a long note during which the elves decide to end the party (do the humans return or is it nearly morning?) and hide. They can practice hiding shapes and choose whether to hide alone or with their partners. Now the elves can start from the beginning and show the whole story.

THE LITTLE CHINOOK
6 to 8 Years
Gigue from Sonata Op. 5, No. 9: Corelli

Music pattern	Music emphasis	Action emphasis		Dynamic emphasis	Spatial emphasis
A	*(drawn notation)*	Bounce, bounce, bounce, spin, skip	1	Mainly a contrast between light, lively movements and firm, sudden ones. As the droplet of water ventures off alone (section A), the bounces are light and springy, the spin quick and smooth, and the skips light and playful. This contrasts with the freezing of isolated body parts, which is firm and sudden as the droplet turns into ice. The rushing of the little chinook is light and sudden. While melting, the body parts that were frozen suddenly lose tension and flop as the chinook blows warm air directly onto each part (section B). The runs of section C are light and carefree. As the droplet attempts to creep away, the tension is fine, but fairly quick. The chinook runs quickly to catch up (section D).	The focus is on pathways. The bounces are in a zigzag pattern as the droplet of water goes over rocks, the spin (in a whirlpool) is on the spot, and the skipping is in a meandering pathway as the droplet flows downstream. It freezes in personal space. The chinook rushes directly to the droplet and explores levels as it melts the droplet. The running downstream (section A) is again an interesting weaving pathway.
		Freeze 6 counts			
B	*(drawn notation)*	Rush	2		
C	*(drawn notation)*	Blow, melt	1 and 2		
	(drawn notation)	Run	1 and 2		
A	*(drawn notation)*	Bounce, bounce, bounce, spin, skip	2		
		Freeze 6 counts			
B	*(drawn notation)*	Rush	1		
C	*(drawn notation)*	Blow, melt	1 and 2		
	(drawn notation)	Run	1 and 2		
D	*(drawn notation)*	Creep 4 counts	1		
	(drawn notation)	Rush	2		
D	*(drawn notation)*	Creep 4 counts	2		
	(drawn notation)	Rush	1		

Music pattern	Music emphasis	Action emphasis		Relationship emphasis	Image or sequence
	D repeats twice			A partner dance, but one where they change roles. Child 1 bounces, spins, skips, and freezes alone as child 2 watches (section A). Partner 2 runs to rescue partner 1 and blows on each body part to thaw it out while 1 melts (section B). During section C, the pair travel together. For the next repetition of ABC, the two children switch roles. In section D, child 1 creeps away, 2 rushes to catch up, but then 2 creeps away, 1 rushes to catch up, and so on. The pair dance together for C^1 at the end.	Winter is approaching and the stream is becoming cold enough to freeze a small droplet of water if it ventures off alone. But, the tiny drops of water are bored with flowing slowly downstream. They want the excitement of splashing on the rocks and spinning in whirlpools all alone. Look out! At this time of year, a drop of water straying too far from its friends will freeze instantly! Luckily, there is a kindly little chinook in the area—a warm little wind who will blow a nice puff of air onto the icy drops to thaw them out so that they can continue to flow downstream. Sadly, the little droplets are slow to learn their lesson, and each one thinks it is strong enough to creep away alone. Luckily they are scolded just in time: "No no no no no no!" Eventually the little drops of water have learned their lesson: Stay with a friend and then you won't freeze.
	A repeats				
	C repeats				
C^1	*(drawn notation)*	Run and freeze	1 and 2		

From S. Carline, 2011, *Lesson plans for creative dance* (Champaign, IL: Human Kinetics). Used with permission of Jackie Best-Walushka.

THE LITTLE CHINOOK

Gigue from Sonata Op. 5, No. 9: Corelli

TEACHING PROGRESSION

You can build the lesson plans based on this suggested progression:

1. Bounce, bounce, bounce, spin, skip } (section A)
2. Freeze 6 counts

3. Blow, melt } (section B)
4. Rush, blow, melt

    Link 4, 3
    Run } (section C)
    Link 1, 2, 3, 4

5. Creep 4 counts } (section D)
    Rush

DANCE SEQUENCE

1. Bounce, Bounce, Bounce, Spin, Skip (First Part of Section A)

Starting in their own spaces, the children can explore bouncing. Bounces are jumps that use a two-foot takeoff and a two-foot landing. They need to practice bouncing high and landing lightly with bent knees. If the children are bouncing on the spot, suggest that they travel and then extend this to bouncing from side to side. After a little practice, with reminders for improving the quality of the action, ask them all to be ready to bounce in a zigzag pathway, using only three bounces (give a clear rhythm with drum or claves). You can give a hint of the story by mentioning that a tiny, light drop of water is bouncing from rock to rock to rock.

Next, explore a whirlpool spin. This needs to be a wide-open spin on the spot. The children should start in a ready-to-spin shape and then spin quickly and smoothly for about 4 beats, freezing their shapes at the end. Over time, you may wish to introduce levels also—a whirlpool that starts high and spins lower—as long as they remain on their feet because of the skipping that will eventually follow. At this point it's a good idea to link the phrase of three bounces with the whirlpool spin and then play with skipping along a weaving pathway. Link the sequence of those three actions, giving the children a rhythm close to that of the music (see figure 9.9).

Now they need to hear the music, at which time you can explain the first part of the story about the little drop of water daring to go off alone. It's a good idea to let the second part of section A play too (see figure 9.10) so that the children know what comes next and that they are going to freeze! Then, back in the space, they get ready to bounce and try the phrase with the music a few times.

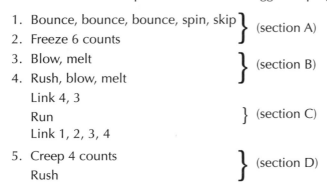

Bounce   bounce   bounce   spin   skip

FIGURE 9.9 The breakdown of actions to section A of the music.

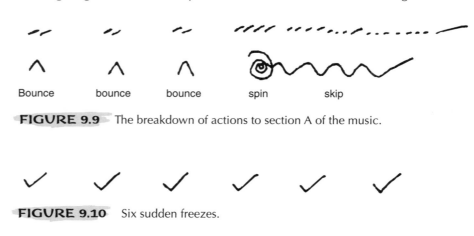

FIGURE 9.10 Six sudden freezes.

2. Freeze 6 Counts (Second Part of Section A)

While they are working in their own spaces once again and starting from a standing position, tell the children that when they hear a sudden beat (claves or drum), bend an elbow suddenly and hold that shape tight. To encourage variety, ask them to stand straight again, and this time suddenly to bend the elbow but put it in a *different* place in relation to their bodies. Pointing out a few interesting ones (e.g., in front of the body, very high) should help them with ideas. Now, holding that shape, ask them to add to it by suddenly bending another part (head, knee, other elbow). Then ask them to stand straight again, tell them that they will have 6 beats for the drop of water to freeze, one body part at a time. Look at the results, which should be angular shapes at a variety of levels, probably looking quite awkward and uncomfortable, but frozen! Try it again a few times so that the children can consciously decide which part to freeze, where, and in which order. Now they can link the whole A phrase of the music (see figure 9.11).

The little chinook blowing to thaw a frozen droplet of water.

3. Blow, Melt (First Part of Section B)

This is a good time to explore the melting process, because like the freezing, it happens one part at a time. From their frozen shapes, tell them that you are going to blow a warm wind on *one* body part (their choice) and that as you do, *that* part will suddenly flop because it has thawed. This takes a bit of practice, as it is hard to maintain a firm tension in some parts of the body while allowing another part to lose tension, but it is fun, and they will succeed, especially if they see a couple of clear examples. Try again, freezing for 6 beats, then thawing for 6 beats.

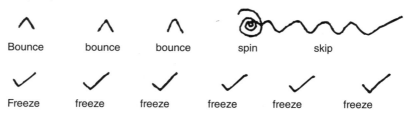

Bounce	bounce	bounce	spin	skip
Freeze	freeze	freeze	freeze	freeze	freeze

FIGURE 9.11   Linking the actions of section A.

4. Rush, Blow, Melt (Second Part of Section B)

Now the children need to find a partner, and instead of the teacher being the chinook that thaws the frozen drop of water, one of them will do it! One child (1) needs to freeze (for 6 beats) and the other, starting a little way from the partner (2), sees what has happened and rushes quickly and lightly straight to the rescue and gently blows directly toward, for instance, an elbow (which flops), then a knee (which flops), a hand (which flops) and so on, 6 times until the thawing process is complete. Let them try that again a couple of times, then switch roles and practice some more.

Next, the children can gather to listen to the music from the beginning while you expand the story line and they dance with their fingers. Partner 2 starts in a shape watching 1 as he or she bounces, spins, skips, and freezes; then 2 rushes to the rescue and blows to melt 1. (This sounds complex, but it seems logical to the children in the context of the story.) When 1 has thawed, the two partners run happily, weaving close together through the space as they travel downstream.

Let them listen again as you watch for understanding, verbalizing the action in the context of the story, and then let the music run on as the whole process starts again, but this time 2 is the one to bounce away on his or her own!

Now with their partners, they can go back into the space, one with feet together ready to bounce, the other one watching closely, and try the first two ABC sections in sequence.

5. Creep 4 Counts, Rush (Section D)

At this point in the story, the individual droplets of water *still* haven't learned that it's not a good idea to go off alone in really cold weather. This time, however, they creep away, so the children need to explore this action in the context of the story.

(continued)

The creeping is light, quiet, but fairly quick, so the children can practice by focusing on raising a knee and placing the foot quietly down, then the next, and so on. As they show control of their knees and feet, suggest that they might step to the side sometimes so that they have to think about where they are traveling as well as how. You may introduce this during another lesson. Starting again, tell them that they have only 4 beats to creep away, then pause (see figure 9.12), and practice it to that rhythm.

Now they can work with their partner again, and 1 will creep away, then 2 rush toward her or his partner, saying, "No no no no no no no!" This causes a fair amount of excitement as one droplet of water creeps mischievously away and the other tries to prevent it. *But*, the second time, which is immediately, 2 creeps away and 1 rushes in admonishing with "No no no no no no no!"

This whole sequence happens again (see figure 9.13). They take turns being sensible, then brave (or foolish).

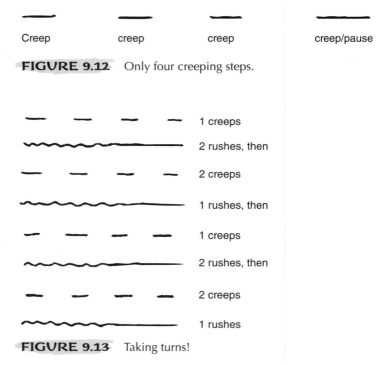

Creep   creep   creep   creep/pause

FIGURE 9.12   Only four creeping steps.

1 creeps
2 rushes, then
2 creeps
1 rushes, then
1 creeps
2 rushes, then
2 creeps
1 rushes

FIGURE 9.13   Taking turns!

After they explore this section and you explain the music and story and have them practice in the space, the children will have played with all the movement ideas in the dance.

The final part of the music is ABC again, and *still* little droplet 1 hasn't learned that unless it stays with another droplet, it will freeze! So, they repeat the original sequence until, at the very end, with section C^1, the two droplets run close together a long way down the stream.

Once you really know the music for this dance, it is logical! The children, as usual, learn the music sections quickly, helped by the story. The unusual partner relationship in this is exciting.

BATTLE OF THE SEASONS

6 to 8 Years

Excerpt from The Snowman: *Howard Blake (track 6, 0:43 to 2:39)*

Music pattern	Music emphasis	Action emphasis	Dynamic emphasis	Spatial emphasis
A		Skip change of step 4 times, bounce, hop 3 times, turn 1 and 2 Skip change of step 4 times, bounce, hop 3 times, turn	The skip change of step, bounce, hop sequences are sudden and light on feet. The spiraling turns of section B are sustained, but winter is firm and powerful, contrasting spring's fine movements. The sparkle jumps are sudden and firm in body, though light on feet.	Winter and spring part and meet with direct pathways in section A. The focus in section B is levels: turns taking the season from high to low, low to high. The sparkle jumps cover as much ground as possible; spring aims to replicate winter's pathway.
B		Turns 1 and 2		

Music pattern	Music emphasis	Action emphasis	Relationship emphasis	Image or sequence
A¹		Skip change of step 4 times, bounce, hop 3 times, freeze 1 and 2	This is a partner dance between winter and spring. Section A is parting and meeting; section B is contrasting levels on the spot. In section C, winter takes the first and third phrases, and spring the second and fourth while following winter's path.	It is that time of year when winter is losing its grip and small signs of spring emerge. Although winter has had a long season, it is reluctant to give way and tries to overpower spring with strength. Gentle spring is determined to erase the last traces of winter. Which season will prevail?
C		Sparkle jumps, freeze 1 Sparkle jumps, freeze 2 Sparkle jumps, freeze 1 Sparkle jumps, freeze 2		
A		Skip change of step 4 times, bounce, hop 3 times, turn 1 and 2 Skip change of step 4 times, bounce, hop 3 times, turn		
B		Turns 1 and 2		
A²		Skip change of step 4 times, bounce, hop 3 times, freeze 1 and 2		

From S. Carline, 2011, *Lesson plans for creative dance* (Champaign, IL: Human Kinetics). Used with permission of Jackie Best-Walushka.

BATTLE OF THE SEASONS

Excerpt from The Snowman: *Howard Blake (track 6, 0:43 to 2:39)*

TEACHING PROGRESSION

You can build lesson plans based on this suggested progression:

1. Skip change of step, bounce, hop pattern (section A)
2. Spiraling turns (section B)
   Link 1, 2
3. Sparkle jumps (section C)
   Link 1, 2, 3
4. Skip change of step, bounce, hop pattern and decide who wins! (section A^2)
   Link 1, 2, 3, 4

DANCE SEQUENCE

1. Skip Change of Step, Bounce, Hop Pattern (Section A)

Each child starts in an open space. Ask them to travel with a skip change of step, keeping the footwork light and lively. After some practice, try a pattern of four skip change of step, traveling as far as possible in a direct path. Use a clapping beat or drum or claves to keep the tempo, which should be as close to the tempo of the music as possible. Next, explore a rhythmic hopscotch pattern, alternating the bounces (2 feet) and hops (1 foot). Encourage light, springy transfer from 2 to 1 to 2 to 1 to 2 to 1, freeze. Suggest that they might like to try hopping sometimes on one foot, sometimes on the other (2 right, 2 left). Some of the children will latch on to this idea, while others might have enough to deal with alternating from two feet to one foot!

From a standing start in the space, link together the four skip change of step into the bounce, hop, bounce, hop, bounce, hop, freeze.

Ask the children to find a partner and start in a space together, standing back to back. Give them the rhythm so they do the pattern as they part: skip change of step 4 times; bounce, hop 3 times; freeze. Run back together, ready to start again, but this time, instead of the freeze at the end of the phrase, they can try a sudden half turn (so that they are facing their partner), then repeat the whole pattern as they travel toward each other and end up face to face. Let them experiment with this a few times, giving reminders for quality as they adjust the distance they travel so that they meet at the end of the second phrase.

Gather the class together to listen to the A section of the music, and indicate that there is no introduction. As soon as the music starts, they will be off! Let them try the pattern using their hands to get a feel for the pace. Send them quickly back into the space, back to back in pairs, and try this part to the music.

2. Spiraling Turns (Section B)

Ask the children, on their own again for a few minutes, to make a high shape that looks as if it is about to turn. Point out examples that show this—good focus and a twist in the trunk indicating a turn is about to happen. Guide them through trying a long sustained turn, with a firm body, as if they want to push and spiral down toward the floor, and once low, to spiral firmly back up to high.

Now try the opposite. Start in a low shape that is about to turn toward a high level. This time, the turn is very fine and gentle but still sustained. Let them try both low to high and high to low. Let them play with these turns for a few minutes so that they can feel the difference in tension.

Ask the children to reunite with their partners and to decide who will be winter (firm) and who will be spring (fine). They start close together with winter high, ready to turn, and spring low, ready to turn. At the same time, winter will spiral to low and spring will spiral to high.

Gather again to listen to section A, and review the skip change of step, bounce, hop sequences as they part and meet, quickly get into their high or low positions for the spiraling of section B. Each pair will have time during section B to turn at least twice. Introduce the story about the time of year when two seasons seem to be occurring at the same time. Send the pairs back to their starting places, ready to try the first two parts of the story. They may wish to switch seasons this time. Give cues as necessary as they work with the music.

There is one phrase of section A immediately after section B, and for this, winter and spring repeat the skip change of step, bounce, hop sequence into a space away from their partner and freeze.

3. Sparkle Jumps (Section C)

This is probably an introduction to sparkle jumps for this age group but appropriate for the story. With these jumps, winter spreads frost and spring attempts to thaw it. Ask the children to find a space, then jump, shooting their arms and fingers upward and outward. A demonstration of this will help, showing that they can push off both feet and extend one a little way behind the body while in the air. The arms quickly pull back toward their shoulders as they land. Let them experiment, always with the intent of shooting either frost through their fingertips (winter) or warmth (spring). Try a series of sparkle jumps, traveling into space.

Gather together to listen to section C. It is a good idea to start the music at the beginning so that the class can review the preceding parts of the dance and get a clearer sense of the transition. As the sparkles begin, winter and spring are apart, but they need to know where each is in the space. Winter (1s) sparkles first, determined to keep that part of the world cold, and has time for 8 sparkle jumps. Then winter freezes, and spring (2s) follows his path trying to thaw the frost before freezing—then it is winter's turn again, then spring's. Listen a couple of times and ask the children to tell you when it is winter or spring's turn. (I sometimes ask them to shoot their hands up when it is their music and quickly put their hands down when it isn't. This is enjoyable and keeps them alert, and it is helpful for the children who are slower on the uptake!) Ask them to run back into the space, ready to try. If you are able to fast-forward the music to just before section C, the class can try the sparkle jumps in isolation a couple of times. Then it is a good idea to do it from the beginning.

Section A follows the sparkle jump section, so spring needs to have caught up with winter by the end of section C and be back to back again, ready to skip change of step away. By now the children will recognize the B music and the power struggle of the spirals when it happens once more.

4. Decide Which Season Prevails (Section A^2)

The last part of the music starts like section A, so the seasons repeat the skip change of step, bounce, hop sequence *but* change their pathway so that they are close to each other for the variation in the music.

By this point, the class will have explored and developed the movements and the story over parts of several classes. Ask them to decide with their partner how it should end. Will winter win the battle, or will spring? The sustained note at the end of section A^2 allows time for them to find a finishing shape showing which season triumphs. For example, does one finish higher or perhaps in front of a partner?

Let them try the whole dance now, and cue where necessary. When they have achieved a measure of fluency, it is a good idea to have half the pairs dance while the others look for certain features (sprightly traveling, contrast in power between winter and spring as they turn, a clear sense of freezing and thawing during the jumps) and then have the other half dance. Brief sharings allow for a lot of learning if the children are looking for positive aspects of what they are seeing, and they come to appreciate each other's work.

Dances for Ages 7 to 9

THE ARCHERS

7 to 9 Years

Jagdlied: Schumann

Music pattern	Music emphasis	Action emphasis	Dynamic emphasis	Spatial emphasis
A	*(notation)*	Gallop, leap	The galloping and leaping are firm, sudden actions, and the archers freeze in a strong shape as soon as they have landed from the leaps off their horses. The stepping and turning of section C are lighter and more sustained as they listen for the whereabouts of their victims.	The gallops use short, straight pathways; the leaps take the archers high into the air before landing. The main spatial focus of the dance is on levels as the archers freeze with their bows drawn. Body bases can be developed here as they try kneeling, standing, sitting, and lying shapes ready to release their arrows. You can place emphasis on the angles of their ready-to-fire positions: high, either side, behind, diagonally.
B	*(notation)*	Freeze		
A	*(notation)*	Gallop, leap		
B	*(notation)*	Freeze		
A	*(notation)*	Gallop, leap		
B	*(notation)*	Freeze		
A	*(notation)*	Gallop, leap		
B	*(notation)*	Freeze		

Music pattern	Music emphasis	Action emphasis	Relationship emphasis	Image or sequence
C	*(notation)*	Step, turn	This is an individual dance as each archer pursues an imaginary escapee from the castle.	Dangerous traitors have escaped from the castle, so the king's archers have been sent in hot pursuit. Armed with a quiver full of arrows and a bow each, they gallop over the drawbridge and into the forest. Each time an archer spots one of the traitors, he leaps off his horse and draws his bow, ready to release an arrow, but the traitor has moved on! A relentless pursuit follows as the traitors hide up in trees or behind bushes and rocks. For a few moments the archers think that they have lost track of their victims, then suddenly spot a movement or hear a sound, and the chase continues.
	(notation)	Step, turn		
A	*(notation)*	Gallop, leap		
B	*(notation)*	Freeze		

From S. Carline, 2011, *Lesson plans for creative dance* (Champaign, IL: Human Kinetics).

THE ARCHERS

Jagdlied: Schumann

TEACHING PROGRESSION

You can build lesson plans based on this suggested progression:

1. Gallop and leap (section A)
2. Freeze in archer shapes (section B)
   Link 1, 2
3. Step and turn (section C)
   Link 1, 2, 3

DANCE SEQUENCE

1. Gallop and Leap (Section A)

Starting in their own spaces, the children can practice galloping. This can be either forward or sideways (experiment with both) with the emphasis on strong bodies but light feet. Give a galloping rhythm on drum or claves. As their movement improves, ask them to be ready to gallop and to look directly at where they want to go, then gallop powerfully in a straight pathway for 4 counts, then freeze. Experiment with this a few times so that the children can practice galloping with intent yet be able to stop suddenly (bent knees, strong legs) after the fourth gallop. Next, ask them to change their routes for each gallop so that each child is zigzagging through the space as if going down pathways in a forest. Often, drawing a pattern of pathways on the chalkboard helps to clarify this idea and makes them conscious of where they are going (see figure 10.1). Having discussed this, try it again in the space.

Now, with the children in their own spaces, ask them to experiment with the idea of leaping or throwing themselves off a horse. Let them try for a few moments, then ask them to make a ready-to-jump shape and give 3 beats, telling them to hold their landing shapes. At this point, much of the information can be drawn from the children. Watch for a child who shows a high and strong leap, one who kicks the legs up as if getting over the saddle, one who turns in the air to land facing another direction, and one who lands in a strong, powerful shape. If the children watch some clear examples while you or they verbalize the strengths of those jumps, they will add to their own ideas. Let them all try a few more.

Next, they need to join the powerful galloping with the leap off the horse. Starting in their own spaces, ready to gallop, explain that they will have four gallops, followed by the leap off the horse, then freeze tight.

Give a clear rhythm for this (see figure 10.2).

Let them practice this so that the movements become clear and they are using the space well. This is a good point for the children to sit and listen to the music while you tell them about the escaping traitors and the

FIGURE 10.1 Drawing two contrasting pathways.

Gallop 4 times   Leap and freeze

FIGURE 10.2 The timing of gallop, leap, and land for section A.

(continued)

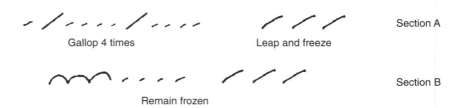

Gallop 4 times	Leap and freeze	Section A
Remain frozen		Section B

FIGURE 10.3 Listening: gallop, leap, freeze for section A; stillness for section B.

pursuing archers. For the moment, the focus is on the gallop and leap phrase, so they will just freeze for the B sections of music (see figure 10.3). Let them listen to the first four AB sections of the music as you verbalize the action, then go back into the space and try it.

2. Freeze in Archer Shapes (Section B)

This is an exciting idea for children of this age. A Robin Hood type of existence has great appeal, and they love to discuss the strength required for pulling the string of the bow, the quiver for the arrows, and so forth. First ask them to show you a shape where they have pulled the bowstring as far as possible but haven't released the arrow. The results will probably be fairly uniform—standing shapes with the focus directly in front of each child. However, several children will likely show a wide base with strong legs, and you can point out that these features are necessary for an accurate shot. Ask them if they have to be on their feet to use a bow and arrow and immediately a whole range of ideas will start to emerge. They can explore, with your guidance and clear examples from the class kneeling and aiming, lying, sitting, and standing in a low position. Give the "And freeze" beat and let them have lots of practice. Exploring bases (stand, sit, kneel, lie) is enough information for one day, but over the next few classes, you can add to the possibilities by exploring the angles as well. Can you freeze with the lower part of your body facing one way, but be twisted so that the bow faces another? Is it possible to be in a very low shape but shoot up diagonally? (Where is the traitor?) The children become very brave in their attempts, and I often get the feeling that the boys and girls would make excellent candidates for the band of merry men in Sherwood Forest.

Now the trick is to sequence the leap off the horse into these marvelous archer shapes, so they can practice the whole sequence of gallop four times, leap, and freeze in an archer shape. Do this first as you give a rhythm, encouraging them to land in a different shape each time. At first, the quality and variety of the jumps may be somewhat lost as they focus on the archer shapes, but with reminders and practice they will be able to remember and execute the whole sequence with full effort. At this point, the children are ready to dance the first four AB sections of the music.

Exploring body bases: a sitting archer shape. The archer is looking toward the escaping traitor.

3. Step and Turn (Section C)

This section will probably be reached during a second class after a review of the previous material. Just for a few moments, the archers lose sight and sound of the traitors, so they step slowly and carefully, turning occasionally so that they are watching all parts of the forest around them. It will be necessary to emphasize the sustainment of this part—no jerky movements, placing the feet carefully, the whole body showing watchfulness. After exploring the ideas, again gather to listen to the music from the start (good review) so that the children are ready for this new part in the sequencing and so that they can learn how long this part lasts before they spot a traitor and gallop off once more.

They can practice the stepping and turning in isolation back in the space, then put it into the whole dance. A good idea that emerged from the children the first time I experimented with this dance was the finger action for releasing the arrow—so as a class we adopted it. At the end of each B section (freeze in an archer shape), the children released the arrow by sharply extending the fingers that had curled around the bowstring and arrow. It takes awareness of timing as they freeze for 7 beats, suddenly release the arrow, then gallop away. These sorts of fine additions develop if children are allowed to build a dance over a series of classes.

Interesting discussions arise from this dance about the design of castles, the narrow slits of windows for the archers, the portcullis, drawbridge, moats, and so on. Associated work in social studies and art could accompany the work on the dance.

THE WIZARDS

7 to 9 Years

Excerpt from The Snowman: *Howard Blake (directly preceding the song "Walking in the Air")*

Music pattern	Music emphasis	Action emphasis	Dynamic emphasis	Spatial emphasis
A		Read, look, turn, rise, shake	Section A is light and sustained as the wizards turn, rise and shake. The runs of section B are quick and firm (but light on feet). The turns and zaps of section C are full of power, the zaps being sudden, firm and direct. Power builds from fine to firm in section D, and the zaps of section E are sudden, firm and direct.	The runs are in straight pathways. The main spatial emphasis is on prepositions as the zaps are direct extensions into space above, below, in front, behind, and to either side.
B		Run 1 Run 2 Run 1 Run 2		
C		Turn Zap, zap Zap 5 times		
	B repeats			

Music pattern	Music emphasis	Action emphasis	Relationship emphasis	Image or sequence
D		Walk Sit Look, turn, rise	The wizards work as individuals, but half the group are 1s for the runs, and the other half are 2s.	An extraordinary thing has happened—time seems to be stuck at 11 o'clock, and it is up to the wizards to find the spell to correct it. They sit and leaf through the book of spells, but when they reach the appropriate page, it is missing! The wizards begin to panic, and run, their bony knees much in evidence. They try a number of spells, but it is still 11 o'clock, so sadly they walk away and have another look at the book, to see if they can remember what was written on the missing page. Suddenly, the recipe for the spell falls into place, so the wizards turn, gathering power and ZAP! They have remembered the order of the spell, so time can progress as usual.
E		Zap Zap Zap Zap Zap Zap		

From S. Carline, 2011, *Lesson plans for creative dance* (Champaign, IL: Human Kinetics).

THE WIZARDS

Excerpt from The Snowman: *Howard Blake*

TEACHING PROGRESSION

You can build lesson plans based on this suggested progression:

1. Run   (section B)
2. Turn, zap   (section C)
   Link 1, 2
3. Read, look
   Turn, rise, shake   } (section A)
   Link 3, 1, 2
4. Walk, sit, read, look } (section D)
   Turn, rise
   Link 3, 1, 2, 4
5. Zaps   (section E)
   Link 3, 1, 2, 4, 5

DANCE SEQUENCE

1. Run (Section B)

It is a good idea to start with the running, even though it isn't the first part of the dance, because it has high energy and occurs twice in the story. In addition, this may be a new way of running for the children.

Starting in their own spaces, ask the children to run quickly and lightly but kicking their feet behind them with each step. After a few moments, stop them, then try it again, keeping their heads and chests up (they have a tendency to lean too far forward), and check that their feet are nearly kicking their buttocks as they run. Look for children who are running lightly on their toes and kicking well behind, and let them run as the others watch, pointing out the clear features. Then let the rest join in once more. Now tell them that you will give them a rhythm so that they know how much time they have for the running and that you want them to run as far as they can and in a straight pathway (see figure 10.4). Then try it again, but freeze tight on the last run so that they maintain body tension and balance on the spot.

Now try a run where the knees are raised high in front of the body with each step, still in a straight line, again freezing at the end of the phrase. Practice this a few times. Tell the children that you are going to give them two phrases: On the first, they will run with feet behind, and on the second with knees in front (see figure 10.5).

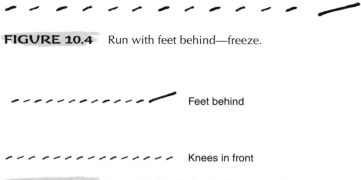

FIGURE 10.4 Run with feet behind—freeze.

Feet behind

Knees in front

FIGURE 10.5 Run with feet behind, then run with knees high.

After a few practices, with reminders about the quality of the run and use of the space, divide the group in half (1s, 2s) and muddle them up in the space. This time, 1s will run with feet behind and then freeze, while 2s will freeze (ready to run) and then run with knees in front.

Give them four sets of the phrases (see figure 10.6). Practice this several times, encouraging each group to start their phrase immediately, so that they take over from the other one (exciting). At this point, gather to listen to the music (listen from the start, then into section B) and introduce the story of the lost spell and wizards in a panic. Go out and practice the runs to section B.

(continued)

2. Turn, Zap (Section C)

In this part, the wizards attempt to make a spell. The most important part of any spell is the zap. Ask the children to start in a shape where their elbows and fists are drawn in toward the center of the body, and then give them a cue to shoot their arms out suddenly and with strength. Try this again, focusing on the speed of the action, telling them to freeze tight at the end of it. Now ask them to be sure that their arms shoot directly out and that they are very strong, sending power far away from the ends of their fingers. Many of the children will zap forward, possibly from standing, so now it's time to explore other possibilities. This time, ask them if they have to zap in front of them, or can they zap somewhere else? Tell them that they are going to do several in a row and that each time, you want to see if they can zap into a different place (above, below, behind, to the side). Do they have to be standing to do this? As you offer possibilities, they will become quite inventive. As they work, point out interesting and clear features, such as those with the whole-body shape helping the zap, those who try from different body bases (knees, back, buttocks), and those who have clear intent or focus. The children enjoy this because they love changing shape quickly.

(The second phrase is longer.)

1s feet behind
2s knees in front
1s feet behind
2s knees in front

FIGURE 10.6 Taking turns, section B.

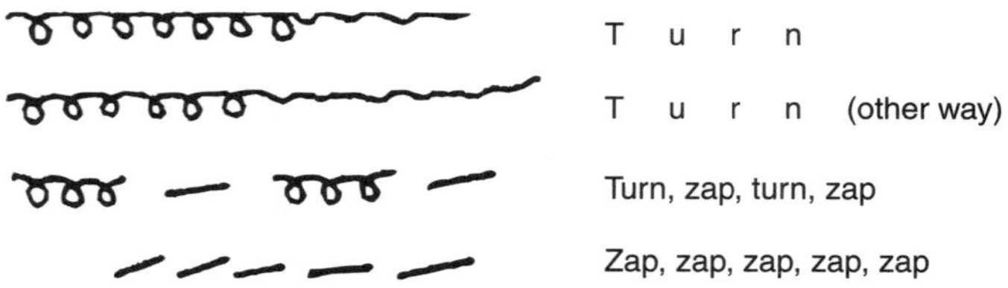

T u r n
T u r n (other way)
Turn, zap, turn, zap
Zap, zap, zap, zap, zap

FIGURE 10.7 The actions for section C.

Now tell them that wizards have to gather power for spell making and that this time, they will turn, really slowly and firmly, then suddenly zap. Practice this, continuing to encourage changing where they zap, then gather to listen to section B (runs) into section C of the music (see figure 10.7). Go back into the space, ready for the runs, then into the turns and zaps.

3. Read, Look, Turn, Rise, Shake (Section A)

This is the beginning of the dance, so the children need to know a little more of the story. Tell them that something peculiar has happened: Time has stuck at 11 o'clock and the wizards have been asked to make the spell to put it right. (*Note:* When I introduced this idea and talked about the consequences—it would never get to be lunchtime, it would never get dark, and so on—the children just looked at me, and I thought that my idea wasn't really exciting to them. I decided to make a few alterations to the story for the next session, but the next time we worked on it, they were full of ideas about time being stuck and the dire consequences, so I didn't change anything. It was obviously a new idea, and it took time to have an effect!)

Ask each wizard to take his or her (imaginary) book of spells and go into the space and slowly look through it to find the one to change time. Many of the children will sit to look through the book, but some may stand. Some will have large books, others small ones. The important thing is that you can see them reading it and turning the pages. As they read, mention that when they get to the place in the book where the spell should be, they find out that it's missing! At this, the wizards look up and around in alarm—what will they do? They slowly rise, turn as if to see the missing page, then gradually stretch high onto their toes with their arms reaching high and shake or vibrate in fear.

Gather to listen to the first part of the music so that they have a sense of how long they have for reading, looking, rising, turning, and shaking (they will hear the high-pitched trill in the music), then go out and try it. Now, tell them that they can dance the story so far through sections A, B, C, *and* B again.

4. Walk, Sit, Read, Look, Turn, Rise (Section D)

This part is similar to section A, so it doesn't require a great deal of exploration. At the end of their efforts to make the spell (section C), the wizards realize that they failed—they didn't get the spell in the right order, so they run in a panic once more.

Now they don't know what to do. Ask the children to show you a sad walk (they excel at this) as they weave slowly among each other. Point out features such as drooping heads and relaxed arms as they walk. Ask the wizards to remember where they left their book of spells and to walk sadly over to that spot and sit down and have another look through (just in case). Then, suddenly, the wizards remember the order of the spell and look up, but this time with hope instead of fear. Slowly, and with increasing power, they rise and turn, ready to perform the important spell!

Listen to this part (section D), elaborating and questioning the children about the story and movements. Then try it to the music. At this point, you may want to practice this at the end of the whole dance so far or go on to the final spell.

5. Zaps (Section E)

The secret of the missing spell that the wizards have finally remembered is the *order* of zaps! Here is the order: a zap above, a zap below, a zap in front, a zap behind, a zap to one side, a zap to the other! Again, in their own spaces, practice this, reminding them of the movement concepts, cueing them, and giving a beat on drum or claves for each zap. Then let the children practice on their own so that they can each develop a clear sequence, making sure that they change body bases now and again. Watch a few clear ones, pointing out or asking the children why they are interesting. Practice again and then listen to the final part of the music (see figure 10.8).

Go straight back into the space and practice with the music several times, encouraging strong direct zaps, use of the whole body, focus, and the right order spatially. Now that the wizards have found the solution, they can dance the whole story!

As usual, this dance is better if developed over time. The children have a chance to become involved in the story and each find his or her wizard personality. It is an exciting dance for them because the movement and the music have clear contrasts. Most children would like to be able to cast spells!

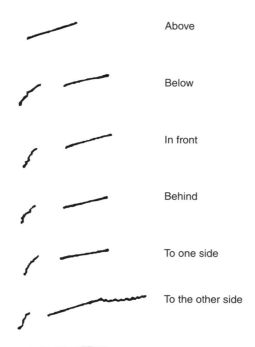

Above

Below

In front

Behind

To one side

To the other side

FIGURE 10.8 The order of the spell.

A strong, direct "zap" in front of the body as part of the spell sequence.

THE SPACE STEALERS

7 to 9 Years

Forrest Gump Suite: Alan Silvestri

Music pattern	Music emphasis	Action emphasis	
Intro	*(notation)*	Ready	
A	*(notation)*	Rush, run, turn, stretch, balance	1
A	*(notation)*	Rush, run, turn, stretch, balance	2
A	*(notation)*	Rush, run, turn, stretch, balance	1
B	*(notation)*	Rush, run, shrink, sink	1, 2
A	*(notation)*	Rush, run, turn, stretch, balance	2
A	*(notation)*	Rush, run, turn, stretch, balance	1
A	*(notation)*	Rush, run, turn, stretch, balance	2
B[1]	*(notation)*	Rush, run, shrink, sink	2, 1
	A, A, B[1] repeat		

Dynamic emphasis

The rushes, runs, and turns are light and fast, contrasting with the stretching, sinking, and shrinking actions, which are light but sustained.

Spatial emphasis

The runs and rushes are along curved pathways through the general space. The stretching uses body extensions into 3-dimensional shapes in personal space at high, medium, and low levels.

Relationship emphasis

A leading-and-following partner dance. Child 1 travels and stretches into a 3-dimensional shape, then 2 travels to 1 and complements 1's balance by helping to steal more space. During the B section of the music, the partners rush apart and shrink in a space alone.

Image or sequence

A group of aliens from a very crowded planet visit Earth and are delighted to find plenty of open spaces. They run as fast as they can in curved pathways, then stretch (something they haven't done for a while at home) into shapes that steal the space above them, below, in front, behind, and to either side.

Every now and again the space stealers feel guilty about taking up so much room and hide away in the tiniest space possible.

From S. Carline, 2011, *Lesson plans for creative dance* (Champaign, IL: Human Kinetics).

THE SPACE STEALERS

Forrest Gump Suite: Alan Silvestri

TEACHING PROGRESSION

You can build lesson plans based on this suggested progression:

1. Rush, run, turn, stretch, balance (section A)
2. Rush, run, shrink, sink (section B)

   Link 1, 2

DANCE SEQUENCE

1. Rush, Run, Turn, Stretch, Balance (Section A)

Starting in their own spaces, ask the children to take a deep breath, rise up onto their toes, then run and rush quickly and lightly, weaving in and out of each other—and stop. (Give a rhythm of fast taps with drum or claves.) Try again, but this time ask them to see if they can run in really curved pathways, as if they want to travel over every part of the floor before they stop. As they run, remind them to use the balls of their feet rather than heels and to be as quick and light as possible. Keep an eye open for any children who are fast, light, and making clear pathways. Usually these children have a fine tension throughout the body and are in control of how and where they go. Stop again and ask a few to run in and out of the rest, pointing out the qualities of their actions. Then ask all the children to join in. The next time, tell the children that they are going to rush and run again, but this time when they stop, they will pull up into a balance high on their toes and freeze there. Let them practice a short, curved rush and balance a few times. Ask the children to find a partner and decide who will be 1 and who will be 2. Starting in a space again, but this time with partners, 1 will rush through the space and balance and freeze, then immediately 2s will rush and balance and freeze next to 1. Cueing them, and giving a rhythm, let them practice this a few times. Gather to listen to the introduction and first three A sections of the music (see figure 10.9). At this point, discuss what it would be like to live on a crowded planet with very little room to move and absolutely no room to run. Introduce the idea of aliens visiting Earth and seeing open spaces!

Go back into the space and try it to the music. This is an appropriate moment to explore the three-dimensional stretches into balance that will take the place of balancing on their feet.

Tell the children that you are going to give them a sound on drum or claves and that you want them to get into a shape where each part of the body is reaching into space. Ask them to try again, reaching into different areas. Now ask them to make a shape where they have a part of the body reaching into space above, behind, in front, to the sides, and below. This is tricky at first but really good for helping each child to become aware of

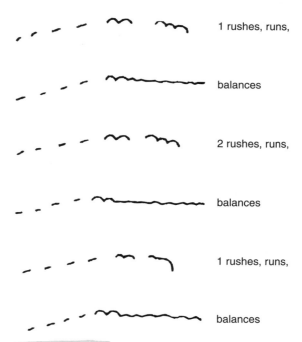

FIGURE 10.9 Partners alternating the phrases in section A.

1 rushes, runs,

balances

2 rushes, runs,

balances

1 rushes, runs,

balances

A three-dimensional shape stealing space above, below, behind and in front.

(continued)

137

exactly where each limb is in relation to his or her trunk (not just the limbs that are where they can see them). You are aiming for three-dimensional shapes, so point out good examples as they occur. With several goes, the children will start to catch on to the concept. If they are all on their feet, ask them to try a shape balancing on a knee instead—this will cause other body bases to be discovered. Give positive feedback to those who are fully extended, showing stretched spines and necks as well as limbs. During another class, after a brief review of three-dimensional shapes, the focus could be on levels as well.

Now tell them that they will get into a three-dimensional shape again, but this time stretch into it slowly—give a phrase of about 4 slow beats for this. Again look for clear stretches with awareness right through to the ends of their fingers and toes. Try stretching into new shapes several times, telling the children that the aliens want to steal as much space as possible. Now link the stretch and balance with the rush and run explored previously. Starting on their feet in a space, give a cue to rush in a curved pathway, then turn and slowly stretch into a three-dimensional shape. Turning into a shape seems to produce more interesting results than running into one. Now, without their partners for a moment, they can try the whole action sequence to the music (see figure 10.10).

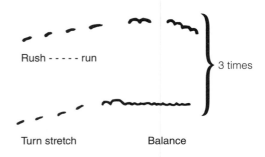

FIGURE 10.10   Linking the three-dimensional shapes to the rush-and-run phrase.

The children can find their partners again, remember who is 1 and who is 2, and try the sequence with the music. Now, 1 has to hold a three-dimensional shape while 2 travels and then turns to stretch into a shape near 1. The next idea to explore is how 2 can complement 1 and help to steal even more space. This is usually more easily explained visually than verbally. Select two children and give the rhythm of the music. Ask 1 to rush (curved), turn, and stretch into a three-dimensional shape. Then explain to 2 that she or he is going to rush and then turn and stretch into some spaces over, under, and to the side of 1. The children who are observing can see the choices that the demonstrating pair make. Now, let the children return to the space and practice this idea for a couple of minutes while you circulate, giving feedback. Next, starting in one of these stealing shapes together with a partner, they can try it to the music.

2. Rush, Run, Shrink, Sink (Section B)

The children are already familiar with the rush and run of this sequence. But this time, feeling guilty about stealing so much space, 1 and 2 both rush and run at the same time but away from each other. Let them try this, then once they are in a space, ask them to shrink (pull body parts into the center) and sink very slowly until they are in tight, closed shapes. Try this several times, looking for whole-body involvement and a variety of finished shapes—suggest that they can end up twisted or on a different part of the body so they don't just sink or shrink symmetrically. Link it now so that rush and run lead into shrink and sink. Next, gather to listen to the music from the beginning, verbalizing the action and warning the children when the new part is about to happen (see figure 10.11).

Now they are ready to practice AAAB and can continue into the next AAAB as the sequences are repeated. Because 1 has had more action than 2, it is a good idea (and another challenge) for 2 to take the A phrase that follows the sinking and shrinking so the roles are reversed. This also allows 1 to have to adapt the stretching three-dimensional shape to the partner's shape, as 2 has done in the first part. Notice that the shrinking and sinking music is longer the second and third times. The children will quickly get used to this and learn to sustain their movements even more.

There are choices that the children can make as a group as they become immersed in the idea of aliens stealing space and fluent with their movement. For the third repetition of A, AAB, all the aliens could decide to steal a massive amount of space between them: A few at a time the children could rush,

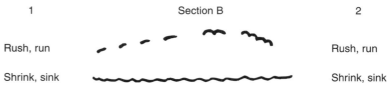

FIGURE 10.11   Feeling guilty: into a closed shape.

run, and stretch in a chosen area of the room. This would make them think about using all sorts of levels and stretched shapes, stealing the space as a group instead of in twos. They love this kind of task and learn to see which spaces aren't filled and if someone is needed higher or lower. At the end, for the final shrink and sink, they could all hide away (guiltily) into a tight mass.

THE VOLCANO MAKERS
7 to 9 Years

In the Hall of the Mountain King: Grieg

Music pattern	Music emphasis	Action emphasis	Dynamic emphasis	Spatial emphasis
Intro	(line)	Ready	Contrast between sustained creep and sudden pounce. Sudden, light-footed running, sudden leap and turn. Contrast between firm, sudden explode, shoot, tumble and sustained, fine drifting.	Use of directions and level changes for creep, pounce. Curved pathways for rushing. The final volcano uses all the space with changing levels.
A	(wavy line notation)	Creep, pounce, freeze or Push, turn Push, turn		
	A repeats twice		**Relationship emphasis**	**Image or sequence**
B	(wavy line notation)	Rush, leap, turn Rush, leap, turn	The whole group of trolls work as individuals, but half of them are 1s, and the other half are 2s.	In the heart of the mountain, trolls are preparing for a volcano. They select the best rocks, push them loose, then rush down the mountain carving pathways for the lava. The volcano explodes!
	B repeats twice			
C	(curly line notation)	Explode, tumble, shoot, drift, scatter, hide		

From S. Carline, 2011, *Lesson plans for creative dance* (Champaign, IL: Human Kinetics).

THE VOLCANO MAKERS

In the Hall of the Mountain King: Grieg

TEACHING PROGRESSION

You can build lesson plans based on this suggested progression:

1. Creep, pounce, freeze, push, turn (section A)
2. Rush, leap, turn (section B)
   Link 1, 2
3. Explode, tumble, shoot, drift (section C)
4. Scatter, hide (end of music)

DANCE SEQUENCE

1. Creep, Pounce, Freeze, Push, Turn (Section A)

First, develop possibilities for where the trolls are looking for good volcano boulders.

Action words: creep, pounce, freeze, push, turn

Dynamics: contrast between sudden pounce and sustained push

Spatial awareness: directions for creeping, levels for pushing

Relationship: group 1, group 2 using alternating phrases of the music but independently using the whole space.

(continued)

Start the children in their own spaces and work on a creeping action, focusing on using the legs and lifting the knees and the reaching and soft placement of the foot. Encourage stepping to the side and behind. The upper body will help with balance as the leg reaches. This works best if done in short phrases (give rhythm like that in the music) with reminders of use of direction and focus on body parts (arms, knees, feet) as they work.

Still in their spaces, ask the children to try a pouncing action (it means up, over, and down). Encourage whole-body use to get height, landing on feet, but with hands touching the floor as well. As they practice, watch for children who get good height, clear shapes in the air, and light, clear landing shapes. Observing a few with clear features can help all the children to improve at least one aspect of their movement. Now, giving a rhythm on drum or claves, link together the creeping and pouncing (see figure 10.12).

As the children work, encourage sustained creeping varying their directions, and sudden pouncing. Next, divide the class into two groups, 1s and 2s, then mix them up in the space and freeze, ready to creep. As the 1s creep and pounce, the 2s remain frozen. Immediately 1s have pounced, 2s start to creep, then 1s, then 2s, and so on. The children love this sense of being quick off the mark. Gather the children to listen to section A of the music. Talk about the trolls inside the mountain and their task of preparing for a volcanic eruption. During this part of the story, the trolls are looking for large boulders. After this, the children should go back into the space, 1s ready to creep immediately, 2s frozen (see figure 10.13).

The next part is where each troll sees its ideal boulder and tries to loosen it. Starting in their own spaces, ask the children to make a shape where you can see that they are pushing something very heavy (a boulder). Test them to see if they have strong bodies—you can do this by pushing against a child's back or arm to see if he or she can hold a shape. Try this again, but suggest pushing from a kneeling shape or a low standing shape. Some children may sit and try pushing with their feet instead of hands, and if you point out new ideas, others will emerge. As they (cued by you) try new pushing shapes, encourage pushing at different angles as well.

Now with drum or claves, give them the rhythm to push hard, then suddenly change shape by turning to face a different part of their boulders and push again (see figure 10.14). Now try the pushing and turning to push again to the first part of the music, still alternating 1s and 2s.

Next, they are ready to alternate a phrase of creeping with a phrase of pushing. Group 1 will creep and pounce, then push and turn while group 2 will push and turn, then creep and pounce (see figure 10.15). Try it first to a rhythm, then with the music.

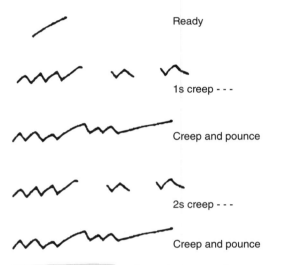

FIGURE 10.12 One phrase of section A showing creeping with a pounce at the end.

FIGURE 10.13 Taking alternating phrases to creep and pounce.

A volcano-maker in a kneeling shape as she pushes firmly against a boulder.

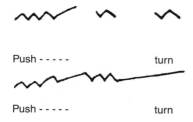

Push - - - - -   turn

Push - - - - -   turn

FIGURE 10.14 The same
music, but now with push and turn.

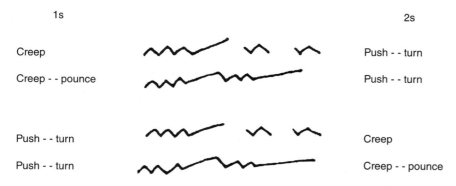

1s   2s

Creep   Push - - turn

Creep - - pounce   Push - - turn

Push - - turn   Creep

Push - - turn   Creep - - pounce

FIGURE 10.15 Now one group pushes and turns while the other group
creeps and pounces.

2. Rush, Leap, Turn (Section B)

The trolls prepare the lava pathways and leap and turn to see what they have done.

Action words: rush, leap, turn

Dynamics: sudden, light footed, rushing, sudden leap and turn

Spatial awareness: curved pathways

Relationship: the same grouping of 1s, 2s, alternating

The children enjoy this because it means *speed*. From their own spaces, they practice rushing, weaving in and out of each other, and suddenly stopping. Repeat, but focus on curved pathways and sudden total stopping. Repeat the rushing, but instead of stopping, leap and turn (180 degrees) so each troll ends up facing where it came from. You can practice the leaping now, introducing ways of landing with the body at a different level each time with a clear body and eye focus on the path just created. Then put it back into the phrase of rush, leap, turn so that the trolls rush to create a pathway for the lava and then leap and turn to examine it.

Try this, again alternating groups 1 and 2 to the second part of the music, which is a little higher and faster than the first. Now the children can start from the beginning of the music and practice these two sections of the dance.

3. Explode, Tumble, Shoot, Drift (Section C)

The volcano erupts!

Action words: explode and tumble (boulders), shoot—sudden upward jumps (sparks), drift—sustained
flexible movement (smoke)

There is room for many possibilities here. It pays to explore each action word separately before allowing the children to form their own sequences. *Explode and tumble* can be turning leaps using huge body shapes in the air, spinning down to tumble over the floor. (Although the actions are big and strong, landings must be

(continued)

controlled.) Sudden, upward jumps with the arms and fingers extending as far as possible represent sparks and flames. The children might want to do two or three quickly, then travel to a new spot for more. Sustained, gentle curved movements using the whole body provide both the smoke of the volcano plus a chance for the children to catch their breath.

Once all the actions have started to develop, let the children (individually) decide on the order in which the smoke, sparks, and boulders occur. In this way, among the class, everything is happening at once and it can be visually exciting.

Listen to the third section of the music, discuss possibilities, and try them out. Then join 1, 2, and 3.

4. Scatter, Hide (End of Music)

For the end of the story, which is a brief part of the music after the volcano has erupted, the children can decide what to do. Do the trolls rush off to hide in another mountain? If so, how, when, and where? Do they disappear from the scene completely? Again, how?

Landing from a turning leap to examine the pathway created for the lava.

During the development of this dance, allow a few moments every now and again (while gathered to listen to the music) to talk about volcanoes. The children tend to be quite knowledgeable about the scientific aspects, especially if they have been studying rocks in science. In one class, a child brought a lovely book to show us, with clear pictures taken at night, of the glowing red lava flowing down the mountainside. It flowed in long curves and reinforced the concept of running in fast, curved pathways, which we had been exploring.

The children know a lot about volcanoes and of course are excited by such a powerful force of nature. At the same time, they are delighted to become the imaginary trolls who cause the volcano to erupt!

The volcano erupts!

Dances
for Ages 8 to 10

THE WARRIORS

8 to 10 Years

Dance of the Warriors: Hanson

Music pattern	Music emphasis	Action emphasis	Dynamic emphasis	Spatial emphasis
A		Gallop, freeze Gallop, freeze Gallop, freeze Gallop, freeze	Firm and fine contrasts. Strong, energetic, powerful gallops. Fine, quiet, sustained turns. Rhythmic, powerful steps and leaps for war dance.	Use linear floor patterns for galloping. The turns are in personal space. The tribal dance is toward, away from, around a group focal point.
B		Turn, watch Turn, watch Turn, watch Turn, watch	**Relationship emphasis** This is a group tribal dance. Each tribe can gallop to all phrases of A, or take turns within the group. The same applies to the spins. The war dance takes place around a central focus.	**Image or sequence** Alert, powerful warriors are hunting for food for their tribe. They travel on search, listen, and finish with a celebratory tribal dance.
A¹		Gallop, freeze Gallop, freeze		
C		Step, leap, tribal dance		
D		Ready, lean, throw		

From S. Carline, 2011, *Lesson plans for creative dance* (Champaign, IL: Human Kinetics).

THE WARRIORS

Dance of the Warriors: Hanson

TEACHING PROGRESSION

You can build lesson plans based on this suggested progression:

1. Gallop, freeze (section A)
2. Turn, watch (section B)
   Link 1, 2
3. Step, leap, jump (section C)
   Link 1, 2, 3
4. Ready, lean, throw (section D)
   Link 1, 2, 3, 4

DANCE SEQUENCE

1. Gallop, Freeze (Section A)

With the children scattered in the space, explore a strong sideways galloping action in fairly straight pathways. Emphasize strong bodies but light feet. Now give them a phrase of 8 beats with drum or claves. They should gallop powerfully but be able to stop abruptly on the 8th beat. Repeat this, each time traveling off on a new tangent. Explain to the children that they are each carrying a spear and to hold it high with two hands above their heads. They should start in a space in a ready position, holding the spear, and looking toward the pathway that they are going to gallop. Gallop for 8 beats, freeze, sharply alter the position of the head, then gallop for 8 beats on a new direct pathway. When they are showing strong, direct gallops, clear halts, and sudden changes in head position, gather to listen to section A of the music and explain the first part of the story—that they are warriors who are hunting with their spears and traveling along tracks in the forest. Listen again, but tell them that they will gallop for the first 8 beats, freeze for the next 8, gallop for 8, freeze for 8 (see figure 11.1).

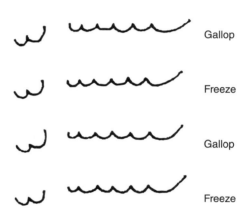

FIGURE 11.1 Galloping on alternating phrases of section A.

Go back into the space and try this once or twice so that they are able to anticipate the sudden starting and stopping. Next, divide the class into two groups, 1s and 2s. Muddle them up in the space and explain that 1s will travel for the first 8 beats, freeze, travel, freeze (as before), but 2s will freeze for the first 8 beats, travel, freeze, travel. Try this, cueing where necessary so that they start and stop powerfully. Then switch so that they can practice doing the opposite pattern.

2. Turn, Watch (Section B)

With each child in a clear space, ask them to show a watchful, ready-to-turn shape. (Now they can hold the spears in one hand.) Point out features of watchfulness, such as total stillness, the head position, and use of a fine whole-body tension in the shape. Work now on an extremely sustained turning action, maintaining the feeling of watchfulness and listening evident by the tension of the body. The children need to practice the slow turn, being careful to place their feet quietly and gently with no sudden movements. Try turning one way, then the other, listening for any sounds of prey in the area.

Gather to listen to the music from the beginning, and verbalize the action, stressing the contrast between the strong, sudden galloping and the fine, sustained turns. Let the children decide whether to be a 1 or 2, then go back into the space and practice from the start, also alternating the turns: 1–2, 1–2, 1–2, 1–2. Let the music continue as two more phrases of galloping are repeated.

As this point (possibly next lesson after a review), discuss the idea of warriors hunting and listening for sounds of prey. Let them form groups of 4 or 5 so that there are several tribes. Now each tribe can decide how to use

(continued)

the first 4 galloping phrases: Do they all travel together, or do they send out a scout for one phrase, then the rest of the tribe catches up? How will they use the space? With a little guidance, the children quickly realize the range of possibilities and can start to develop their own tribal traveling. Let them sort it out and practice for a while, then play the music a few times so that they can see if their ideas work. The same principle applies to the turning section—where are they in the space, who turns, and when?

3. Step, Leap, Jump, Tribal Dance (Section C)

This part of the dance will become the tribal celebration around the fire. Each tribe will develop its own patterns—but the ideas need to be generated individually at first. In their own spaces, ask them to try to develop a short, rhythmic pattern, possibly using a combination of steps and hops. This takes some trial and error but works well if you circulate, reinforce good ideas, help to modify possible patterns, and so on. Sometimes I spot

a pattern that has potential and we all try it. As they pick up the rhythm and pattern, remind the warriors about strong bodies because they might have turned back into children while learning something new! Then let them practice again. To give it more form, I suggest that they try using forward and backward or side to side with their patterns. When they begin to get a grasp of this idea, the children can return to their tribes, each tribe choosing a space on the floor for their fire area. There they can show each other the ideas they have. Then as a tribe they choose one, or a combination of several, and develop their celebration dance moving toward and away from or around the central fire area. The development of this group work needs to take place over part of several lessons so that the children have time to modify, refine, and polish their ideas.

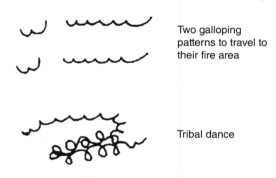

Two galloping patterns to travel to their fire area

Tribal dance

FIGURE 11.2 Transition into places for the tribal dance.

Gather to listen to the music so that they can hear how long the celebration part lasts and what precedes it (see figure 11.2). Let them practice the tribal section a few times, then start from the beginning of the dance so that they can work on their spacing and make any necessary adjustments.

Ready, lean, throw

FIGURE 11.3 Prepare . . . and throw!

4. Ready, Lean, Throw (Section D)

This last section is a strong throw of the spear and requires practice to ensure a good preparation position, transfer of weight, and a strong hold after the throw. It occurs at the very last moment (see figure 11.3).

When you are all satisfied that the dance is well done, it is a good idea to have half the tribes watch the other half, then vice versa. The observers can watch for strong and quietly moving warriors, clear focus, the way in which a tribe decided to use the first four galloping phrases, and of course the celebration part. The children are eager to point out clear and interesting ideas. This process can affect their present and future dance because they can be helped to recognize not only high-quality movement but exciting group relationships as well.

THE ABANDONED CARTWHEEL
8 to 10 Years
Air Gai: Gluck

Music pattern	Music emphasis	Action emphasis	Dynamic emphasis	Spatial emphasis
A	*(musical notation)*	Extend, freeze Extend, freeze Extend, freeze Extend, freeze Extend 4 times	This dance explores the ability to make firm, *extremely* sudden extending actions and holding the resulting shapes. The spinning actions of section B and circling group work of section D contrast this, because they are light with a sense of speedy continuity.	Wheel shapes: The center of the body as the hub; arms, legs, and head as spokes. The rim is suggested as a result of clear shaping. The limbs extend into space forming parts of an old cartwheel, leaning at various angles, so involving the use of levels and body bases.
B	*(musical notation)* B repeats	Spin, freeze 1 Spin, freeze 2		The D section involves circling floor patterns.
C	*(musical notation)*	Extend, turn Turn, extend		

			Relationship emphasis	Image or sequence
D	*(musical notation)* D repeats twice B repeats	Skip, gallop, run, jump circling patterns	Sections A, C, E of the music are cartwheels moving individually. The first two B sections involve 1s and 2s spinning and freezing alternately. Section D is group work where groups of about 5 children develop a circling pattern. Each group may use one or more repetitions of section D. All spin and freeze for the last D section. Section E is individual.	Several old cartwheels are leaning against crumbling stone walls, dilapidated sheds and rusty gates. Not one of them is whole. Parts of each are broken or worn away so that some spokes and sections of the rim are missing. Weeds and long grasses partly obscure them from view. They are a product of a time gone by—before the era of tractors, trucks, and combine harvesters. Just for a few moments, these cartwheels appear to come to life, powerfully emerging to spin, circle, and be of use—but soon return to their original places of abandonment.
E	*(musical notation)*	Extend, freeze Extend, extend Extend, extend		

From S. Carline, 2011, *Lesson plans for creative dance* (Champaign, IL: Human Kinetics).

THE ABANDONED CARTWHEEL

Air Gai: Gluck

TEACHING PROGRESSION

You can build lesson plans based on this suggested progression:

1. Extend, freeze (section A)
2. Spin, freeze (section B)
   Link 1, 2
3. Skip, gallop, run, jump circling patterns (section D)
4. Extend, turn (section C)
   Link 3, 4 and then 1, 2, 3, 4
5. Extend, freeze (section E)
   Whole dance

DANCE SEQUENCE

1. Extend, Freeze (Section A)

With the children starting in their own spaces, explain that when you give a sharp sound with a drum or claves, they need to move quickly and strongly into an extended shape and hold it there. Do this a few times, asking them to change their extended shape each time, being aware of where in space they are reaching each limb and that they are fully stretched. Look for examples of shapes where a child may have balanced on a hand and a foot instead of one or two feet. Now explain that these shapes are wheel shapes, so they must be flat (in one plane) but can be tipped at any angle. Try a few more.

To clarify the concept further, I draw part of a cartwheel on the board for them, explaining that parts of it are missing. I draw a complete one first, then erase parts (see figure 11.4).

I explain that their bodies are the hub and their limbs are spokes, and although they can't form the rim, if their shapes are clear, we can see where it would be. The children should go back into the space and experiment with more wheel shapes, finding out which parts they can balance on, at what angles they can lean, and so on. After some experimentation, ask the children to make their own sequences of three sudden, firm shapes in a row, making sure that each is very different: parts to balance on, angle of lean, level. Give 3 sharp beats, with a space in between each so that they can practice and learn their individual sequences. Gather to listen to section A of the music so that they can hear the sudden quality of the extensions and the length of each freeze (see figure 11.5).

For the last phrase, they repeat their sequences but this time without the long freeze between each. They have time for 1, 2, 3, and back to 1 (just to be different).

Now they can go back into the space and start in an altogether different shape, because on the first chord of the music they go *into* shape 1. Watching half the class

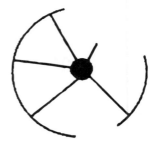

FIGURE 11.4   The missing sections of the rim are suggested.

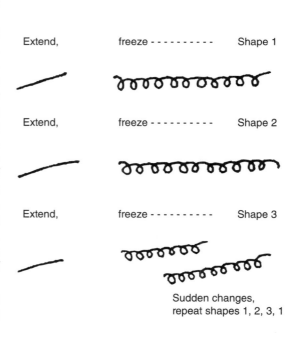

FIGURE 11.5   The timing of the movements.

at a time may help to reinforce the idea that radical changes of level, front, and angle are more interesting, and strong body tension is necessary.

2. Spin, Freeze (Section B)

At this point the wheels really get moving and there are various ways to go. One challenging method for this age group is to start in a closed shape, then fling open to create a wide spin, but hop on one foot so both arms and one leg are extended as the child turns. This takes a bit of trial and error, but it's worth it. They learn to be brave, to lean at daring angles but still maintain balance. After a little practice (remember to try this both to the right and to the left), ask some children to be 1s, some to be 2s, and all to get in a ready position. With drum or claves, give the appropriate length of phrase (see figure 11.6).

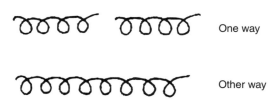

#1s spin - - - - - freeze

#2s spin - - - - - freeze

#1s spin (opposite direction) freeze

#2s spin (opposite direction) freeze

FIGURE 11.6   The 1s and 2s spinning to alternating phrases of section B.

Practice a few times so that they are really quick at picking up their cues to start spinning each time. Listen to the music from the start (mentally review their shape sequences), hear this new part, then go out and try it to the music.

During the next few sessions, as you review and improve ideas, the children can think about an interesting starting scene for the cartwheels. (Tell the story.) Do they all start separately? Could there be some individual ones, and others in groups of three or two at different levels and angles?

3. Skip, Gallop, Run, Jump Circling Patterns (Section D)

In this part of the story and music, the children can play with the idea of several of them forming one wheel. The wheel will travel in a circle. It can be in groups of three, four, or five (or some of each). More than five makes it difficult to maintain a wheel shape and possibly to agree on their course of action. For many relationship situations, it is better to work individually first and then, once each child has ideas, to form a group. However, in this dance, since each group member has to do the same thing to form one wheel, they need to work together from the start. The objective is for the group (wheel) to circle. Let them try a variety of actions such as gallop, skip, run, or even put a jump or two in rhythmically. They can maintain the wheel shape by holding hands or shoulders or through any other means that doesn't inhibit traveling. Can the circling of the wheel change direction? As a group forms a clear pattern, let the others watch and determine *why* it works (keeping tension between them so that the circle stays circular). When they have ideas, give a rhythm that is the length of one D phrase so they know when to change direction (see figure 11.7).

One way

Other way

FIGURE 11.7   The group wheels change direction.

Gather to listen to section D of the music, which happens three times consecutively. The children can make lots of choices. Could some groups circle on the first and third repetitions, freezing their wheel during the second? Could some circle on repetitions 1 and 2, freeze their wheel on repetition 3, and so on? Have them go back out, knowing exactly where in the space their own circle is and where they are in it (this is important for the transition into the circle beforehand), and try it to the music.

4. Extend, Turn (Section C)

This part uses some ideas previously explored, so it won't take long to create. It serves to take the individual wheels (spin, freeze in section B) to their starting places for the big circling wheels. Send the children back into their own spaces, and ask them to extend into a new wheel shape, then spin toward their big wheel location, extend again, spin, and so on. There is a contrast between the sudden, complete extension of the body and the fast spins that allow them to travel toward their destination. Let them listen to section C of the music so that they know how much time they have to travel (some might have to go a long way, and others might need to make a zigzag pathway if they haven't far to go). From their own places, try it to the music until they are fairly good at reaching their circles, then continue into the circling part.

(continued)

At this point, they can go back to the very beginning and dance right through ABBCDDD, then *all* repeat their spins of B to get a feel for the sequencing and transitions.

5. Extend, Freeze (Section E)

The final section of the dance is where the cartwheels return to their original abandoned starting places. The movements are similar to those of section A: sudden, bold wheel shapes that contrast each other. As each child goes from one shape to another, she or he can gradually return to the starting spot. There are many ways to finish the dance. The children might have ideas of their own now that they know the whole story. This section of the music has lots of strong shape-changing sounds, and it would be difficult for each child to change shape on each one. It can be done differently each time, as long as the wheels return to their original positions.

Forming a wheel, circling.

8 to 10 Years

Toota Lute from Fresh Aire II: *Mannheim Steamroller*

Music pattern	Music emphasis	Action emphasis	Dynamic emphasis	Spatial emphasis
A	*(notation marks)*	1s run, kick 5 times, freeze 2s run, kick 3 times, freeze 1s run, kick 5 times, freeze 2s run, kick 3 times, freeze	Sections A and B develop sudden, light, energetic actions, but the step and turn and contract actions of section C contrast with sustained, sad movements.	Primarily traveling into general space, working in personal space, with contrasts in level in section A as the jesters freeze together. Section A: running far, angular kicking actions on the spot. Section B: jumping high in personal space, steps and bounces in general. Section C: stepping into general space, turning and contracting in personal space.
B	*(notation marks)*	Jump, jump, step and bounce Jump, jump, step and bounce or Step and bounce, jump, jump Step and bounce, jump, jump	**Relationship emphasis**	**Image or sequence**
C	*(notation marks)*	Step, step, turn and contract Step, step, turn and contract Step, step, turn and contract Step, step, turn and contract	This can be developed in several ways. Section A is a lead–follow relationship where 1 goes and freezes followed by 2, who joins 1 at a contrasting level. Sections B and C can be each jester working independently or separated into 1 and 2. The main relationship is with the jester sticks.	Historically, a jester had to be agile, lively, and cheerful to fulfill the job as court entertainer. Sections A and B of the music reflect this as the jesters show their quick footwork, rhythms, and jester shapes. Section C is a contrast as the jester reveals the sadder side of life.
D¹	*(notation marks)*	Slide 4 times		
	A, B, A, C, A repeat			

From S. Carline, 2011, *Lesson plans for creative dance* (Champaign, IL: Human Kinetics).

THE JESTERS

Toota Lute from Fresh Aire II: *Mannheim Steamroller*

TEACHING PROGRESSION

You can build lesson plans based on this suggested progression:

1. Run, kick on the spot, freeze (section A)
2. Jester shaping

   Link 1, 2
3. Jump, jump, step and bounce patterns (section B)

   Link 1, 2, 3
4. Step, step, turn and contract (section C)

   Link 1, 2, 3, 4
5. Slide, slide, slide, slide (section D)

(continued)

DANCE SEQUENCE

1. Run, Kick on the Spot, Freeze (Section A)

Start the children in their own spaces and work on light but lively running, covering as much space as possible. Introduce the idea of bringing the feet high behind the body (almost touching the buttocks), then bringing the knees high in front of the body while traveling. They need to be light on their feet but with enough tension to make quick movements.

Giving a phrase of 6 beats, challenge them to travel lightly with the feet sometimes behind, sometimes ahead (any combination). Then, using that pattern, cover as much space as possible. At the end of the phrase, they should freeze very suddenly. Notice the focus on quick actions, changes in the angles, and placement of knees and feet.

Still in their own spaces, experiment with the same kind of leg actions, but now on the spot, kicking the feet and knees high in front, behind, and to the side. It will help to use the arms for balance. Give a rhythm of 6 beats for this, with freeze as the 6th beat.

Now link together the travel for 6 beats, and the kicks on the spot for 6 beats, emphasizing the contrast between traveling far and then staying in one place. Repeat this but with a phrase of 4 beats for the on-the-spot section. (See section A of music.)

Divide the children into 1s and 2s spread randomly in the space (see figure 11.8). Practice this so that 2s learn to go immediately after 1s and vice versa. Then change roles and practice. All listen to this part of the music, detecting the difference in the length of the kick phrase for 1 and 2. Then have them go straight back into the space and try it.

2. Jester Shaping

At this point, a brief discussion about jesters would be beneficial: what they did, what they wore, and so on. Children usually tell me about their outfits with the two- or three-point hats. If it doesn't emerge from the children, I introduce the idea of a jester stick that the jester held, and this leads nicely into the next part of the exploration.

In their own spaces, try the pattern of kicks again, but this time, on the 6th beat, freeze in a shape holding an imaginary (for the present) jester stick and clearly looking at it. Then practice getting quickly into a variety of freezes, pointing out jester-like features, such as clear angles of the body and placement of the jester stick above, below, to the side of the body. Someone will probably make a shape on a body part other than feet, and this opens up a whole new range of possibilities for body bases (standing, sitting, kneeling, lying). Encourage brave shapes rather than boring standing straight ones.

Reintroduce the travel for 6, kicks for 5, incorporating these new jester freezes at the end of each phrase. Remember to practice the kicks for 3 and freeze as well.

Now the children have lots of ammunition to use in pairs. In twos, each pair in its own space in jester shapes, they can do section A so that 1 travels, kicks, and freezes and then 2, who freezes in a contrasting shape close to 1. There are many possibilities for

A jester brings a knee high in front of her body.

1s take the first phrase

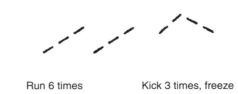

Run 6 times   Kick 5 times, freeze

2s take the second phrase

Run 6 times   Kick 3 times, freeze

FIGURE 11.8 The 1s have a longer kicking phrase.

the relationship to contrast (high and low, above and below). If you point out a few clear ones, the children will start to experiment.

3. Jump, Jump, Step and Bounce Patterns (Section B)

Still clearly with the jester image in mind, ask the children to try jumps with an upward looking focus. Limit this to jumping up with no running preparation, making two consecutive jumps on the spot. Contrast this with a series of steps and bounces, where the jesters step lightly and rhythmically, focusing on clear legs and feet. Then join the sequence of two upward jumps on the spot and travel to a new space.

Listen to section B of the music (see figure 11.9), then let the children try their patterns. Experiment to see if the pattern can be done in reverse (step and bounce, jump, jump) because some children hear it better that way. They can experiment, then choose which each would like, then practice and learn their own pattern so that it can repeat four times in a row.

This section follows the one explored earlier, so now, starting back with their partners, the class can go from the beginning through ABA of the music, stop and listen through section C, but be ready for A again. This gives them a sense of the sequencing and enables them to think ahead.

4. Step, Step, Turn and Contract (Section C)

This part of the jester dance is a contrast to the previous sections because it is sustained movement rather than sudden and lively. With the children in their own spaces, explore starting in a fairly wide shape, where they are holding up and looking at the jester sticks, then contracting slowly so that the body, starting from the center, closes and they draw the stick inward. Try this several times, then add the idea of turning slightly as the contracting occurs (as if turning away sadly).

Now add two slow steps to the start of this (see figure 11.10). Explore the idea of the steps being open (body high, focus on jester stick), taking the jester to a new place and the contracting taking place on the spot.

Listen to the music and discuss the sad side of the jester—how hard it was for them to appear cheerful and lively all the time, and that in unguarded moments, they were sad. The sadness is something that children of this age can express beautifully in dance, and now they have the action phrase of step, step, turn and contract it will become more sustained by adding the sad quality.

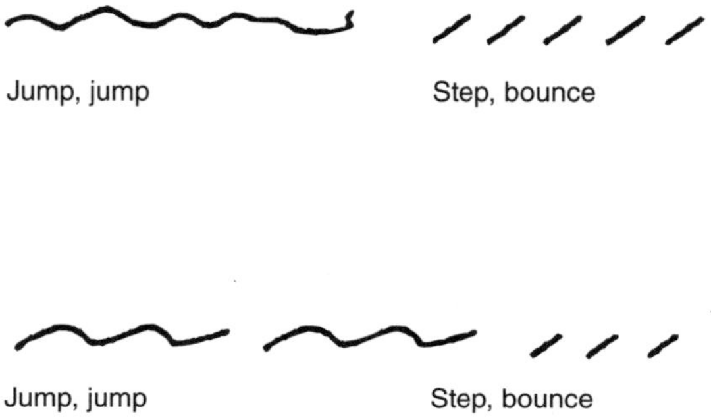

5. Slide, Slide, Slide, Slide (Section D)

At this point, all the sections have been explored with the exception of D (see figure 11.11), which occurs once only in the music. It is a good opportunity to respace using a clear step, slide feet together, step while holding a focus on the jester sticks. From here on, it's a matter of improving the quality of the dance. Over time, the children seem to become more "jesterish" as they become involved with the idea. If there is room in the curriculum, the children can make jester sticks with a dowel about 18 inches (45 cm) long and a head of either Styrofoam or fabric, which is stuffed. They can dress this with a two- or three-point hat, a collar, and a face (but *no* pins).

It is better to introduce the use of the real jester sticks in the dance after all the initial exploration has taken place and their bodies have absorbed the jester's qualities. At that point, you can introduce the sticks, which the children will use skillfully, greatly adding to the dance. Used too soon, the sticks, not the children, do the dancing.

Jump, jump   Step, bounce

Jump, jump   Step, bounce

FIGURE 11.9 Jump and step pattern for section B.

Step, step,   turn, contract

FIGURE 11.10 Actions of the sad jester.

FIGURE 11.11 Section D of the music: side step slowly into a space.

8 to 10 Years

Sunrise from Also Sprach Zarathustra: *Richard Strauss*

Music pattern	Music emphasis	Action emphasis	Dynamic emphasis	Spatial emphasis
Intro		Rush	The contrast is between sudden and sustained movement. The rises and sinks are strong and sustained, and explosions strong and sudden. The steps are strong and rhythmic.	Curved floor patterns for all the rushing and running. The rise goes from a low to high level, then higher for explosion. The sink goes from high to low and then to high for the explosion.
A		Rise, explode or Sink, explode Step, step		
A		Sink, explode or Rise, explode Step, step	**Relationship emphasis**	**Image or sequence**
B		Rise, explode, tumble	An awareness of the individual in relation to the actions and use of space of the whole group. The initial rushes are individual but have a sense of timing with others. The last rush is the group led by one member.	The powerful creation of planets. Individual bolts of energy rush through space but are drawn together to explode into being. The whole then runs, jumps, and rushes to carve its place in the universe.
C		Run, leap Rush		

From S. Carline, 2011, *Lesson plans for creative dance* (Champaign, IL: Human Kinetics).

PLANETS

Sunrise from Also Sprach Zarathustra: *Richard Strauss*

TEACHING PROGRESSION

You can build lesson plans based on this suggested progression:

1. Rush (introduction)
2. Rise, explode, step; or sink, explode, step (section A)
   Sink, explode, step; or rise, explode, step (second section A)
   Link 1, 2
3. Rise, explode, tumble; or sink, explode, tumble (section B)
   Link 1, 2, 3
4. Run, leap, rush (section C)
   Link 1, 2, 3, 4

DANCE SEQUENCE

1. Rush (Introduction)

Starting in their own spaces, explore the idea of rushing in curved pathways, weaving in and out of each other. Try it again, asking the children to take a deep breath, and rush as fast but as silently (quiet feet) as they can.

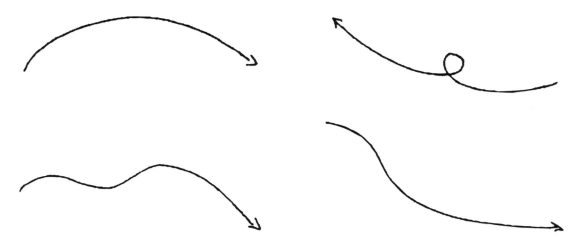

FIGURE 11.12 Some ideas for curved pathways.

After a few moments, stop them. If two or three children are traveling in evident curves with speed and appropriate body tension, let the rest of the class watch this as you point out the clear movement features. Immediately, let the whole class practice once more. Now ask the children to stand at either end of the space, spread out along the two walls. This time, a few at a time, they can rush from one end of the space to the other in a curved pathway. Practice this a few times, encouraging speed, lightness, and clear curves. Some children will pick up the idea of the curved pathways quickly, but a visual demonstration can help others and also introduce more complex ideas. Ask the children to gather

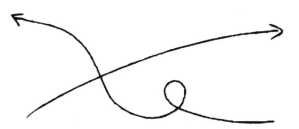

FIGURE 11.13 Entering the space at different times.

by a chalkboard and show them a few possibilities, and ask for their suggestions (see figure 11.12).

The dance is based on filling a void. At any given time, at least one person needs to rush through the void—but not everyone at once! Therefore, all the students must be ready to enter at different times (see figure 11.13). Let them go back to the sides and try again—it takes a little practice. You can start this in silence because the introduction to the music is short and might not accommodate a large group.

2. Rise, Explode, Step; Sink, Explode, Step (Section A)

Children need to explore these action words so that they develop exciting individual sequences. To explore *rise*, start with a variety of strong, fairly low shapes (on feet, knees, buttocks). Using a drum, provide a steady, quiet beat as the children rise from their starting shapes in a sustained movement—no jerking. This is quite difficult because a child might have to transfer weight from buttocks to feet while rising. Explore which parts of the body can lead the movement, always focusing on drawing upward. Remind them to keep the body strong and sustained, as if they are a powerful force being pulled upward. At the height of the rise, notice the variety of body shapes and which parts of the body are high. Teach a similar process for *sink*. The children need to find ways of starting the body high and strong, then sink in a sustained action to a low finish.

Explore the word *explode*. Students at this age are strong jumpers and can readily involve their arms in a powerful upswing, create strong shapes in the air, and land quietly on their feet before possibly transferring their weight to the floor for a tumbling action. Encourage turning in the air as they explode. Once they see a child turning, they will agree that it gives a much better impression of exploding. Now let each child choose whether to start low (therefore rise, explode) or high (sink, explode). With a drum accompaniment, try their sequences. Then, try the opposite sequence so that they are familiar with both.

For the stepping that follows the first two exploding actions, work with the children on making large, strong stepping actions (but light on feet), again to the beat of a drum. Explore making the body travel through space by stepping backward and sideways as well as forward. The children will need to practice reaching a little with each step so that they cover as much space as possible.

(continued)

Gather to listen to the music from the beginning. Verbalize the rushing introduction, and tell them that toward the end of it, each of the children will rush and freeze *in* the void, either high or low ready for their new sequences. At this point, you can discuss atoms and particles rushing through space, eventually being ready to form something larger: planets. Each child will have a sequence that goes one of two ways:

Rise, explode, step; sink, explode, step; rise, explode

Sink, explode, step; rise, explode, step; sink, explode

From the beginning, practice thus far.

3. Rise, Explode, Tumble; Sink, Explode, Tumble (Section B)

The children have already explored the first two words of this action sequence, but now the music changes and the newly formed planets tumble about in the space to find their positions. To explore tumbling, ask them to roll over the floor, but keep their bodies in large, curved shapes so that they have spaces or holes. At this age they should be quite capable of transferring their weight comfortably with a variety of curved shapes and changing direction at times. Encourage a focus on appropriate body tension so that no parts flop. Link this with rise and explode so that now, as they land, they tumble instead of step. Also try sink, explode, tumble. Again, each child can choose which sequence to use—rise, explode, tumble; or sink, explode, tumble.

Next, they can link the introduction and sequences with sections A and B, which will help them to anticipate the order of the music and action. At the end of the tumbling, ask all the children to freeze.

4. Run, Leap, Rush (Section C)

Now try choosing one child as leader who runs among the group (choose a different child each time until they have a finished version they like). As the leader passes a student, that person follows, then the next, and so on, until the individual elements have grown into one vast traveling mass that rushes and leaps in a curved pathway.

The children enjoy the idea of joining in or being pulled into traveling as the leader passes by. With practice they improve their reaction time so that eventually it does look as if the leader and those she or he has collected have the power to draw everyone into the fast-moving mass of bodies (a little like a magnet with iron filings).

Listen to section C so that they know how much time is available for this—but of course, like the beginning, part of it can occur in silence.

To finish the dance, discuss and experiment with a few ideas. Does the mass of moving planets exit completely? Does the whole thing explode, scattering the individuals back into random spaces?

To practice the complete dance, start in silence with the particles rushing through the void. Then once the first drawn-out sounds of the music are heard, the students rush into the space ready for the rest of the dance.

Dances
for Ages 9 to 11

DAY O

9 to 11 years

Day O (Traditional): Raffi

Music pattern	Music emphasis	Action emphasis	Dynamic emphasis	Spatial emphasis
A	*(music notation)*	Yawn, stretch, rise, sink, rise	Impulse (sudden into sustained) yawns.	Changes of level for yawn sequence and lean–flop sequence.
B	*(music notation)*	Step–close 4 times, rise, swing Step–close 4 times, rise, swing	Lively, confident step–close pattern. Firm jumps. Sustained lean, rise, sudden flops.	

			Relationship emphasis	**Image or sequence**
B	*(music notation)*	Step–close 4 times, rise, swing Step–close 4 times, rise, swing	Relationship in 2s and 3s, of supporting partner's weight for lean, flop, rise, flop sections.	The beginning of a working day for the banana pickers who wake reluctantly but fall into the rhythm of work. They have the bananas weighed and then take a break, during which they keep falling asleep. Finally, when the shift is over, they return home.
C	*(music notation)*	Jump, jump, jump, reach, shake Jump, jump, jump, reach, shake		
D	*(music notation)*	Lean, flop, rise, flop		
B	*(music notation)*	Step–close 4 times, rise, swing Step–close 4 times, rise-swing		
C	*(music notation)*	Jump, jump, jump, reach, shake Jump, jump, jump, reach, shake		
D	*(music notation)*	Lean, flop, rise, flop		
B	*(music notation)*	Step–close 4 times, rise-swing Step–close 4 times, rise-swing		
E	*(music notation)*	Stagger, drag Collapse		

From S. Carline, 2011, *Lesson plans for creative dance* (Champaign, IL: Human Kinetics).

Day O (Traditional): Raffi

TEACHING PROGRESSION

You can build lesson plans based on this suggested progression:

1. Step–close pattern (section B)
2. Yawn, stretch, rise, sink, rise (section A)
   Link 2, 1
3. Jump, jump, jump, reach, shake (section C)
   Link 2, 1, 3
4. Lean, flop, rise, flop (section D)
   Link 2, 1, 3, 4
5. Stagger, drag, collapse (section E)
   Link 2, 1, 3, 4, 5

DANCE SEQUENCE

1. Step–Close Pattern (Section B)

It is easier to learn this working pattern if the children spread out in the space, all facing in the same direction (front). Facing front, they take a step to the right, then bring the left foot together with the right. Repeat this several times until the children have picked up the rhythm. Do the same thing to the left. Now try it again, establishing a series of four step–closes to each side. (I usually face the class as I step with them, but lead with the opposite leg so we are mirroring. As soon as they are confident, they can do it alone.) Next, try a huge circular swing, as if each child were standing in a hoop, and the fingers trace the circle of the hoop. The action is led by the arms, but the whole body is involved, stretching up at the height of the swing and knees bending at the lowest point. Try it several times, encouraging the children to be relaxed but in control and to follow the movement of their hands with their eyes. Now, from a standing position, do two circling actions in a row, one counterclockwise and the second one clockwise. Add this to the stepping pattern (see figure 12.1). Then repeat to the left side.

Step-close, step-close, step-close, step-close

Circling swing counterclockwise, clockwise

FIGURE 12.1   The working pattern, section B.

Gather the children together. Before listening to the music, explain that this is the working pattern of banana pickers in a plantation and that the workers are exhausted and waiting for sunrise when their shift will end. The idea of working a night shift in a plantation might be difficult for some children to imagine, so encourage group discussion. The children are genuinely interested in learning about the working conditions: a hot and humid climate, the insects, and the fact that the workers are often paid for the quantity of bananas they pick instead of an hourly wage. Listen to the brief section A, ready to verbalize the step pattern for section B, which occurs four times in a row at the start (it occurs only twice in a row later in the music). Go back into the space and try it a couple of times to the music. During another class, after a review, the students can decide in small groups to develop their own floor patterns and relationships as they do the working pattern.

2. Yawn, Stretch, Rise, Sink, Rise (Section A)

The next step is to explore how to fall asleep standing up. Explain to the children that they need to have a strong base but let the top part of their bodies relax, as if they have fallen asleep. Look for interesting examples, pointing out to the children necessary features such as totally relaxed arms and head tipped at an angle. Encourage asymmetrical sleeping shapes, such as tipping to one side or with a slightly twisted trunk. Let them try two or three different ones, then suggest that they experiment with sitting sleeping shapes (as if leaning against a tree trunk) or kneeling or lying. Once they have experimented a little, ask them to stay asleep, and tell them that you are going to give a sharp sound (drum or claves) and that they will suddenly be startled awake from their

(continued)

deep sleep. Try this several times until the children react quickly to the sound. Now do it again, but this time, after they have been startled, they will *very slowly* sink back into either the original or a different sleep shape. The children enjoy experimenting with this and can be encouraged to sustain the motion of falling back to sleep more each time. Now each child can put together a sequence of two wake–sleep actions, except that the second time, they *must* slowly stumble to their feet because they have to get back to work!

At this point, they can get into a sleeping starting shape (later some of them may decide to lean against another banana picker) ready to try the waking-up part followed by the working pattern to the music. Another time, encourage the children to look at the whole picture. Are all the banana pickers asleep at one level? It is more interesting if some are standing, some sitting, and so on.

3. Jump, Jump, Jump, Reach, Shake (Section C)

Discuss with the children the size and weight of a bunch of bananas, called a hand, as it grows on the tree in comparison to the small bunches that they see in grocery stores. It is also interesting to discuss how the banana pickers are paid for their labor—possibly by the amount of bananas they pick rather than by the hour. Now ask them to stand facing the front again and jump a little off the floor to land with their feet apart, holding their arms in front with palms up to suggest that they are carrying a bunch of bananas. Now take a second jump to land with their feet farther apart, knees bent more, arms wider, a bigger bunch. The third jump is wider again and with knees bent even more. Come back to standing and do the sequence again, encouraging strong jumps (heavy bananas) but light landings: wide, wider, widest and heavy, heavier, heaviest. After the last jump, they drop the bananas on the floor, slapping the floor with their hands as they do so; they jump high, clap their hands in the air, shake their bodies out, and do the sequence again (see figure 12.2). Listen to section C of the music and try the jump pattern a few times. Then they can practice from the beginning so that they anticipate the transitions from one part to another.

4. Lean, Flop, Rise, Flop (Section D)

This section relies on partner work. One of the easiest ways to give the children a starting point from which to go away and develop their sequences is to ask one student to try something with you, the teacher. The idea is for one person to be in a strong, balanced position so that he or she can gently receive the weight of the partner.

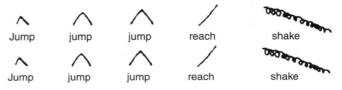

FIGURE 12.2 The weighing pattern, section C.

The student volunteer can start standing with his or her back to you and lean back (like a dead fall) while you reach, catch the student under the arms, and step back lowering her or him gently to the floor. Commentary about a strong base and balance should accompany this. Next, ask the student to stand with a strong base and lean the top half of the body over (or to the side) and you can rise up and lower head and shoulders onto the student's back, explaining that you are not really leaning your full weight but making it look like you are (relaxed arms, head). The students can then go with a partner and experiment. The idea is to develop a couple of these weight-taking ideas and cleverly link them together, making it appear that the two banana pickers are literally asleep on their feet or knees). When they have some ideas, let them try them to the music. Also, let them all watch a couple of examples that seem to be working quite well. This partner work will not be complete during one session. It is another of those ideas that improves and develops over time.

At this point, all the sections have been introduced with the exception of the very end. The students need (by practice) to become familiar with the sequencing of the music so that they can develop good transitions from one part to the next.

5. Stagger, Drag, Collapse (Section E)

After a long, hard shift, the banana pickers may go home. Let them decide with their partners if they do stagger away, or if they fall asleep right there, or if one falls asleep while the partner pulls him or her off. They will have lots of ideas of their own. These ideas will develop over time and with cooperation as a group. It is more interesting if some workers do manage to leave the space while others fall asleep. Some children show a lovely sense of timing as they stagger toward the side and collapse just as the music ends.

SKELETONS AND GHOULS
9 to 11 Years
Danse Macabre: Saint-Saëns

Music pattern	Music emphasis	Action emphasis	Dynamic emphasis	Spatial emphasis
Intro	*(notation)*	Stillness	Contrast between sudden and sustained movement. The skeleton skips (section A) involve sudden actions of the knees, elbows, and head to produce disjointed, angular skipping. The ghoulish rise, sink, and turn and reach are sustained actions.	Use of levels: The skeletons start lying in their graves and rise to begin their mischief. The skips travel as high as possible at times, with the knees and elbows flung into the air. At other times, they drop to a lower level. The ghouls rise up and over, sink down and under in space, and turn at a medium level.
		Rise		
		Rise 6 counts		
		Freeze		
A	*(notation)*	Skip		
		Skip	**Relationship emphasis**	**Image or sequence**
		Skip	Many possibilities. The dance can start with 3 groups of skeletons in lines or circles in their graves. Group 1 takes the first section A of the music, working in 3s within their group. Group 2 is individual ghouls but weave in and out of one another. Group 3 takes the second section of A and repeats group 1's actions. Each group is absolutely still while the others work. At the start of the second section A, wildness begins. All ghouls and skeletons break loose from their groups and work individually through ABA, using the whole space. Near the end of the last A, they skip back to their gravesites, ready to sit, then lie suddenly back in their graves.	For 1 hour, starting at midnight, October 31, the skeletons rise from their graves to do a little haunting and exercise their bones before lying down for another year.
		Skip		
B	*(notation)*	Rise, sink 2 times, turn and reach		
		Rise, sink 2 times, turn and reach		
A	*(notation)*	Skip		
		Skip		
		Skip		
		Skip		
	A repeats			
	B repeats			
	A repeats			
End	*(notation)*	Sit, lie down!		

From S. Carline, 2011, *Lesson plans for creative dance* (Champaign, IL: Human Kinetics).

SKELETONS AND GHOULS

Danse Macabre: Saint-Saëns

TEACHING PROGRESSION

You can build lesson plans based on this suggested progression:

1. Skeleton skipping (section A)
2. Rise, sink, turn and reach (ghouls) (section B)
   Link 1, 2
3. Rise and freeze (introduction)
   Link 3, 1, 2
4. Sit, lie down (end)
   Link 3, 1, 2, 4

DANCE SEQUENCE

1. Skeleton Skipping (Section A)

By this age, skipping should be a mature skill, but skipping like a skeleton requires a purposeful *un*coordination that requires instruction and practice. Starting in their own spaces, briefly work on large, energetic skips that travel through a great deal of space. Then work on large skips still, but try to put the knees in places where they do not usually go—for example, out to the side, higher than usual, across the center of the body, behind the body. This will require some experimentation and use of the whole body. Next, work on making the skipping unpredictable so that no two knee placements are the same. The image of a skeleton helps here: a frame that doesn't have muscles to keep the limbs restricted or organized.

As they work, encourage similar displacement of the elbows so that the arms remain fairly angular but an elbow may be above the shoulder, in front of the body, and so forth. The spine will have to stretch and curl to accommodate all these displaced limbs! Watching a few clear examples will help to complete the picture.

Listen to the first A section of the music, and let them do skeleton skips to it.

Now, in groups of three (with a couple of pairs if necessary), join right hands together, use the skeleton skips, and travel in a circle. As they practice, encourage purposeful use of levels so that as one skeleton is high, another may curve the body down a little. In this way, the group appears more random and skeleton-like. Do the same with left hands attached. Organize this by skipping clockwise (right hands in) for about 8 skips, then, without losing the flow, turn so that the action is counterclockwise (left hands in). Listen again to section A of the music to hear where changes can occur, and try again.

2. Rise, Sink, Turn and Reach (Ghouls) (Section B)

Once again, the children need to start in their own spaces. This time, the movement is smooth, sustained and controlled. With hands leading, explore rising as high as possible, then with a sense of going over the top, the hands lead in a sinking action, then almost brush the floor before the rise starts again. This can involve traveling over a short distance (see figure 12.3).

FIGURE 12.3 The movement of the ghouls: up and over, down and under.

The body needs to extend fully at the top of the rise, then the hips and knees bend at the bottom of the sink. As they get the idea of this continuous movement, encourage use of pathways so that those are curved, too.

With the same sustained movement, explore a turning action where the arms reach as far away from the body as possible. Then link a series of rise, sink, rise, sink, and turn and reach.

Rise, sink, rise, sink

Listen to section B of the music, then go into the space and practice (see figure 12.4). At this point, it is a good idea to put the contrasting actions of the skeletons and ghouls into the sequencing of the music, so the children can be ready in their groups of 3, dance through the skeleton part (A), change to slimy sustained individual movement for the ghouls (B), then return to the sudden actions of the skeleton for section A when it repeats.

Turn and reach

FIGURE 12.4 Linking rise, sink and turn and reach.

3. Rise and Freeze (Introduction)

By this time the children will be well into the images of Hallowe'en. They need to lie flat on their backs, arms at their sides, absolutely still. From this position (in their graves) the skeletons sit up slowly with their skulls tipped slightly up, eyes staring at a distant point. This takes a little practice because only the trunk moves, so their abdominal muscles do the work. Again, watching one or two who rise smoothly with eyes totally focused (no darting eyeballs) helps to establish the image. Try this again, then from this sitting position, explain that they will have to get to standing, but by making a series of sudden, angular actions, one body part at a time (the skeletons are stiff from so much lying in the grave). Allow some practice, then start again, lying flat, rising smoothly to sitting, then in a jerky fashion for 8 beats to standing, in the group of three, hands attached ready for the skeleton skipping. Listen to the introduction of the music, noting that there is no action at all until the clock has chimed 12 times (midnight), then the sustained rise occurs.

From this point on, the children can make a lot of decisions. I divide them into three groups and they experiment with various organizations for their graves (see figure 12.5). On their own, they need to practice the rise to sit, then jerky rise to feet, ending in starting shapes for the skeleton skips in groups of three.

They can decide as a class whether to all do section A, then B, then A (tiring, considering what follows) or have group 1 take the first section A while the rest remain totally still in their starting shapes, group 2 takes section B (ghouls), and group 3 takes the second section A—because then the whole lot break loose!

As section A comes for the third time, all the children do skeleton skips individually and wildly over the whole space.

As section B repeats, all turn into ghouls over the whole space.

As section A comes for the last time, all revert to skeletons but start to return to their gravesites for the surprise ending.

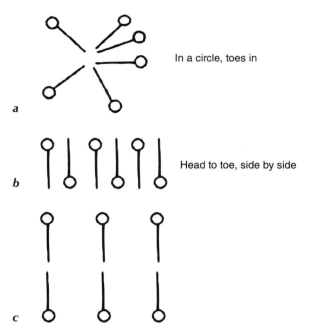

FIGURE 12.5 Possible starting positions.

a — In a circle, toes in

b — Head to toe, side by side

c

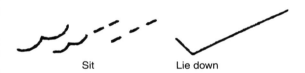

Sit   Lie down

FIGURE 12.6 The precisely timed end.

4. Sit, Lie Down (End)

Once they are in their gravesites (still on their feet), there is a short but vital piece of music (see figure 12.6) during which all sit and suddenly lie down as if nothing ever happened.

Here is a recap:

Introduction: All rise from graves

A: Group 1 or all groups, skeletons in 3s

B: Group 2 or all groups, weaving ghouls

A: Group 3 or all groups, skeletons in 3s

A: All skeletons, individually, whole space

B: All ghouls, individually, whole space

A: All skeletons, individually, return to gravesite

End: Sit, lie down

THE MIRAGE

9 to 11 Years

Theme Two: The Flame Trees of Thika: Ken Howard/Alan Blaikley

Music pattern	Music emphasis	Action emphasis	Dynamic emphasis	Spatial emphasis
A		Surround, rush, surround Rush, surround, whirl, hide Surround, rush, surround Rush, surround, whirl, hide	The main contrast is between sudden and sustained movement. Each surrounding of space is a firm, sudden impulse action that fades into a finer sustainment. The whirl into hiding is firm and sudden (section A). The runs (section B) are fine and sudden, and the rise and sink are fine and sustained.	The dance is based on the spatial prepositions below, above, and behind. In section A, the intent is to capture the enormity of a desert space. The visitor surrounds the space below, the space above, and the space behind before feeling overwhelmed by it and whirling to hide. The runs in section B are direct, freezing suddenly with the focus on a distant oasis. Body bases are used as child 1 is joined by 2, then 3, then 4 in a group with one focus. The oasis turns out to be a mirage, so the rise and sink change level slightly as the mirage blurs, then dissolves.
B		Run, freeze (1s) Run, freeze (2s) Run, freeze (3s) Run, freeze (4s) Rise, sink, rise, sink Rise, rush		
A		Surround, rush, surround Rush, surround, whirl, hide Surround, rush, surround Rush, surround, whirl, hide		

			Relationship emphasis	**Image or sequence**
	B repeats		All A sections are individual. In section B, groups are formed as 1 runs to choose a focus (the oasis), followed one at a time by 2, 3, 4, all of whom share the same focus.	A visitor to the wide open spaces of an African desert feels very tiny and attempts to surround the space that is everywhere—below, above, and behind—before feeling overwhelmed and hiding away from the space. The visitor's attention is drawn toward a distant oasis that unfortunately becomes hazy and blurred and eventually dissolves—a mirage. Finally the visitor has to decide whether to deal with the big space or to hide away.
A¹		Surround, rush, surround Rush, surround, whirl, hide Surround, rush, surround Rush, surround, whirl, hide		

From S. Carline, 2011, *Lesson plans for creative dance* (Champaign, IL: Human Kinetics).

THE MIRAGE

Theme Two, The Flame Trees of Thika: Ken Howard/Alan Blaikley

TEACHING PROGRESSION

You can build lesson plans based on this suggested progression:

1. Surround, rush, whirl, hide (section A)
2. Run, freeze; rise, sink (section B)

   Link 1, 2, 3

DANCE SEQUENCE

1. Surround, Rush, Whirl, Hide (Section A)

First, the children need to learn or review the concept of an impulse movement. This is a movement that starts with a sudden, strong burst of energy and then fades into a lighter, sustained movement. There are various ways of introducing this. Start the children in a group and ask them all to make a tight fist with one hand, fairly close to the body. Suddenly, with a bursting feeling, open the fist and let the hand rise away from the body, continuing to rise as the speed and weight of the action get slower and lighter. Try with the other fist, watching it as the action occurs and letting it move far enough away that the body begins to be involved in the movement.

In their own spaces, ask the children to imagine the vastness of a desert with nothing in it but miles of sand. Experiment with surrounding a portion of the space with the trunk and curved arms, using an impulse movement and curving the spine (contracting the center of the body). Try this several times, as if each person has an enormous wingspan that he or she attempts to wrap around the space and enfold it. Encourage the children to pull their centers (bellies) in and curve the spine rather than just bend at the waist and then pause when the action is complete. Now try, using the same impulse movement, to surround some of the space below so that the focus is either directly below or slightly to either side (the spine will be twisted). It is easier to do this from a fairly high standing position. This time, tell the children to take a deep breath and lightly rush a short distance before surrounding a space below them, then rush again to a new space and surround another piece of space below.

An impulse movement into surrounding the space below.

Next, try surrounding a space above. This time the focus will be upward, either directly or slightly to either side. Now the impulse movement takes the arms out and upward. To get under this space, the shoulders and chest will face upward too. Once the children have the idea of this, again try letting them rush and then surround space above. Suggest that they try this from kneeling (one or two knees) as well as from standing. Point out clear features of any children who are capturing the idea because this might help others. Now tell them that they will rush into a space and surround space below them, pausing as the movement fades, and then rush into a different space and surround the space above them, pausing again. This helps to build transitions from one movement to the next and allows them to feel the contrast between sudden and sustained movements.

(continued)

The third area to surround is the space behind the body. This time, the impulse movement takes the arms slightly forward and outward, reaching and fading behind the body (almost like a very wide breaststroke action). The head follows the movement, so the children end up looking over one shoulder. Again, they should try this on their feet and on one and two knees. Try rushing into this: The children will find that they need to rush forward, then do a half turn to surround the space behind them. Next, link rush, surround space below, rush, surround space above, rush, surround space behind. Encourage good use of the floor space.

Last, the space is so big that each person feels the need to hide away from it. Ask them to start in a shape that is about to spin, then very suddenly, whirl around and tuck themselves away, hiding. Try this again, encouraging full speed as they whirl, which comes to a sudden stop as they wind themselves into a hiding shape. Notice the hiding shapes on various bases (back, side, knees), all with a sense of being not there. Some children need practice in order to whirl from feet (possibly traveling) and then transfer their weight swiftly and safely down to other body parts on the floor. Let them experiment. Now link this movement to the previous three.

Gather to listen to section A (finally!), and possibly discuss sandy deserts where nothing grows. The music has clear impulses in the phrasing, and the children have no trouble in hearing when each action occurs (see figure 12.7).

Notice that the whole sequence happens twice in a row in section A (see figure 12.8).

Now, back into the space. The children can choose which of the surrounding shapes to take as their starting positions, then try the whole thing to the music with a cue from you. Encourage them to visit different areas of the desert for each surround so that they also focus on where they are going. This will become easier once the order of the sequence becomes automatic. Also encourage changing level for some of the surround actions.

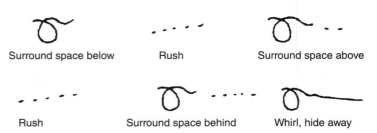

FIGURE 12.7   One complete phrase of section A, which then repeats.

FIGURE 12.8   The entire sequence for section A of the music.

2. Run, Freeze; Rise, Sink (Section B)

During this section, each person in the desert thinks that he or she sees an oasis in the distance. Starting in their own spaces, the children choose a point in another part of the room and run straight there quickly and lightly. Try this again several times, encouraging them to get the feeling of running far toward a distant point. This time, run again, but on reaching the place, stop in a shape where the body is leaning and focusing on the distant oasis. After a few attempts, point out some clear shapes, where the whole body is part of the shape and the tension in the body helps the focus on the oasis. Some of the children might have been making standing shapes while others have been kneeling and looking or lying and looking. Now, without the run for a moment, explore possibilities within each of these so that the children build a vocabulary from which they can choose later. Practice low, medium, and high standing shapes (with a distant focus) and kneeling, sitting, and lying ones.

Now the group work begins. It helps if the children have a clear picture of what they are trying to do in this case, so

Focusing on the distant oasis, which proves to be a mirage.

often they learn through a demonstration. Sit the children in a group and ask one child to run and freeze (as practiced). Notice whether he or she is standing, kneeling, lying, or possibly sitting. Now ask another child to run, ending up behind child 2, and focus on the same distant point but with the body at a different level. Now child 3 runs to add to the picture, again at a different level or base, then child 4. All their eyes are focused on the same distant point. Do this with a different group, building the picture as each child joins the first one. Ask the children to get into groups of four (with one group of three or five if necessary). Decide among themselves who is 1, 2, 3, 4 (if there is a group of five, have two children as 4). Give a sound on drum or claves for each of the 1s to run into an empty space, freeze, then all the 2s. Remind them of focus, levels, and being close enough together that one can tell that they are a group. Try this several times. Each time 1 should stop in a different shape so the rest have to react to a new situation. At the conclusion of one practice, when the groups of four are in position, ask them to imagine that the oasis in the distance is becoming fuzzy, hazy, blurred. Very gently the whole of each group starts to rise a little, sink a little, rise a little higher, still maintaining their group shape. Let this continue for a few moments, ensuring that their whole bodies rise and sink, not just parts. Then suddenly they all rise and scatter as individuals back in the desert! It was only a mirage. Try this again, then gather to listen to section B (see figure 12.9).

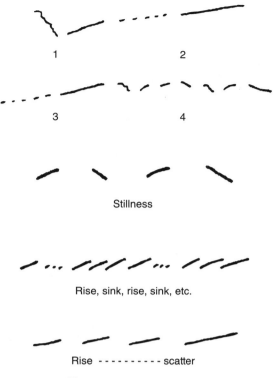

FIGURE 12.9 A breakdown of the action for section B.

Now go back into the space and practice this part a couple of times.

The music is ABABA, so all the concepts have been explored. Now it is a matter of practice so that the children can move well from one kind of movement into another, use the general space well, and explore all possibilities within each movement.

The last A section ends a little differently, so the children can have the choice of whether to conquer the space (to finish over, under, or behind) or to be conquered by it (hide away).

Although this is an abstract idea, children of this age are able to get the feeling of the vastness of space—the spatial quality of the music really helps. Much discussion occurs about oases, mirages, heat, haze, and so on.

CHANGES

9 to 11 Years

Titles from Chariots of Fire: *Vangelis*

Music pattern	Music emphasis	Action emphasis	Dynamic emphasis	Spatial emphasis
Intro	*(wave notation)*	Open, extend Expand, rise	The main contrasts are between sudden and sustained actions and movement and stillness. The introduction is fine, sustained extending and expanding, opening and rising. The first section A uses contrasting actions within each pair as they firmly and suddenly open and close, expand and contract, rise and sink outside the rubber band. Section B is surges of movement powerful in the body but light on feet as 1 rushes and soars past 2 and then drops, causing 2 to rush, soar, drop past 1. The second A repeats the actions of the first A but this time the movement is light and sustained inside the rubber band. The third A is sustained but stronger as the pairs reach and link together. The end is firm and sustained.	The A sections occur in personal space and involve contrasting levels between the partners and rubber band. The B sections travel in a leap-frogging manner as 1 soars, rushes past 2 stretching the rubber band, then drops, causing 2 to overtake in turn.
A	*(notation)*	Open and close, freeze Expand and contract, freeze Rise and sink, freeze Open and close, freeze		
B	*(notation)*	1s rush, soar, drop 2s rush, soar, drop		
B	*(notation)*	1s rush, soar, drop 2s rush, soar, drop		

Music pattern	Music emphasis	Action emphasis	Relationship emphasis	Image or sequence
A	*(notation)*	Open and close Rise and sink Expand and contract Open and close	The children work in pairs, each pair having a rubber band (about 3 meters). The pairs are numbered 1 to 6, each with certain phrases of the first A of the music where they open and close, freezing for other phrases. Between them, they cause the rubber band to change shape. During the B sections, they use the stretch of the rubber band to cause a leapfrogging (or over-taking) sequence. In the final A, all groups link together.	The dance explores the possible changes in shape that can happen with a rubber band manipulated by two children, at times outside and at times inside it.
	B repeats twice			
	A repeats			
End	*(notation)*	Reach, extend, link Rise, vibrate, hold		

From S. Carline, 2011, *Lesson plans for creative dance* (Champaign, IL: Human Kinetics).

CHANGES

Titles from Chariots of Fire: *Vangelis*

TEACHING PROGRESSION

You can build lesson plans based on this suggested progression:

1. Open and close
   Expand and contract } (section A first time)
   Rise and sink
2. Rush, soar, drop (section B)
   Link 1, 2
3. Open and close
   Expand and contract } (section A second time)
   Rise and sink
4. Reach, extend, link (section A third time)
5. Rise, vibrate, hold (end)

DANCE SEQUENCE

1. Open and Close, Expand and Contract, Rise and Sink (Section A, First Time)

Although the dance is in pairs with large circular rubber bands, the children need to explore the movement concepts individually and without bands first. Starting in their own spaces, the children start in a folded and closed shape. Then, giving a cue on drum or claves, tell them to open very suddenly so that at least two limbs are extended, leaving the center of the body exposed. Then close again suddenly into a different shape, open,

Contrasting expand and contract with a rubber band.

(continued)

169

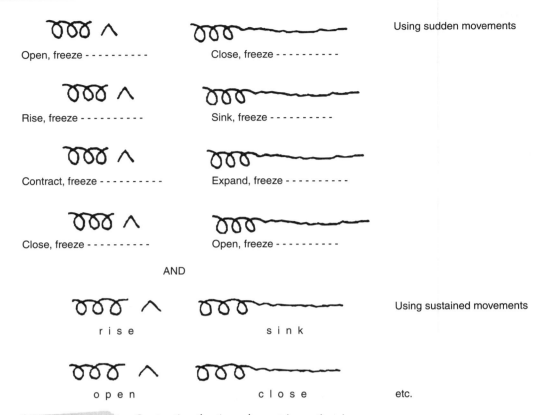

FIGURE 12.10 Contrasting the time element in section A.

close, and so on. To further develop the concept of opening from the center of the body and closing around it, ask the children to stand with their arms extended to each side with feet apart, and tell them to imagine that you are going to punch them in the stomach! They should react by contracting their abdominal muscles, causing the extensions of the body to close around their centers so that the spine curls. Start open again and try this several times so that they concentrate on pulling the muscles of the abdomen in and curving around the center of the body. Now explain that they don't have to be symmetrical but can contract around the center and twist to one side so that the arm and leg on one side of the body close over the other side. Gradually extend this idea so that they learn to open and close on feet and on knees and buttocks, opening to face a slightly different place each time—still using sudden movements. Encourage them to pull hard in their centers each time they close; each time they open, they should open as far as possible.

Now change the time aspect. Tell them to start either open or closed and that you are going to give a few beats so that they open and close in a sustained manner, taking the whole length of the phrase to complete the movement. Encourage the leading arm each time. Again explore this at different levels on different bases.

Repeat this process with expand and contract and rise and sink so that they can move both suddenly between each opposite and gradually in suspension.

Gather to listen to the first A section of the music, helping them to hear when the movements will start and stop (see figure 12.10).

Go back into the space and practice once using sudden movements, then again but with sustainment.

Now, the rubber bands! About 3 meters, or just over 9 feet of 1 cm (3/8 inch) black sewing elastic tied into a circle provides enough stretch for one child to fully expand, rise, or open while the partner contracts, sinks, or closes. Ask the children to find a partner (have a group of three if necessary) and give a large rubber band to each pair. For a few minutes, let them play with the bands with an open task such as this: "Hold the band in your hands so that you are both outside the circle, and see how you can make it stretch and change shape as you open and close, rise and sink, expand and contract."

They will need to find out what the rubber band will do in relation to what they do. Gradually encourage them to try very sudden movements so that it changes shape suddenly, then very sustained ones so the change is gradual. They will start to discover what happens if one person rises and the other sinks, and so on.

Now let them start with the band fully stretched, then try sudden changes to section A.

At this point, move on to explore the ideas for section B to give them a change of pace. However, another day, after a review of the concepts previously explored, you and the children can decide on the phrasing of this first A section of music.

Number each pair as 1, 2, 3, 4, 5, or 6. (There will probably be two or possibly three pairs of each number.) Explain that each number will move for some phrases of section A and freeze for others. It is easier to draw this as you explain (see figure 12.11).

Let them listen to section A several times. Those who are about to move shoot their hands up each time their particular phrase comes up.

Once they understand, send them back into the space, making sure that the numbers are fairly evenly distributed. Choose a starting shape outside the bands, again encouraging each pair to start differently from each other so that levels and angles are interesting. Try the sudden open and close, expand and contract movements to the music (cueing them at first), and be sure that they can freeze the rest of the time.

On another day, use the introductory part of the music as a prelude to this.

Each pair will start closed and close together or overlapping so that the rubber band is bunched. During the introduction music, they gradually open, extend, rise, and expand into a starting shape for section A.

2. Rush, Soar, Drop (Section B)

Again, first without bands, explore the movement ideas. Starting in their own spaces, the children take a deep breath and rush lightly to another space. Do this several times, encouraging speed, light feet, and good use of the space. Now ask them to start on feet but crouched, then rise quickly to full stretch and rush again, then drop suddenly back to a crouch. Again, have several tries. This time, from a crouch, ask the children to rise as they travel and soar as high as they can but start to get lower as they return (still traveling) to a crouch. Their air patterns will resemble a curve (see figure 12.12).

Tell them to imagine that they are holding the band in one hand. As they start to soar, they pull it up over their heads, travel with it high, then bring it over to the front of the body as they finish in another crouch. After a few practices, gather to listen to section B (see figure 12.13).

Within each pair, there will be a 1 and a 2, who will take alternating phrases (see figure 12.14).

Now go back into the space, each 1 starting a little behind 2, and try it to the music without the rubber bands.

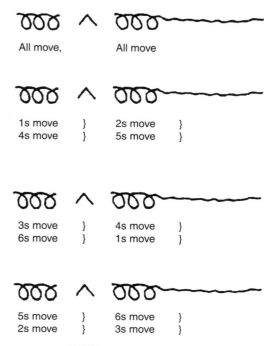

All move,   All move

1s move }   2s move }
4s move }   5s move }

3s move }   4s move }
6s move }   1s move }

5s move }   6s move }
2s move }   3s move }

FIGURE 12.11   Each pair takes different phrases of section A.

FIGURE 12.12   The rubber band travels up, over, and down.

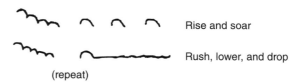

Rise and soar

Rush, lower, and drop

(repeat)

FIGURE 12.13   The movement for one phrase.

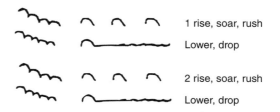

1 rise, soar, rush

Lower, drop

2 rise, soar, rush

Lower, drop

FIGURE 12.14   The partners travel on alternating phrases.

(continued)

Next, bring back the rubber bands! Now, the same movements occur, but the children need time to experiment on their own to find out how 2, holding the band in one hand, can, by raising that hand, cause 1 to rise, soar past him or her, and drop, which in turn makes 2 rise, soar past, and so on. They will need to explore to see how far or fast they can travel with the length of band while staying away from the pathways of other pairs. Try this part to the music. (It will improve over several classes.)

Now the children can practice from the introduction through section A, section B, section B, and ready for the second section A.

3. Open and Close, Expand and Contract, Rise and Sink (Section A, Second Time)

The children already explored the sustained movements for this, but you need to introduce one new idea. For this repetition of section A, the children, in pairs, will work inside the circle of rubber band. Starting with the band wrapped around their backs and holding it with extended arms, they explore how their opening and closing and other contrasting movements, this time with sustained movement, can change the shape and level of the band. By being aware of each other's movement, they can create exciting contrasts with their bodies and the band. Over time, some children might want to manipulate the band with a foot and a hand—they need time in short practices to develop ideas and quality. Now try this to the second repetition of section A. All the pairs use the whole section so the movement is continuous from start to finish.

4. Reach, Extend, Link (Section A, Third Time)

By the end of the last B section, the children will be distributed all over the space. Now, for this last section A, each pair reaches slowly, extending to link with other pairs. This must be slow and gradual until each child is connected to his or her band and that of another pair. This is fun, but it takes practice and awareness of the group to create levels and angles as they join together. Each time they practice this part, it will be different.

5. Rise, Vibrate, Hold (End)

Once the children have completed the previous section, they are in position for the end. For this last part of the music, they rise slowly. With tiny hand movements, they cause the rubber band to vibrate until the last note, when they hold still.

Using props such as rubber bands is exciting. If the children have a good movement background and vocabulary, they will be able to handle this idea well because the movements of the whole body cause the band to change shape.

Dances
for Ages 10 to 12

THE SHERIFF AND THE COWBOY

10 to 12 Years

Bonanza: Livingston and Evans

Music pattern	Music emphasis	Action emphasis	Dynamic emphasis	Spatial emphasis
Intro	*(hand-drawn wavy lines)*	Ready	Firm, sudden gallops and leaps come to an instant stop, binding the flow. The clapping patterns of the shootout are sudden too. The stepping and watching of section C are sustained and light, contrasting with the urgency of the rest of the dance.	A clever cowboy is attempting to escape from a sheriff who has a good opinion of himself but is slow on the uptake. The cowboy leaps obstacles to hide from the sheriff. They come face to face for shootouts and the ending can be written in many ways.
A	*(hand-drawn wavy lines)*	Gallop 4 times, jump, hide — Gallop 4 times, freeze, look, look		
A	*(hand-drawn wavy lines)*	Gallop 4 times, jump, hide — Gallop 4 times, freeze, look, look		

			Relationship emphasis	**Image or sequence**
B	*(hand-drawn angled lines)*	Clapping patterns for shootout	The most important feature of this dance is the tongue-in-cheek relationship between the cowboy and sheriff. Section A is a lead–follow relationship as the cowboy escapes, only to be followed by the sheriff, who practically trips over him but fails to notice his prey. The B section of the music, the shootout, is a pattern worked together by the two opponents. In C, the two circle each other warily before the cowboy makes good his escape again.	A clever cowboy is attempting to escape from a sheriff who has a good opinion of himself but is slow on the uptake. The cowboy leaps obstacles to hide from the sheriff. They come face to face for shootouts and the ending can be written in many ways.
	A repeats 3 times			
	B repeats			
	A repeats			
C	*(hand-drawn lines with loops)*	Step, watch		
	A repeats 2 times			
	B repeats			
	A repeats			
D	*(hand-drawn line rising)*	Collapse, flee, freeze		

From S. Carline, 2011, *Lesson plans for creative dance* (Champaign, IL: Human Kinetics).

THE SHERIFF AND THE COWBOY

Bonanza: Livingston and Evans

TEACHING PROGRESSION

You can build lesson plans based on this suggested progression:

1. Gallop, jump, hide (section A)
2. Gallop, freeze, look (section A)
3. Clapping patterns for shootout (section B)
   Link 1, 2, 3
4. Step, watch (section C)
   Link 1, 2, 3, 4
5. Design the end: collapse, flee, freeze (section D)

DANCE SEQUENCE

1. Gallop, Jump, Hide (Section A)

Starting in their own spaces, to a galloping rhythm, briefly practice a high, vigorous sideways gallop, ensuring that the children can travel easily with both the left and right sides of the body leading. Now, maintaining the strong galloping action, see if they can lower the body by bending the knees and turning them out, a bit like a cowboy who has just jumped off his horse. Keep the galloping phrases short so that they practice freezing often, still in the cowboy shape with prominent knees and elbows.

The jumping in the context of this dance is jumping over, which should produce differences in body shapes in the air from jumping. Making sure that they have plenty of space, experiment with jumping over an imaginary object, encouraging use of the arms to gain height and soft landings. Watch for children who give the impression of clearing an obstacle by having tucked-up legs, or focus on the object being cleared. Watching a few and recognizing features appropriate to the task often help. Now put the jumps into a sequence of gallop 4 counts, jump over, freeze. You can ask for suggestions of obstacles in Western towns (the story gradually emerges), such as cattle troughs, tumbleweed, and cacti. Now is the time to work on hiding behind shapes so that the freeze at the end of the sequence takes form. The children can experiment with a variety of appropriate body shapes and at different levels, matching the shape of the objects they are hiding behind. The next step is to link the gallop 4 counts, jump, hide. Then listen to section A of the music (see figure 13.1), go back into the space, and try it.

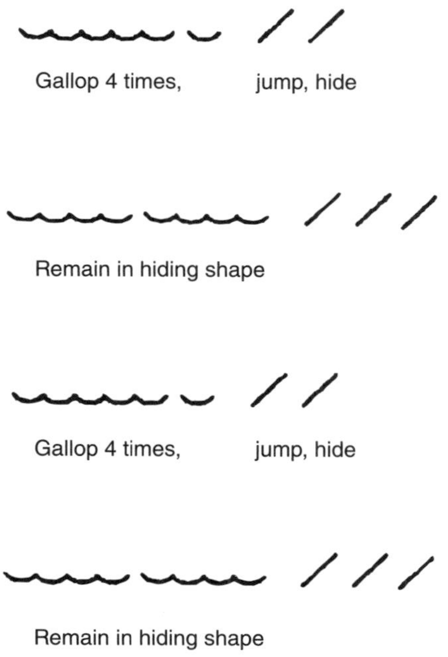

2. Gallop, Freeze, Look (Section A)

Having suggested a cowboy theme, it is easy to explore the sheriff's role and explain that this sheriff is keen but not too observant! Work on a phrase of gallop 6 counts and freeze, making the freeze "gallop shaped." Then explore how, with feet remaining still, they can look with the whole body—behind, up, down, to a diagonal, and so on. Again, point out clear examples of children whose whole body shows directional focus and tension. The trick now is to do two of these looks very suddenly one after another but show total contrast in shape and level or direction: low looking behind to high looking to the other side. Now link gallop 6 counts, freeze, look, look; try it to the second phrase of section A (see figure 13.2).

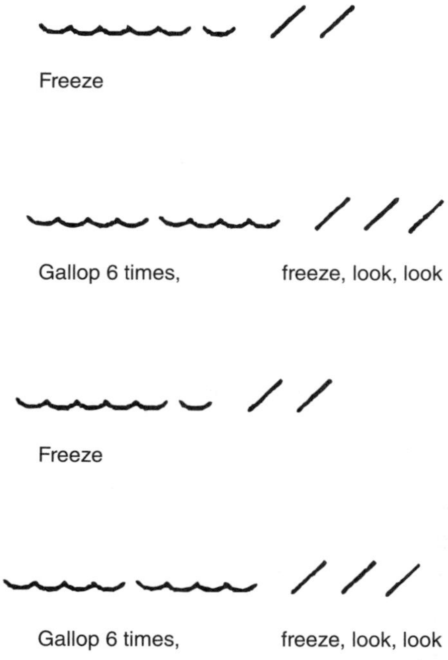

By this point, the children have begun to experiment with the vocabulary for both the cowboy and the sheriff, and it will improve in character and quality over time. The children are ready to get into twos and decide who will be each character (if there's an odd number, have a group with one cowboy and two sheriffs). Starting close to their partners, but in such a position that the sheriff can't see the cowboy (back to back, one peering into the distance with the other close to his or her feet), practice the sequence to a rhythm (claves or drum): The cowboy escapes with gallop 4 counts, jump, hide; the sheriff immediately gallops 6 counts toward the cowboy partner, freezes very close but without seeing him or her, then does the two looks so that he or she fails to spot the cowboy at all! This sequence repeats immediately and requires the children to be quick off the mark either escaping or pursuing. Have the children switch roles, practice, then do it to the music, letting it play into the B section so they can hear what comes next.

Gallop 4 times,   jump, hide

Remain in hiding shape

Gallop 4 times,   jump, hide

Remain in hiding shape

FIGURE 13.1   The cowboy's actions to section A.

Freeze

Gallop 6 times,   freeze, look, look

Freeze

Gallop 6 times,   freeze, look, look

FIGURE 13.2   The sheriff's actions to section A.

(continued)

3. Clapping Patterns for Shootout (Section B)

There are many ways to do this, and excellent shootout episodes will occur if the dance is developed over time. I start by teaching a clapping pattern in twos, facing each other (see figure 13.3).

Try this to section B of the music. Once they are fairly fluent, reinforce the characters. They need to stand farther apart, knees bent, elbows bent, glaring at each other (this *is* a shootout!) and do the clapping pattern in this manner.

Now they can start right from the beginning, working through sections A and B and section A again (three times this time) to get a feel for the sequencing. Generally I leave the shootout as the clapping sequence for the first session but add suggestions for development during the next class. For example (always keeping the same rhythm), what other parts can clap (elbows, ankles, fists)? Can they change levels at some point? Given some time to practice with your input and watching the exploration of other pairs, the children come up with better ideas than I could invent. For those who are slower to find their own patterns, the security of the original clapping pattern is always there.

4. Step, Watch (Section C)

Section C occurs once in the music, in between two A sections. At this point, it looks as though the sheriff has caught the cowboy, and they circle each other quietly, watchfully, like two boxers in the ring—then suddenly the cowboy escapes again. Once the children have worked on the sustainment and relationship of this section, they have explored the material for the whole dance except the end. I often leave this until they have fully developed the characters and their own story ideas have emerged.

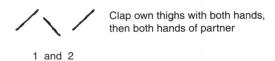

Clap own thighs with both hands, then both hands of partner

1 and 2

Clap own thighs with both hands, then both hands of partner

1 and 2

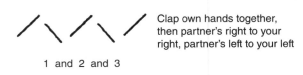

Clap own hands together, then partner's right to your right, partner's left to your left

1 and 2 and 3

FIGURE 13.3 The original clapping pattern for the shootout.

5. Design the End: Collapse, Flee, Freeze (Section D)

The children need to listen to this little bit of music and then discuss the options. Will the cowboy escape? If so, how can we tell? Perhaps the short-sighted sheriff does capture him. Occasionally two children choose a fatal ending where they simultaneously shoot each other down. This is fine, as long as they can work it well to the music, because the whole dance is quite a caricature of the two characters.

Once they have decided and worked on their endings, the children can do the whole dance. It's a good idea to have half the class watch the other half and vice versa. To make this a positive experience, discuss features that they can look for, such as clear jump-and-hide sequences, interesting shapes between the cowboy and sheriff, and original shootout patterns. In this way the watching becomes a learning experience and the children appreciate others' ways of moving. I find that they often store up original ideas to use at a later date in another situation.

This sheriff holds a dejected finishing shape—the cowboy escaped!

RENDEZVOUS
10 to 12 Years
Fourth Rendez-Vous: Jean Michel Jarre

Music pattern	Music emphasis	Action emphasis	Dynamic emphasis	Spatial emphasis
Intro	~~~~~~~		Light yet purposeful runs and bounces, firm spinning, and sudden, firm freezing.	Floor patterns. Curved pathways through a space: run, bounce, spin along a clear curve. Changes of levels during the spin and freeze.
A		Run (8 beats)		
		Bounce (8)		
		Rise (4)	**Relationship emphasis**	**Image or sequence**
		Run (8)	This is a dance for groups of 3 to 5. Changing leaders for each entry, each group follows a pathway in space as they enter and exit.	This can remain purely as a sequence of actions or develop into ideas about the movement of asteroids (or other things) in space.
		Bounce (8)		
		Rise (4)		
		Spin (8)		
		Freeze (8)		
	A repeats twice			
B		Rush, run		
	A repeats twice			
	B repeats			

From S. Carline, 2011, *Lesson plans for creative dance* (Champaign, IL: Human Kinetics). Used with permission of Gina Almquist and Jackie Best-Walushka.

RENDEZVOUS

Fourth Rendez-Vous: Jean Michel Jarre

TEACHING PROGRESSION

You can build lesson plans based on this suggested progression:

1. Run, bounce, rise, run, bounce, rise, spin, freeze (section A)
2. Rush, run (section B)

   Link 1, 2

DANCE SEQUENCE

1. Run, Bounce, Rise, Run, Bounce, Rise, Spin, Freeze (Section A)

Starting the children in their own spaces, practice a run to a clear, even rhythm given by drum or claves. The run is light, on the balls of the feet, *one step per beat* with the feet kicking behind. The upper body needs to be kept high. Let them practice for phrases of about 16 runs, then stop. Remind the class about light feet and moving into open spaces, and practice again. Now introduce the idea of really covering ground with the runs so that they are lightly and purposefully moving as far as they can, still keeping one step per beat.

Next, practice the bounces in much the same way (bounces are jumps from and to two feet), keeping the rhythm and allowing the bounces to travel. As they bounce in and out of spaces created by the rest of the group, the children can try leading with the side of the body. It is important that they maintain a light tension in the rest of the body so that they don't flop.

Join phrases of 8 runs with 8 bounces with the emphasis on the first beat of each 8 so that the children move clearly through the transition. As they work, remind them to move into open spaces and continue the sense of going far.

In the dance, *rise* means an action through the body that finishes in an entirely stretched shape on the spot. The children need to feel what complete extension is from the toes through to the head (which looks up) and stretched fingers. Although the phrase (4 beats) is short, they can learn to control the body and fully extend each time. Add the rise to the run and bounce, back into run, bounce, and rise again. So now the sequence is run, bounce, rise, run, bounce, rise.

They can do spinning in many ways, but in this instance it is a traveling one. Explore with the children powerful wide spins that take them from one spot to another. Next, add the idea of changing level so that as they spin, they gradually get closer to the floor. As they improve (not necessarily on the first day), they can be challenged to add turning over the floor, which is a large tumbling action. This is good for them because they start at a medium level, spin, gradually lower the center of gravity, and then smoothly transfer their weight down to the floor. Try this again so that the whole sequence occurs within 8 beats. Now put the spinning phrase into the sequence with the other words:

Run 8, bounce 8, rise 4, run 8, bounce 8, rise 4, spin 8

Freeze comes right after the spin, so it is an effective way of stopping or binding the movement very suddenly. This needs practice so that they are in control of their movement and brave enough to be able to spin fast, tumble fast, and bind the tumble abruptly rather than slow to a stop. It is fun and challenging, and the children may be helped by watching one or two who master this idea quickly. The freeze shape is held for the remainder of that phrase:

Spin 2, 3, 4, 5, 6, 7, 8; freeze and hold 2, 3, 4, 5, 6, 7, 8

With practice over time, the children will be able to hold their tumbling shapes at a variety of angles with some shapes higher than others on different body parts. The big question is whether they can get from the held shape quickly back into a run without struggling to their feet. This transition requires anticipation of the next phrase and practice.

Once the children are aware of the order and duration of the complete action sequence, they can sit and listen to the music. There is a brief introduction, then the sequence begins. The next step is to go back into the space and work with the music. The whole action phrase is repeated three times in a row before the music changes to something new.

I would tend to stop here, then review and develop the sequence during the next several classes. Over a series of classes, you can introduce the following ideas as the children are ready:

1. Moving through a stage space. Have most of the gym space as the stage space. Two of the edges are resting space (see figure 13.4). Now, instead of using the space randomly as before, each child travels across the stage space with the action sequence, focusing on a curved pathway. Using a chalkboard, show the children possibilities for pathways, and ask for their ideas (see figure 13.5). Discuss the idea of asteroids (or other things) traveling at speed, in curves, through blackness. Now the children don't all need to travel at once. Start about half the class in each resting place, and ask seven or eight children to enter with the first sequence, more with the second, and so on.

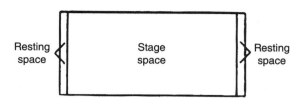

FIGURE 13.4 Creating a stage space.

FIGURE 13.5 Examples of curved pathways.

2. You can add the relationship aspect. Try the previous idea but with the children traveling in pairs, one behind the other (this can be extended to threes or fours later). Now two students (one leading, one following) travel on the same pathway. Each time they enter, there is a new leader.

3. Now the tricky one, but exciting for older or more experienced children! In the music, the action sequence is always done in order, each action to its own particular phrase of music, but a group could decide to enter with bouncing. To do this, they would wait for the run phrase to be over, then enter bouncing. Similarly, they can enter on any given part and likewise exit on any part. Some children pick up this idea readily, whereas others need a little time, so it pays to ensure (subtly) that each group has a fairly rhythmic member.

At first they may lose the clear pathways because their entire focus is directed toward when to enter, but over time and with reminders they can deal with the timing, complex curved pathways, a sense of purpose in traveling far, and not having too many or too few groups in the stage space at any one time.

2. Rush, Run (Section B)

Toward the end of the third repetition of the previous action sequence, all groups should have exited or are about to exit so that the stage space is empty. The music changes and takes on a rushing quality. The children work as individuals again and rush about the space, weaving in and out of each other. They enjoy this because it means traveling and curving very fast pathways. After a few seconds, one child abruptly comes to a halt and remains in one spot, still running but kicking his or her feet behind. Randomly but spaced out over this music section, each child does the same, always stopping in a space. So, at any given time, some children are on the spot while others are rushing among them. Eventually, all are running on the spot. Practicing this is great fun because they have to become sensitive to what the rest of the group is doing, when to stop, and where to stop. As soon as the run, bounce music returns, they fall back into the pattern, using it to travel back into their linear groupings and continuing with the entrances and exits.

At this point, the children have explored all aspects, and it is a matter of improving the quality of their movement and anticipating the order and duration of each section of the music and use of space. This idea takes time and practice in short doses. It is fast paced and requires the children to keep their energy level and body tension up. There are many ways to develop this (as in most ideas), depending on a variety of factors, especially the children's own ideas.

SEASCAPE

10 to 12 Years

The Voyage from On the Threshold of a Dream: *The Moody Blues*

Music pattern	Music emphasis	Action emphasis	Dynamic emphasis	Spatial emphasis
A	*(wave-line notation)*	Open and close Close and open Open and close Close and open	The most important focus for this dance is working with extreme contrasts of firm, sudden opening and sustained closing or sustained opening and firm, sudden closing actions in the A sections.	The opening and closing movements in the A sections focus on extensions into areas of personal space.
B	*(wave-line notation)*	Turn, rise, sink	Section B is fine, as sustained as it is possible to be without actually coming to a stop, a drifting feeling using a variety of actions.	The advancing and retreating of C sections use forward-and-backward movements.
C	*(music notation)*	Advance, retreat Advance, retreat Advance, retreat Advance, retreat	Section C explores the gradual increase of force in the advancing, retreating, building to rushing, jumping, retreating, and whirling of the incoming tide.	The whirlpool of section D uses a spiraling floor pattern.
C	*(music notation)*	Rush, jump, retreat, whirl Rush, jump, retreat, whirl Rush, jump, retreat, whirl Rush, jump, retreat, whirl	Section D is strong and relentless as the whirlpool forms.	

	Music emphasis	Action emphasis	Relationship emphasis	Image or sequence
	C repeats		Many possibilities. The sea anemone can be individual or in 2s or 3s with a sense of being attached to rocks. B is individual. For C sections, the children can be divided into 2 groups: 1s and 2s. They can work as pairs so that as 1 retreats, 2 advances, or they can be randomly divided. In section D, the whole group rushes, whirls, leaps in a huge spiral, with a feeling of centrifugal force.	The image is of the changing forces of the sea and some of the life below. The sea anemone open and close to catch their food, and in the deepest parts, flotsam and jetsam drift in the slow-moving currents. The tide is coming in gently at first with small advances on the shore but with increasing speed and distance as the waves get bigger. Finally, the stormy water is pulled into an enormous whirlpool.
	A repeats			
	C repeats 3 times			
D	*(whirlpool notation)*	Rush, leap, whirl, spin, anchor		

From S. Carline, 2011, *Lesson plans for creative dance* (Champaign, IL: Human Kinetics).

SEASCAPE

The Voyage from On the Threshold of a Dream: *The Moody Blues*

TEACHING PROGRESSION

You can build lesson plans based on this suggested progression:

1. Open and close (section A)
2. Turn, rise, sink (section B)
    Link 1, 2
3. Advance, retreat (section C)
    Rush, jump, retreat, whirl
    Link 1, 2, and 3
4. Rush, leap, whirl, spin, anchor (section D)
    Link 1, 2, 3, 4

DANCE SEQUENCE

1. Open and Close (Section A)

In their own spaces, the children need to find a closed, tucked-up shape. The shapes can be on knees, buttocks, or part of the trunk. Warn them that when they hear a strong beat on the drum, they will suddenly open into a strong, stretched shape. To another beat, they close in tightly again very quickly. It is likely that the children will open into somewhat uniform symmetrical shapes, so the focus needs to be on where in space the nonsupporting limbs can extend. Work on suddenly opening, thinking about putting the arms into a different area of space so that the spine might be arched or twisted to one side. The neck should be extended too, and a leg if possible. The body should show strong tension and be open to the maximum: stretched elbows, hands, knees, feet. This time, close into a different tucked shape, because this will allow a new open shape for the next movement. After a short practice, encouraging variety, let the children listen to a series of about 8 softer, faster beats on the drum. Now, starting closed again, they can open, but gradually, taking all 8 beats to reach full extension—then close suddenly on one beat. Try this the other way around, opening suddenly, firmly on one beat, and closing gradually for 8. Then, with an alternating rhythm of 1 strong beat, then 8 faster and softer, let each child choose whether to open suddenly and close gradually, or open gradually and close suddenly. The ability to open and close with the center of the body initiating the movement takes practice over time with your guidance and is aided by watching clear examples.

Listen to the music of section A, reinforcing the idea that they can choose when to move and whether to be sudden and sustained or sustained and sudden, but you must see the contrast. At this point, you could talk about creatures like sea anemones, which open and close to feed. Try this to the music. Eventually, the children could choose to be alone on a rock or in groups of two or three to provide an interesting start.

2. Turn, Rise, Sink (Section B)

This part occurs only once in the music and explores the difficulty of controlling one's movement so that it is as sustained as it is possible to be without coming to a stop. The image is of debris (content to be discussed!) at the very bottom of the sea where slow currents cause drifting. From the last sea anemone shape, explore turning over the ground, making sure that no body part moves suddenly. This involves maintaining enough tension in the body to hold the shape and also requires thinking ahead so that the body weight can be transferred slowly. From this, introduce action words like *rising, turning,* and *sinking* in a long, continuous movement so that the debris changes level and location. Listen to the music (it is very quiet) and try this part, using the whole space. Then, go from the beginning so that the children practice the transition from the strong movement of the sea anemones with their varying time changes to the sustainment of the jetsam on the floor of the sea.

3. Rush, Jump, Retreat, Whirl, Advance, Retreat (Section C)

At the end of the B section of the music, a faint rhythm emerges and the transition is made into section C. Explore the idea of the body being drawn forward gently (no foot movement as yet), then being pulled back, with the upper body leading the movement. Build the intensity so that the feet start to become involved with

(continued)

little rushes forward and back. You can discuss the way the tide encroaches on the shore: almost imperceptibly at the beginning of the flood tide but building in strength, size, and distance traveled. Listen to the first C section of the music and focus on the pull forward and back. Then try it to the music, showing how the movement starts very small and subtle, building as it goes. By the second C section, the tide is truly on the way in and the waves are getting higher. The rush forward and back becomes a rush into an upward jump, which starts to be pulled back immediately on landing (remember the undercurrent!). The children need to experiment with this and find ways of jumping and being pulled back. To make each wave action flow together, try rush, jump, retreat by whirling to gather strength for the next rush forward.

Now, for relationship, and to have waves coming in as other water recedes, randomly divide the children into 1s and 2s. The waves will now overlap, giving a lovely sense of timing and movement (see figure 13.6).

This music happens again right away, allowing a build-up of power that is very exciting. Then section A recurs, so the children are flung back to the opening and closing of the sea anemones. Section C builds again, 3 times in a row (hence the need to divide into 1 and 2).

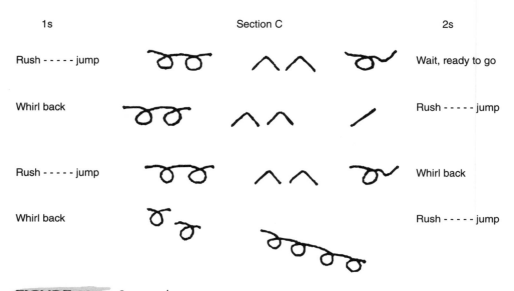

1s	Section C	2s
Rush - - - - - jump		Wait, ready to go
Whirl back		Rush - - - - - jump
Rush - - - - - jump		Whirl back
Whirl back		Rush - - - - - jump

FIGURE 13.6 Staggered waves.

4. Rush, Leap, Whirl, Spin, Anchor (Section D)

The last section of the music loses the clear rhythm of the tide but increases in pace and power. Various things could happen here. By the time the class has progressed to this point, they will probably have their own ideas of how to finish the dance.

An idea that works well and is enjoyable is the formation of a giant whirlpool and incorporation of some of the previously explored actions. To move from the last part of the tide coming in, the class simply starts to travel in a loose clockwise direction: leaping, whirling, and rushing with the circle becoming tighter and tighter. Right at the end, it is possible for the whirlpool to draw them in and down or to spit them out so that they scatter, leaping, whirling, and rushing out to anchor alone.

The quality of the movement, the building of crescendo for the tide, and the smooth transitions come over time as the children internalize the ideas.

THE MINERS
10 to 12 Years

Working Man: Rita MacNeil

Music pattern	Music emphasis	Action emphasis	Dynamic emphasis	Spatial emphasis
	Introduction	Sink: elevators	There are many contrasts in this dance, and the most important one is between sustained and sudden movement. It is very much an effort dance. The sinking of the introduction is sustained, as are the push and pull of the carts, the lifting of the coal, the rescue after the explosion, and the rising of the conclusion. The pickax motifs are sudden and firm and so is the explosion and the spin and hold of chorus 5.	Each section of the dance focuses on different aspects of space. The pickax motifs involve driving the ax into all areas of rock surrounding the miners. The push-and-pull cart section involves clear pathways. The main focus throughout is on levels, especially contrasting high and low for the youth motifs of verse 1, the explosion and rescue of chorus 4, and use of all levels for the pickax motifs, push-and-pull carts, and the spin-and-hold section.
	Chorus 1	Pickaxes		
	Verse 1	Spring, run, turn: youth motifs		
	Chorus 2	Push-and-pull coal carts		
	Verse 2	Tableau		
	Chorus 3	Lifting coal		
	Chorus 4	Explosion and rescue		
	Chorus 5	Spin, hold		
	End	Rise: elevators		

Relationship emphasis	Image or sequence
Different for each section. The miners descend into the mine and are lifted to the surface in unison. The pickax, push-and-pull carts and lifting coal choruses involve a variety of relationships with groups of 4 to 6. The youth motifs are based on partner work and the spin and hold of chorus 5 are individual.	The dance follows the spirit of the lyrics of "Working Man." The miners start their shift as they descend in the elevator to the lower levels of the mine (introduction). Once there, they chip away at the rock face, trying to release the seams of coal (chorus 1). The youths of 16 years (verse 1) express their exuberance and intent of finding jobs outside the mine: They have no intention of working underground all their lives. In chorus 2, the miners push and pull the heavy carts of coal to a place where it can be taken to the surface. In verse 2, at the age of 64, one miner leads a stranger through a tableau of his life: men frozen in the act of swinging pickaxes and pushing heavy carts. In chorus 3, the miners lift the awkward lumps of coal out of the way so that they have more room to work, but then unexpectedly at the start of chorus 4, an explosion blasts the miners off their feet, many of them landing injured on the ground. During the rest of chorus 4, the dazed miners rise to their feet assisting those who are too hurt to do so alone. In chorus 5, all the miners spin frantically and freeze, holding their heads and vowing that if any of them ever see the sun or can hold it in mind, they never again will go down underground. They end the shift as the elevator rises to the surface.

From S. Carline, 2011, *Lesson plans for creative dance* (Champaign, IL: Human Kinetics).

THE MINERS

Working Man: Rita MacNeil

TEACHING PROGRESSION

You can build lesson plans based on this suggested progression:

1. Swing and impact: pickaxes (chorus 1)
2. Sink: elevators (introduction)
   Link 2, 1
3. Push-and-pull carts (chorus 2)
4. Spring, run, turn: youth motifs (verse 1)
   Link 2, 1, 4, 3
5. Tableau (verse 2)
   Link 2, 1, 4, 3, 5
6. Lifting coal (chorus 3)
7. Explosion and rescue (chorus 4)
   Link 2, 1, 4, 3, 5, 6, 7
8. Spin, hold (chorus 5)
9. Rise: elevators (end)
   Whole dance

DANCE SEQUENCE

1. Swing and Impact: Pickaxes (Chorus 1)

The dance is based on working actions and rhythms, and the first one is the exploration and development of swinging a pickax against a rock face. Starting the children in their own spaces, ask them to imagine that each of them has a heavy ax that requires a two-hand grip. Let them experiment with swinging the ax and introduce the idea of impact where the action comes to an abrupt, firm stop as the ax contacts the hard rock face at the end of the swing. They need to prepare, swing, and freeze suddenly. Some of the children might understand this and show the impact early on in the exploration—in that case, let the class watch a few examples. As they work, talk about the need for a wide base of support, strong legs, and the transfer of weight from one leg to another as they swing the ax.

Next, ask them to think about where they are swinging the ax (most will likely swing overhand and forward). They can try swinging and ending high, low, diagonally at any level, and also undercutting. (Strong arms are necessary.) Some may try from a one- or two-knee kneeling position.

Now, using a drum or claves, give a rhythm (see figure 13.7) so that they can hear when the sudden impact comes at the end of each swing. Keep the rhythm going so that the children can experiment with using levels, angles, and different types of swings (overhead, undercut) with their axes. Remind them about focus (looking where the ax will contact), strong movement, and stepping forward, to the side, and so on.

Gather the children to listen to the introduction and chorus 1, and introduce the story of coal miners. Let them return to the space to practice using pickaxes to chorus 1 (see figure 13.8).

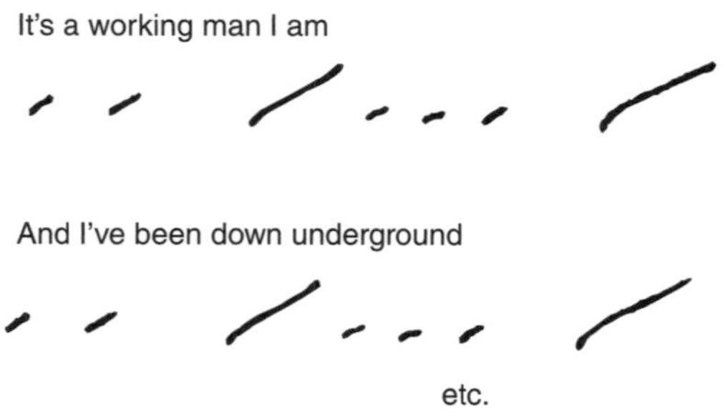

At this point, after they have processed the idea, it is better to leave it and move on to part 2 or another dance. Next time, review the idea and start to develop group

FIGURE 13.7 The strong beats indicate impact: ax hitting rock.

It's a working man I am

And I've been down underground

etc.

FIGURE 13.8 The pickax music.

work. The children can decide in groups of four to six how they will work together for this part. Do they all face the same way, or are they almost back to back in a narrow space? Does each miner swing for each, or do they want to take alternating phrases, freezing on the impact part in between? These ideas need short repetitions over time to evolve as the children become immersed in the mining story.

2. Sink: Elevators (Introduction)

Starting from a standing position, let the children practice sinking very slowly to their knees, keeping the top part of the body upright and still. This takes control. The focus is straight ahead, and the idea is that the miners are going down to the lower levels of the mine to start their shift. Gather the children to listen to the introduction of the music so that they can hear how sustained their sinking action must be, then let them try it to the music. The children can divide into groups, so several elevators are going down at once—these groups could be of four to six students who will work together for the pickax section, or larger groups that will separate later. Each group needs to decide where in the space their elevator is situated. At the very end of the dance, they will go back up in these same elevators.

Let them try it again, this time making the transition from going down in the elevator to stepping into the pickax movements of chorus 1.

At appropriate times during the dance classes, discuss coal mining and the life of miners. I have found that they are eager to know details of what might be a whole new world to most of them. We talked about the blind pit ponies, the caged birds whose live presence assured the miners of adequate oxygen levels, miners' helmets with candles or lamps attached to them, the children who could be sent into spaces too small for the adults, and the fact that the coal dust became ingrained in their skins. I told them about the slag heaps that grew into mountains and overshadowed the villages and of the disaster in Aberfan, Wales, when a slag heap slid, burying an elementary school so that a whole generation died. Without becoming morbid, the children were both interested and curious and understood the spirit of the "Working Man" lyrics. They asked lots of questions! Another good topic of discussion is the mining disaster in northern Chile, in August 2010, when 33 coal miners were trapped underground for 69 days. Because of the efforts of experts from several countries, all were rescued alive.

3. Push-and-Pull Carts (Chorus 2)

By now the children know the pace and rhythm of the chorus. This section is about moving carts loaded with coal. Explore pushing actions by experimenting with using hands, shoulders, or backs to push a low cart and moving forward a little with each push. Let the children develop their own patterns here (see figure 13.9).

Again, emphasize a strong base, firm body, focus, and powerful sustained movement. Try pulling the carts with an imaginary rope over one shoulder, again developing a rhythm, but this time lean away from the cart. Let the children try this to the chorus, and watch some examples for quality and variety, pointing out relevant features of their movement.

Step, step,   push step, step   push

Push   step, push   step

FIGURE 13.9 The rhythm for pushing the coal carts.

At a later date, group the children in threes or fours (a group of six from the pickax section could split into two groups of three). Let them experiment with pulling and one pushing, or one pulling and two pushing, keeping a clear rhythm as they travel. Eventually each group will have to work out its pathway in relation to the other groups.

The order in which the pickax and pull-and-push motifs take place in the dance is up to the children. Here are some possibilities:

Chorus 1: All use pickaxes or all pull and push, or half the groups do pickaxes and half pull and push

Chorus 2: All pull and push or all use pickaxes, or half the groups now push and pull and half use pickaxes

When they have decided, gather in the elevator groups and try from the beginning of the music, working through chorus 1, listening to verse 1, and working through chorus 2.

(continued)

TIP

Each time I have worked on this dance with children, it has evolved differently. It is a long dance, and it needs to be worked on over time (as do most ideas) so that it can develop in depth. Because of its intensity (in parts), it is better if the children are working on other dance ideas as well, especially ones with different actions and movement qualities, or they may become stale. Of all the dance ideas I have worked on with children of this age, this has been the most rewarding, because the children come to learn about, and in a way experience, a completely different aspect of life.

Two "youths of 16 years" convey exuberance in their sequences. They do not envision becoming miners.

4. Spring, Run, Turn: Youth Motifs (Verse 1)

In this section, the youth of 16 years are showing that although they are working in the mines at present, they think that they will be able to leave for other, better jobs. (We discuss the fact that few of them actually had much choice in the matter.) But youth has exuberance, and this is the quality to be incorporated. Various partner work has resulted from experimenting with the children's ideas of 16-year-old behavior: conversations, friendly punches, high-five slaps, and so on. One idea that the children developed evolved from two children starting apart, crouching, and looking toward each other; they then sprang up high, ran together, clasped opposite hands, and spun around, crouching suddenly. Then they sprang back up, ran away, and leapt and turned to land back in a crouch. This motif, practiced by all, led to the idea of timing, which the children love and perform so capably at this age. We decided which pair would go first. As they separated, another pair would spring up, meet, part, then another, and so on. As they became used to the order, their timing improved and the picture of energetic youth became clear. This idea also accounted for an uneven number of children, as one child would meet one partner, then another later on in the series.

Many things could be developed here with your guidance and ideas from the children. As something starts to develop, let them practice it to the music of verse 1. Then start the dance from the beginning so that they learn to anticipate the transitions and accentuate the contrast from the sober work section of chorus 1 into the exuberance of verse 1 and back to the work of chorus 2.

5. Tableau (Verse 2)

This part is in direct contrast to the youth of 16: At the age of 64, a veteran miner will "gently lead you by the arm" as he takes visitors on a tour back through time to tell them of the hardships. For this, all but two of the children will remain absolutely still throughout the verse and can choose in their working groups whether to freeze (making a tableau) in the pickax section or push-and-pull cart section. Obviously the class will have to give and take here so that some groups of each are represented. At the end of chorus 2, they will move into their positions and hold absolutely still. I remind the children to choose a position that they can hold comfortably for a while, but most of them persist in holding a shape that shows hard labor (I say nothing but admire their involvement immensely). Ask a child (who has a sense of quietness) to walk slowly through the tableau and equally slowly collect another child, who follows, quietly looking at the scene inside the mine. The child has to choose a pathway where he or she can look at each scene along the way.

Now practice this first to verse 2, then in the context of the dance so far. In each practice of the whole dance, even though the individual sections may not be complete, the children learn to anticipate the next part and figure out where they need to be and how to get there naturally.

6. Lifting Coal (Chorus 3)

In this section, the miners have to move heavy pieces of rock or coal that have been chipped from the walls. With the children working individually to start with, experiment with the idea of lifting something very heavy, carrying it a little way, and setting it down. Focus on feet being apart, bending at the hips and knees, keeping firm throughout the body, and moving slowly (children have a tendency to move quite quickly). After some practice, let the children go back into their groups and devise methods of picking up and passing this heavy material to each other so that it is eventually put into a pile. They need to find a system of passing coal, keeping to the rhythm of the chorus (well known by now), and checking that each miner receives and passes on a chunk of rock or coal that maintains its size and weight. In other words, they have to be aware of how far apart their arms are. This passing can take many forms: along a straight line, around a corner or curve, two lines feeding toward one miner (this makes for an interesting rhythm). The children can incorporate different levels so that the coal is being passed up or down. Again, let them experiment, then try it to the music.

Groups work at lifting chunks of coal chipped from a seam and passing them along.

7. Explosion and Rescue (Chorus 4)

Starting with plenty of space around each child, tell them that you are going to give them a sound on drum or claves and that you want them to jump as if the blast of an explosion has caused the jump. Try this several times so that they can get the feeling of being blown up and backward and to the side very suddenly with little preparation. They are being jumped rather than just jumping—a reaction movement. As in many learning situations, one or more children may capture this in their movement quite quickly, and watching a few examples often helps the others to see the relevant characteristics of the jumping action.

The children will probably be landing in a variety of positions from such a jump—now the landings can be explored too. Ask them to be blasted again, but this time (carefully) land in an awkward shape, with some parts of the body where they ought not to be as if they are injured. Point out clear ones as they occur: a head tipped back, a shoulder out of place, an arched spine, a leg at an awkward angle, and so on. I am always surprised by the children's capacity to capture this idea. Try the jump, land several times more so that each child can experiment, and find out how to land safely while making it appear to be a pure reaction to an explosion in the mine. Now do it again, and ask them all to hold their landings for a few seconds, then slowly, as if they are dazed and stunned, get to their feet and walk away.

Again, but this time only a few of them will rise and slowly help a more injured miner to his or her feet before walking away alone. Each child will want to try both helping and being helped and over the time in which the dance develops may do each several times. The children become so involved with the idea of this that the explosion and recovery can be different each time—they learn to react and work as a group.

At this point it is useful to listen to chorus 3 (lifting coal) and chorus 4 (explosion and rescue) to learn the exact moment of the explosion. At the end of chorus 3, they continue to shift coal, but the explosion occurs on "It's a—" at the start of chorus 4, so it is completely unexpected.

8. Spin, Hold (Chorus 5)

By the end of chorus 4, all the miners are walking slowly with blank expressions as a result of the explosion. As soon as chorus 5 begins, each miner spins powerfully, so a clear contrast is made between sustained and sudden movement.

(continued)

In their own spaces, the children try a powerful, fast spin, then bring it to an abrupt halt (binding the flow). Try it again, even more powerfully, and stop suddenly (this takes practice and control). Now encourage them to change level as they spin and to freeze at a different level. Next, focus on the position of the head, bringing their elbows up and back, so that their hands are spread out on either side of the head as they freeze. In this final chorus, one can hear a sense of resolution as Rita MacNeil sings a descant above the voices of the miners: "I never again will go down underground." As the children spin and then bring their hands to the sides of their heads as they freeze, angling their heads and upper bodies in various ways, they show this sense of resolution.

The children will naturally spin and hold with the phrasing of the music:

It's a working man I am

(Spin, hold)

And I've been down underground

(Spin, hold)

They will need to work on increasing the power of the spin, traveling a little if they wish, and binding the flow absolutely.

9. Rise: Elevators (Ending)

These last few seconds allow the miners to abandon the frenzy of chorus 5 and walk slowly to their original elevator places. This time, however, they kneel, then rise slowly in their groups until they are standing, looking straight ahead. Like the sinking at the start, rising slowly and smoothly from two knees to feet takes practice!

Now, the children have explored all the ideas and movement concepts within the dance, and from this point they can work out and refine sections as needed. Over time, the children develop their own miner characteristics and small refinements that contribute to the quality and meaning of the dance.

APPENDIX A

Suggested Music for Introductory Activities

Note: For the music files listed here, go to http://education2.uvic.ca/Faculty/thopper/index.htm, the Web site for Dr. Tim Hopper, University of Victoria. Click "Dance," then "Music Files."

Baby Beluga, sung by Raffi; *Baby Beluga*: iTunes and Introductory Music Files

Chanson Pour Petula, André Gagnon; *La Collection Emergence*: Introductory Music Files

L'ouverture Éclair, André Gagnon; *Neiges*: iTunes and Introductory Music Files

New River Train, Raffi; *More Singable Songs*: iTunes and Introductory Music Files

Oats and Beans and Barley, Raffi; *Baby Beluga*: iTunes and Introductory Music Files

Pennywhistle Jig, Mancini and Galway; *In the Pink*: Introductory Music Files

Pennywhistle Song, Hans Zimmer; *Power of One* Soundtrack

Pie in the Face Polka, Mancini and Galway; *In the Pink*: Introductory Music Files

Pour Les Amants, André Gagnon; *La Collection Emergence*: Introductory Music Files

Radetzky March, Johann Strauss; *The Best of Strauss*: iTunes and Introductory Music Files

Second Rendez-Vous, Jean Michel Jarre; *Rendez-Vous*: iTunes and Introductory Music Files

With Kate by the Sea, White Eisenstein: Introductory Music Files

APPENDIX B

Sources for Dances With Music

Note: For the music files listed here, go to http://education2.uvic.ca/Faculty/thopper/index.htm, the Web site for Dr. Tim Hopper, University of Victoria. Click "Dance," then "Music Files."

Changes: Vangelis, "Titles" from *Chariots of Fire*: iTunes and Dances to Music Files

Day O (Traditional): Raffi, *Baby Beluga*: iTunes and Dances to Music Files

Pattern to Cure a Headache: Paderewski, Minuet in G Major: iTunes and Dances to Music Files

Peter Pan and His Shadow: Grainger, Children's March: iTunes

Planets: Richard Strauss, "Sunrise" from Also Sprach Zarathustra; *The Best of Strauss*: iTunes and Dances to Music Files

Rendez-Vous: Jean Michel Jarre, "Fourth Rendez-Vous" from *Rendez-Vous*: iTunes and Dances to Music Files

Rice Krispies (Traditional): Vera Lynn: Dances to Music Files

Seascape: Moody Blues, "The Voyage" from *On the Threshold of a Dream*: iTunes and Dances to Music Files

Skeletons and Ghouls: Saint-Saëns, Danse Macabre: iTunes and Dances to Music Files

Snowdrifts: Maykapar, "The Little Music Box" from Biriulki, Op. 28: iTunes and Dances to Music Files

The Abandoned Cartwheel: Gluck, "Air Gai" from *Iphigénie en Aulide*: Dances to Music Files

The Archers: Schumann, "Jagdlied/Hunting Song" from *Waldszenen: Neun Klavierstücke*, Op. 82: iTunes and Dances to Music Files

The Battles of the Seasons: Howard Blake, Excerpt from *The Snowman* track 6 (0:43-2:39): iTunes

The Full Moon: Alan Menken, "Fireworks and Jig" from *The Little Mermaid*: iTunes and Dances to Music Files

The Ghost: Raffi, "Skin and Bones" from *More Singable Songs*: iTunes and Dances to Music Files

The Jesters: Mannheim Steamroller, "Toota Lute" from *Fresh Aire II*: iTunes and Dances to Music Files

The Little Chinook: Corelli, "Giga Allegro" from Sonata Op. 5, No. 9 in A Major: iTunes and Dances to Music Files

The Miners: Rita MacNeil, "Working Man" from *Mining the Soul*: iTunes and Dances to Music Files

The Mirage: Howard and Blaikley, "The Flame Trees of Thika" Theme II (*Masterpiece Theatre*): iTunes and Dances to Music Files

The Queen's Guards: Tchaikovsky, "March" from *The Nutcracker Suite*: iTunes and Dances to Music Files

The Sheriff and the Cowboy: Livingstone and Evans, *Bonanza*: iTunes and Dances to Music Files

The Snowchildren: Herbert Donaldson, The Snowmaiden: Dances to Music Files

The Snowstorm: Bruce Broughton, "The Boy Who Could Fly" from *The Boy Who Could Fly*: iTunes and Dances to Music Files

The Space Stealers: Alan Silvestri; "Forrest Gump Suite" from *Forrest Gump*: iTunes and Dances to Music Files

The Volcano Makers: Greig, "In the Hall of the Mountain King" from *Peer Gynt Suite No. 1*: iTunes and Dances to Music Files

The Warriors: Hanson, Dance of the Warriors: Dances to Music Files

The Wizards: Howard Blake, Excerpt from *The Snowman* track 4 (at 12:23): iTunes and Dances to Music Files

When I Get to the Fairground: Alexander Faris, "Upstairs, Downstairs" Theme I (*Masterpiece Theatre*): iTunes and Dances to Music Files

ABOUT THE AUTHOR

Sally Carline, MA, qualified as a teacher at I.M. Marsh College of Physical Education in the UK and taught in secondary school before moving to Canada, where she completed her BEd and MA at the University of Alberta. She taught at the elementary school level and then as a sessional lecturer at the University of Alberta until her retirement in 2010. Sally has taught creative dance to children ages 4 through 12 since 1975 and is head of the Children's Creative Dance Program in Edmonton. She has conducted numerous in-services and professional development seminars on creative dance and has a variety of publications in the field of dance and movement education.

Carline has presented both nationally and internationally and has produced several dance videos focusing on both the teaching process and dance performance. She has held memberships with Dance and the Child International, the Fine Arts Association, and the American Alliance for Health, Physical Education, Recreation and Danc

Sally Carline

DATE DUE